FEELING, BEING, AND
THE SENSE OF SELF

FEELING, BEING, AND THE SENSE OF SELF

A New Perspective on Identity, Affect, and Narcissistic Disorders

Marcus West

KARNAC

First published in 2007 by
Karnac Books Ltd.
118 Finchley Road, London NW3 5HT

British Library Cataloguing in Publication Data

A C.I.P. for this book is available from the British Library

ISBN-13: 978 1 85575 412 6

Edited, designed and produced by The Studio Publishing Services Ltd,
www.publishingservicesuk.co.uk
e-mail: studio@publishingservicesuk.co.uk

10 9 8 7 6 5 4 3 2 1

www.karnacbooks.com

CONTENTS

Dedicated to the memory of P. E. W. and J. L. W.,
and to L, E, M, and A

ACKNOWLEDGEMENTS

I am enormously indebted and grateful to my two good friends Gillian Russell and Rob Abbot for their comments on drafts of the book and help in editing, and to Gillian also for her proof-reading (and I acknowledge any peculiar turns of grammar as my own). I am also very grateful to Anne Tynedale, Richard Carvalho, Bob Withers, and Fiona Ross for their very helpful observations and comments on previous drafts of the book. I would also like to thank James Astor, Anna Bravesmith, Joe Cambray, Warren Colman, Elizabeth Gee, Jean Knox, Joe Redfearn, Elizabeth Urban, and Barbara Wharton, who have helped with or commented upon previous papers, drafts of papers, or talks which have become incorporated into the book. This list could also be considerably expanded to include those who have made interesting and helpful comments at the presentation of those papers and talks. The dialogue has always been tremendously helpful and I am extremely grateful to all of the above, although, of course, I take full responsibility for the views expressed herein and any associated errors. Finally, I am grateful to my patients and, in particular, those who have given their permission for me to write about our work together here.

This book has been born out of mistakes, a difficulty in under-standing certain concepts, and hard experience. Many of the mis-takes are documented here, particularly in the first chapter, which gives an extensive clinical example and which serves, from one per-spective, to document my development as an analyst. While some of these mistakes might be seen as inevitable enactments, which came about through naïvety and over-identification with my patients, they are mistakes nevertheless, and I believe important lessons can be learnt from them.

The difficulty in understanding certain concepts—the terms pro-jective identification and the paranoid–schizoid position are good examples—was only addressed, in the end, through the hard expe-rience of analysis, with the theories, many of which are explored herein, serving as guide-posts. I am grateful to my patients for their many, and continuing, lessons. If this book has been written with anyone in mind it is for those who similarly struggle to really understand the meaning of such concepts.

Put at its simplest, I stumbled across a new perspective from which to view things—a perspective based on the variations in the way we experience ourselves and the underlying psychic structure that supports that identity. As time went on I discovered many other elements in other theories that provided similar perspectives to my own, so that the book could be presented as a patchwork of theories. I hope I have done justice to those who have worked on these issues before, in weaving them together with my own experience and perspective.

The notion of perspective explains the illustration on the cover, and a theme that runs throughout the book. It relates to a story that I first met in the form of "The Wise Man and the Elephant", but that I understand has had many forms and incarnations. In the story, a wise man asked a number of blind men to describe what they could of an elephant. They all argued and disagreed about this creature, being able only to describe what each could feel of the elephant, one describing the trunk, one the body, one the leg, and so on. They were all adamant that they were correct and that the others must be wrong. They were, of course, all describing different parts of the same creature.

The link to the analytic field is obvious, and I do not claim to be able to describe the whole analytic elephant, although I hope that I have been able to string a few parts together and show how some perspectives might articulate with some others. In writing the book I have become particularly interested in the fact that, in the story, these are *blind* men. I have come to see that we can only describe things from our own perspective and that any description remains an approximation and a construction. We can only ever approximate to "truth" and therefore always remain, in some sense, blind. This book represents the limited description of what I can feel of the elephant analysis at the present time.

INTRODUCTION

This book aims to show how complex, clinical phenomena can be understood in terms of a few simple mechanisms. It offers a model that is drawn out of, articulates with, and underpins, the main analytic models.

The book weaves together three main threads. The first concerns identity and the significance of variations in the individual's sense of self. The second is an account of the nature and functioning of the non-verbal self, rooted in the nature of affect and the functioning of an "affective appraisal mechanism", located in the brainstem and the right hemisphere of the brain. The third is a theory of narcissism, which is understood to underlie all other psychopathologies, and to follow from the functioning of the affective appraisal mechanism.

While the book's origins and premises are simple, its implications and applications are far-reaching. The simple origins concern observations of certain phenomena, observable primarily in borderline, hysteric, and narcissistic states, although also very much a feature of everyday life: that the more deeply an individual feels something, the more certain, real, and true it feels to him or her, but that, paradoxically, the less of a sense of "I" he or she has. The clinical implications of this are, I believe, enormous, and tell us a great deal about identity and the range of psychic experience and forms of relating.

This book explores these phenomena and follows the perspectives that they open up. They are perspectives that traverse the heartland of analytic theory, so that the scope of the book is both extensive and ambitious. In tracing these threads across the analytic heartland it develops a model that offers critiques of, but also a possible reconciliation between, the major models—Freudian, Kleinian, Jungian, and Lacanian. Specifically, the notion of the unconscious is seen to have evolved, via Freud's development of his second, structural model—the ego, id, and superego—and through the theories of Bion, Matte Blanco, attachment theory, and neuroscience, to a position where it can be seen as an organ for affective processing, not dissimilar to a pared down version of the Jungian self, as outlined in Chapter Six. Similarly, a critique of the Jungian understanding of the ego as overly narrow, also delineated in Chapter Six, could bring the Jungian nearer the psychoanalytic position without, it is argued here, substantially depleting the richness of either model.

The book is, however, primarily clinical in nature. The delineation of the relationship between the different models is not the prime focus, so that the consequences for these models are often only sketched or suggested, rather than fully elaborated.

What follows in this introduction is an outline of the model developed herein, which is further fleshed out and explored in the following chapters.

Regarding those experiences which feel particularly powerful, real, and true but which are accompanied by little or no sense of "I"—this constitutes a paradox, as the individual may feel strongly that he or she is particularly "himself" or "herself" at these times. It can be understood that such intense experiences follow from immersion in one part of the personality only (Redfearn, 1985), or even one feeling only, with the individual being out of touch with the other elements of the personality. At these times the integrative aspect of ego-functioning, which carries the sense of "I", is suspended.

The core thread of the model developed here understands that our sense of ourselves can be separated into a *sense of being* and a *sense of "I"*, though these are not normally distinguished subjectively. We experience our sense of being (in a pure form) when we become *absorbed* in experience, be it a powerful feeling, experience, or sensation or even, perhaps, an activity, such as reading a book, making love, or doing the washing-up. To repeat, at this time we are absorbed in one part of our subjective experience, out of touch with the wider elements of our personality. Christopher Bollas (1992) calls such experience "simple self-experience".

Experiencing only a sense of being, in the absence of a sense of "I", feels powerful, real, and true. It can also be experienced as terrible or sublime, as the experience comes to constitute, subjectively, the *whole* of our being. Such immediate experience is normally framed by the broader sense of self—the sense of "I"—that *contains, filters, links, and puts in perspective*, the current experience. Bollas calls this broader kind of experience "complex self-experience". While the shift to simple self-experience, where there is no sense of "I", is normal, natural, and everyday, under some circumstances it can be intensely problematic because it represents a suspension of integrative ego-functioning.

The sense of "I" is understood, here, to constitute the subjective experience of developed, integrative ego-functioning—the integration of the different aspects and elements of self and object representations. It requires a certain degree of ego-development—Chapter Two, Section I explores the complex nature of the ego and ego-functioning at some length. This stable, developed sense of "I" is different from the narrow and impermanent sense of "I", which is understood to be the self-referential element of subjectivity—the evanescent sense of "I" associated with such actions and senses of being as "I am eating a sandwich" or "I am driving to work".

This book also develops the notion of "flexible ego-functioning", which is both broad and inclusive of all elements of the personality *and* open to the affective core of the individual. This concept, embodying the view of identity developed here, offers a different way of understanding what is sometimes referred to as "ego weakness".

The division of the sense of self into a sense of being and a sense of "I" parallels the two forms of consciousness that the neuroscientist Antonio Damasio (1999) delineates, from a neurological point of view: *core consciousness* (corresponding to the sense of being) and *extended consciousness* (carrying a sense of "I"). These categorizations also correspond, broadly, to Stern's (1985) delineation of the non-verbal and verbal senses of self.

This division of the sense of self throws new light on certain clinical configurations and, in particular, phenomena related to destructiveness. Individuals can be seen to take their (core) sense of being to be their "real selves", and to turn against their integrative ego-functioning, disavowing their sense of "I". Such a disavowal is, in part, in the interests of more powerful affective experience, but it also brings in its wake more complete contact and intimacy with others (an adhesive identification (Meltzer, 1975)). Bollas (1992, p. 16) also describes the way in which the individual in a simple self state is "transformed" into an object *inside* the other. That is to say, the shift in the self-state represents the individual losing his or her distinctness and becoming contained in the other. Bollas's transformation corresponds, perhaps, to a more benevolent form of Meltzer's (1992) claustrum. Issues of identity can, therefore, be seen to powerfully affect and determine the individual's forms of relationship. The issue of identity is a complex one, which is explored in Chapter Two, Section II.

The experience of a sense of being, without a sense of "I", can also be understood in terms of the second thread of this book—affect. When the individual disavows their integrative ego-functioning they become immersed in the experience of affect, centred in the current moment. This can also be understood in terms of primary process functioning (Freud), beta functioning (Bion), the archetypal nature of the unconscious (Jung), or the unbounded nature of affect (Green). Clinical experience demonstrates that such affects are experienced subjectively as "infinite", that is to say, they are experienced as timeless, endless, powerful, eternal, numinous, archetypal, or oceanic, and imbued with truth, beauty, awe, or horror. Such subjective experience is understood, here, in terms of Matte Blanco's (1975) concept of symmetry, whereby, in the absence of ego-functioning, only the *sameness* between experiences is registered. In this way the individual, living intensely in the moment, experiences things as infinite, as one experience is linked seamlessly to the next, with the differences ignored (Chapter Three). The interplay and inter-relatedness of identity and the subjective experience of affect lead to this being understood as an "*identity-affect*" model.

Following Matte Blanco, and drawing on neuroscience, affect theory, attachment theory, and developmental research, this book develops and details a model of functioning of the non-verbal self in the *right hemisphere* of the brain. Integral to the functioning of this hemisphere is the operation of the *affective appraisal mechanism*, which is understood to constantly appraise experience in terms of the *sameness and difference* with/from/to the individual's developing set of preferences. This mechanism is understood to be the primary form of connection with, and relation to, others. The sensitivity to sameness and aversion to difference is understood to underlie the individual's desire for union and reaction to separation, which plays such an important role clinically. This mechanism is experienced subjectively as the sensitive, *"emotional core"* of the individual (West, 2004). Emde (1983) also describes an "affective core" to the personality that he sees as central to the prerepresentational self.

The later development of the predominantly verbal, *left hemisphere* and the frontal lobes of the brain and, thus, the integrative elements of ego-functioning, allow the individual to react to reality from the broader base of the different elements of the personality. The continued functioning of the predominantly affective right hemisphere, however, augments, and is intrinsic to, a proper appreciation of reality. This understanding of the affective appraisal mechanism offers a different frame of reference from which to understand paranoid experience, in terms of it being the veridical (accurate, veracious), though narrow, experience of reality, when ego-functioning is suspended, rather than being, for example, solely delusional or based on phantasy (Chapters One, Two and Four).

Affect is understood to be central to this model of the mind, and the individual's development is understood against the background of the primary caregiver's regulation of the individual's affect and, thereby, his or her sense of self—the caregiver is a *self-regulating other*, in Stern's (1985) terms. This offers an explanation of the profound and continuing significance of the other on the individual's sense of self.

In this book the self is seen as a vehicle rather than as an edifice. Individuals are understood to be continually active in manipulating their experience of themselves and their life, sometimes quite radically (and often with paradoxical and problematic outcomes), rather than seeing the individual as the fixed outcome of a developmental process. In this way the individual's identity and, specifically, his or her sense of self, is seen as an organizing, motivating, guiding, limiting, and sometimes determining factor on the individual and the course of his or her life. These issues have consequences for theories of identity (Chapter Two, Section II), projective identification (Chapter Four), analytic technique (Chapter Five), spiritual experience (Chapter Six), and the Jungian concept of the self (Chapter Six).

One further consequence of these ideas is that a strong, active principle (the preferencing of similarity and aversion to difference) is placed *within*, and is *intrinsic to*, the psyche itself. This offers a perspective *in addition to* that of the individual's particular personal history. This principle/mechanism is understood to be a template for what is significant to the individual—essentially the mechanism for registering change and embodying the individual's own point of view. The mechanism is not understood to be simply internalized from parental figures but is seen, instead, to have influenced the interaction with those figures and to have determined, therefore, what was internalized in the first place.

Finally, the affective appraisal mechanism, with its preferencing of sameness and aversion to difference (in respect to its developing set of preferences), is understood to constitute the basic narcissistic mechanism of the psyche. This model is parallel to the views of Symington (1993), who holds that narcissism is the pathology that underlies all others. Here, schizoid, hysteric, borderline, and narcissistic personality organizations, which will be examined in detail in Part II of the book, are understood to represent different reactions to, and configurations of, this affective appraisal mechanism in response to the challenges and difficulties of meeting reality and developing flexible-enough ego-functioning.

PART I
AN "IDENTITY–AFFECT" MODEL

CHAPTER ONE

The clinical picture

Introduction

An outline of the theoretical picture having been given in the Introduction, this chapter first describes the analysis of a patient, whom I will call Rachel, with whom the themes in this book began to take more substantial shape for me. The chapter then introduces theory relevant to the clinical picture, and outlines the identity–affect model, before returning to complete the clinical narrative, drawing together the theoretical and clinical threads.

Rachel's analysis was far from a model one. It represents, in part, the story of my analytic development from inexperience, struggling with boundary issues, and trying to come to grips with this kind of clinical situation, to a more developed analytic attitude. The "errors" were crucial to the generation of the model developed herein and tell us, I believe, much that is important about the nature and functioning of the psyche.

This chapter is a substantially modified version of a paper that appeared in the *Journal of Analytical Psychology*, 49(4): 521–552 (2004).

Clinical outline

I had been seeing Rachel four times a week for about six years and, despite my best efforts, things were not going well. Rachel had originally sought analysis to help her deal with her many fears and anxieties: she felt she had no substance or resources in herself, she was powerfully reliant on others, and feared she would not survive in the world. She was frightened that she would black out in public and had done so on at least one occasion.

There was an initial period, characterized by a predominantly positive transference, where Rachel was very appreciative of the analysis and fully committed to the work on her difficulties, fears, dreams, and desires. After six years, however, rather than feeling more stable and secure, she was now deeply regressed and acutely sensitive to everything that was going on around her. In particular, she was sensitive to my attitude and position with respect to her— whether she felt I was being, for example, warm and concerned or distant and irritated.

I realized that there were many occasions when Rachel could quite accurately gauge what I was feeling; however, her perceptions and reactions to me seemed, at first, mystifying. These reactions were also becoming increasingly extreme. If she did not experience me as warm, sympathetic, understanding or concerned, she would experience terror, panic, acute pain, and rage, feeling that she was dying or being killed off by me. She would sometimes tell me that she would not survive to the next session, that she would die or would kill herself, or would not be able to stop from harming herself; she would, then, hide all the knives and scissors in her house.

Rachel would also tell me that if I would not hug her or answer her questions she could not continue with the analysis. There were occasions when she would ring me at home, demanding answers to questions that had come up in the day's session. Sometimes these were hypothetical questions about whether I would ever hug her, or what contact there might be between us after the analysis had finished.

If at all possible I would not answer her questions directly, but would rather try to explore these issues with her. Frequently this was not satisfactory for her and a crisis would ensue where Rachel would rage at me, telling me how bad I was. She would make clear what the consequences of my not answering her questions were—her hurting herself, not surviving, or leaving the analysis. On two occasions she threatened to report me to my registering body. As we lived through these crises, Rachel would usually emerge from them apparently feeling stronger and that she had really "got to the point". She would often tell me she was grateful to me for maintaining my line.

There were rare occasions when I did answer directly, as the discussions had become interminable, hypothetical, and seemed, to me, meaningless. I felt I wanted to bring them back down to earth and/or I did not know what else to do or say. Perhaps, sometimes, unconsciously, I wanted to avoid the inevitable further confrontations. Answering such questions often led to a greater sense of confusion and expectation—if I would answer *this* question why would I not answer *all* her questions?

Following the crises things might be all right for a little while, but something else would soon trigger another crisis that would this time come on more suddenly and acutely. Rachel would then experience things more deeply, she would fragment more quickly and express herself more powerfully. She was clearly becoming increasingly deeply regressed.

Over time I was able to see that the trigger for these crises depended on whether I was identifying with Rachel's position—seeing things her way and acting in a way that coincided with what she wanted—or whether, instead, I was maintaining my own, separate position and perspective, which did not coincide with hers.

Much of the pressure she put upon me was to encourage, cajole, or force me to see things the way she did. This was both to experience the security, satisfaction, and gratification of feeling alongside or at one with me (this included wanting me to feel sexually towards her) *and* to avoid the terrible feelings of annihilation, terror, pain, and rage that would occur if I was *not* identified but separate. This situation was underlined by the fact that she felt she had no substance herself, and so relied on me to guarantee that she felt good about herself, to give her some stability, and to provide her with her very sense of existence.

One of the fruits of the first few years' work with Rachel was being able to identify the terrible mix of feelings she experienced:

to recognize them as terror, panic, rage, and so on. Previously, Rachel had been unable to recognize these as her *own* feelings, but had felt that she was being assailed from outside and taken over by a force, like some kind of daemon, that she did not understand and could not bear; she had a series of dreams about just such a daemon.

Rachel was thus in a terrible state, reeling from crisis to crisis— crises that might last a few moments, a session, a day, a week, or even longer. I felt that she genuinely believed, at these times, that she would die. As time passed, however, and she did survive, she and I, in our different ways, seemed almost to get used to living in this terrible way.

She felt that despite, or even because of, the terrible crises we were getting down to the real issues that had never been reached before. She would tell me that she felt very real and alive. I was left hoping, albeit with increasingly less conviction, that something would come of all this, that the regression was necessary, and that it would lead somewhere. Clearly I was under tremendous pressure too, and, as the years passed, and as Rachel's mental state deterio- rated, so the analysis also took its toll on me.

Before looking at the way in which the analysis proceeded, the evolution of the transference and the countertransference, and describing something of Rachel's early life, the question of how what was going on might be understood theoretically is addressed.

Analyses of the clinical situation

There are several main conceptualizations that best capture the picture with Rachel.

Freud would describe the clinical situation described above as a negative therapeutic reaction—a type of resistance born from the fact that certain patients appear to prefer suffering to being cured. Freud linked this to a number of factors: unconscious guilt, and the subject's wish to prove his superiority over the analyst (1923b), masochism (1924c), super-ego resistance (1926d) and, ultimately, the "irreducible nature of the death instinct" (1937c). Although the term "negative therapeutic reaction" is over-determined, in so far as having a number of different explanations associated with it, it is useful descriptively, and shows the ways that Freud was struggling with similar clinical issues.

Michael Balint would describe the situation with Rachel as a malignant regression, where the patient seeks "gratification of (his) instinctual cravings . . . an external event, an action by his object" (Balint, 1968, p. 141). The clinical picture he describes was very similar to my experience with Rachel. He writes:

> . . . it seemed that [the patient] could never have enough; as soon as one of their primitive wishes or needs was satisfied, it was replaced by a new wish or craving, equally demanding and urgent. This, in some cases, led to the development of addiction-like states which were very difficult to handle, and in some cases proved—as Freud predicted—intractable. [*ibid.*, p. 138]

He continues:

> As long as the patient's expectations and demands are met, the therapist is allowed to observe most interesting, revealing events and *pari passu* his patient will feel better, appreciative and grateful. This is one side of the coin, but there is an obverse side too. If the expectations are not or cannot be met, what follows is unending suffering or unending vituperation, or both together. [*ibid.*, p. 140]

Klein (1946) talks in terms of projective identification, and addresses both the pressure put on the other and the patient's lack of sense of self. She sees the depletion of the sense of self as a result of the projection of disavowed parts of the self on to the other. The attempt to harm, possess, or control the other is due to the fact that the individual does not distinguish self from other, and attempts to control those parts of themselves that they have projected into the other by controlling the other. Chapter Four takes up the question of projective identification in detail.

Bion (1959) developed the notion of projective identification, contrasting normal with excessive projective identification, and proposed the theory of container–contained (1962a) where the patient's unmanageable affects (the "contained"—beta elements) are transformed in the container (the (m)other/analyst) into manageable, thinkable, alpha elements. Bion (1959) also described the patient's attacks on any links to objects experienced as separate from the self. He addressed the attacks on the patient's and analyst's thinking capacities, writing that: "[the] lack of progress in any direction must be attributed in part to the destruction of a capacity for curiosity and the consequent ability to learn" (Bion, 1959, p. 101).

Meltzer (1992) developed Bion's theory of the container–contained into the concept of the claustrum, where the individual aims to intrusively take up residence in the other's insides for defensive purposes, just as I felt Rachel wanted to reside inside me.

Betty Joseph (1982) described one group of patients whom she felt were "addicted to near-death", and who were extremely passive and masochistically excited by the patterns of self-annihilating despair and self-destruction in which they wish to get caught up with the analyst. Rachel could also be seen in this way.

The Jungian analyst, Michael Fordham (1974), describes a syndrome that he calls a "defence of the self" where the patient attacks anything that is seen as other than self, describing this as a primitive biological aversion to alien matter. (Britton [1998, p. 58] echoes this same biological aversion to otherness.) Fordham describes how, in the analysis, "not-self" parts of the analyst, "seen by the patient as technique, method etc." are attacked by the patient. He describes these attacks as "violent attempts to attack and do away with the bad object-[which] can reach a level at which one must speak in terms of annihilation" (Fordham, 1974, p. 140). Describing the clinical situation that, on occasion, echoed my experience with Rachel, he writes:

> In its most dramatic form the syndrome may develop so that the interview becomes filled with negative affects and confusion, until the whole of the dialectic seems to break down. The time may be filled with denigrating the analyst's interventions, ending up in loud groans, screams or tears whenever the analyst speaks: the patient uses every means at his disposal to prevent the analyst's interventions from becoming meaningful. [Fordham, 1974, p. 140]

Donald Kalsched (1996), another Jungian analyst, describes a form of defence similar to an identification with the aggressor, which he calls an "archetypal defence of the personal spirit". Here the individual forms a punishing inner object that keeps the core of the individual isolated in order to prevent exposure to further hurt. The daemon that Rachel dreamt of repeatedly would correspond to just such a malevolent object.

Peter Fonagy (1991), investigating borderline phenomena, talks of the vital importance of reflective function—the capacity to conceive of conscious and unconscious mental states in oneself and others—and understands the patient's disavowal of otherness as an "inhibition and defence against conceiving of his own or his objects' mental functioning".

Finally, in terms of categorization and personality type, Britton usefully develops Rosenfeld's views on thin-skinned and thick-skinned narcissism (Britton, 1998, pp. 46ff.), where Rachel could be seen as a thin-skinned narcissist, which Britton calls borderline, reacting hypersensitively to her objects.

Predominantly, however, Rachel could be understood to be hysteric, although she showed marked borderline features. As Khan writes: "the hysteric seeks, omnipotently, to solve new life tasks with sexual reverie and complicity with the adult humans, and beseeches them to take over the necessary and required ego-functions" (Khan, 1975, p. 53).

While Rachel's predominant personality type might have been hysteric, there is much overlap between hysteric, borderline, narcissistic, and even schizoid functioning (see Part II), and further analysis and investigation revealed much about the nature of the psyche itself and the reason for that overlap.

In summary then, Rachel could be seen to be in a malignant regression, employing excessive projective identification, aiming to reside in me in the manner of a claustrum, defended against anything she experienced as not-self, attacking links to anything experienced as separate, and attacking her own and my capacities for thinking and reflective function; in terms of personality type she was predominantly hysteric. I found these views the most clinically accessible, descriptive, and useful.

While these theories were helpful and sometimes illuminating, showing me, reassuringly, that at least people had trodden similar ground before, I felt that none fully reflected the situation before me. The traditional Kleinian picture, in particular, concerning the loss of sense of self being seen as due to parts of the self having been projected on to the other, just did not feel quite right; for example, the depletion of Rachel's sense of self did not seem to be because of parts of herself were being projected into me (although I could see that what I did had a very big effect in determining what she felt)—this explanation did not do justice to the nature of the interaction that was taking place. As the situation stood, I was not sure what to do (or not to do) in order to move on from the impasse in the analysis with Rachel.

The identity–affect model

One of the main elements of the analysis which required particular attention, and which threw particular light on the question of identity, was Rachel's feeling that she was essentially nothing and that she had no substance. This preoccupied her enormously and seemed pivotal in her demand that I stand in for or, at least, stand by her in order to provide her with some stability and solidity. I saw that the more deeply Rachel experienced things, the more real and true they felt to her, and the more certain she was about them. This experience was also mirrored with other patients. It was not simply true of clinical situations, however, but applied across the whole range of "everyday" beliefs and experiences. *The times that Rachel felt that she was more truly "herself" were those which, at the same time, paradoxically, she had little or no sense of "I".*

I came to see that there was a part of her that operated predominantly in an affective manner, by which she was dominated. I understood this to be her "emotional core" (West, 2004)—a term which I hope gets close to the subjective feel of this part of the self.

These affective experiences can be understood to be structured, coloured, and to some extent generated by an *affective appraisal mechanism* operating in the right hemisphere of the brain from the beginning of life. It operates by registering the sameness and difference between what the individual experiences and their set of (developing) preferences. These samenesses and differences are registered affectively as pleasurable or unpleasurable, good or bad, and experience thus becomes affectively toned. The results of such experiences of self-in-interaction-with-the-environment are stored as *internal working models* (Bowlby, 1969; Knox, 2003). The notion of appraisal has a rich history, and the understanding of the affective appraisal mechanism developed here is related to the notions of Arnold (1960), Bowlby (1969), Matte Blanco (1975), Stern (1985), Watson (1994, 1995) and Damasio (1999), as is outlined in Chapter Three.

I came to understand that Rachel was functioning primarily from her emotional core with little, or only sporadic, integrative ego-functioning. As a result, the nature and functioning of affect and the affective appraisal mechanism was prominent. The affective appraisal mechanism is at the heart of a number of essential functions: perception, classification, and appraisal; relating, self-regulation, and affect regulation; distinguishing self from other and developing a picture of the self; orientating the individual to the world; developing a picture of the relations between self and other; generating a sense of being; structuring experiences of infinite affect; and providing the primary link to reality. These functions are outlined below and explored in more detail in later chapters.

Perception, classification, and appraisal

Perception is not neutral. At the core of the perceptual system is an affectively based mechanism for appraising the significance of stimuli. This affective appraisal mechanism is an essential part of an organ of consciousness by and through which we perceive the world. As the neuroscientist LeDoux says, "the core of the emotional system is . . . a mechanism for computing the affective significance of stimuli" (LeDoux in Schore, 1994, p. 287).

The brainstem and the right hemisphere are the first to develop in the life of the infant (Schore, 1994) and are the first elements in the more sophisticated overall mechanism of the brain. The operation of the right hemisphere underlies the operation of the later-developing left hemisphere and the rational functions.[1] When integrated with the ego, the emotional core and the affective appraisal mechanism are experienced subjectively as, for example, intuition, "instinct", or sensitivity.

This mechanism for recognizing sameness and difference means that the individual can begin to classify experiences, at first into the categories of same or different, familiar or new, pleasant or unpleasant, good or bad, frightening or safe. As Matte Blanco (1975) explains, in order to register that this large, hairy, four-legged animal is a horse, we have to be able to recognize the similarities between this and other animals that we have previously recognized in this category. Similarly, in order to register whether a new situation is safe or dangerous, we have to register the similarity of this situation to previous safe or dangerous situations. For the infant, this capacity allows them to begin to distinguish things and orientate themselves towards the world, differentiating, for example, mother from others from the beginning of life.

Due to the suspension of Rachel's ego-functioning (see Chapter 2, Section I), she was acutely sensitive to whatever was going on between us. She experienced things deeply and appraised her experience in terms of good or bad, frightening or safe, and so forth; people were experienced as being either on her side or against her. This was a paranoid form of experience where splitting predominated as she tried to avoid bad, and ensure good, experience.

In the adult whose integrative ego-functioning is operating, and where the affective appraisal mechanism is integrated with other faculties of the psyche, the attunement to the similarity with others gives a sense of kinship and permits empathy, care, and concern, while registering difference allows an appreciation of boundaries and a delineation of the limits on the self.

Relating, self-regulation and affect regulation

The highly-attuned, affective perception allows us to ascertain the state of the other and their relatedness to us. It is the foundation-stone of relatedness. Stern (1985) describes how the caregiver acts as a *self-regulating other*,[2] regulating the individual's sense of self and, specifically, their *sense of being*. "Self-regulation" here refers to another person regulating the individual's sense of self, rather than the individual regulating him or herself, for which the awkward-sounding term *auto*-regulation is used.

Integrative ego-functioning carries the sense of "I" and, when this was suspended, Rachel's *whole* experience was determined by what she was experiencing in that particular moment. She experienced only a sense of being—this could be, for example, a sense of being afraid, a sense of being angry, and so on. At this time, therefore, the regulation of her affects was the same as the regulation of her sense of being—*affect regulation was equivalent to self-regulation*. The infant also experiences the sense of being as encompassing their *whole being* due to the lack of development of their integrative ego-functioning; as Fordham (1987) describes, the experience of whole objects *precedes* that of part objects.

Another way of describing these phenomena is to say that the (m)other acts in order to regulate the infant's feelings/affects—the process of affect regulation. Schore (2001) describes how the mother is almost entirely responsible for regulating the infant's affects for the first six months of life as the infant has not developed the structures necessary for affect auto-regulation. While these structures take rudimentary form at six months, they achieve more substantial form at one year, and greater coherence at 15–18 months with the onset of the verbal self.

Rachel wanted me to take on responsibility for the regulation of her affects and her sense of self; indeed, she felt it was imperative that I do so. The struggle for her to come to regulate herself, to a significant degree, under the auspices of her *own* ego-functioning, was the core thread of the analysis.

Distinguishing self from other and developing a picture of the self

Damasio (1999, pp. 19–23) describes how the infant continually maps the state of the living body, the external world, and the relationship between the two. There is a constant scanning of the inner world, the external world, and their inter-relation, in order to search for sameness and difference; in other words, to register *change*. Damasio understands that the individual thereby develops an internal map of the self, which he calls the *proto-self*, that changes little in relation to the external map. For example, as we simply turn our head through 180° the external map changes a great deal, while our internal map, the proto-self, changes little in comparison. When there is a change to our *inner* world, for example, when we catch a cold or break a leg, this is flagged up in a different (usually more disturbing) way.

Fonagy, Gergely, Jurist, and Target (2002) cite Watson (1994, 1995) who calls the mechanism for registering sameness and difference the *contingency-detection mechanism*. Fonagy and colleagues write of the initial attunement to sameness in the first three months of life: "[This] initial attention bias serves the evolutionary function of developing a *primary representation of the bodily self* as a distinct object in the environment" (Fonagy, Gergely, Jurist, & Target, 2002, p. 167, original italics).

With the development of the left hemisphere, there arises the ability for what Fonagy and his colleagues call *second-order representation*, which allows there to be reflection on the primary affective experience and gives us reflexive self-consciousness. Schore reports on the neuroscientist, Ohman's work:

> Ohman's (1986) studies demonstrate two dissociable modes of processing affective information, a rapid, unconscious, pre-attentive analysis of an emotional stimulus followed by a later conscious assessment of the relevance of the same emotional stimulus. [Schore, 1994, p. 238]

This second-order representation also allows a linking up with the other elements of the personality, thereby affording broader self-representation (an integrated "picture" of the different elements of the self) and, subjectively, a sense of "I". This broader perspective is what Damasio (1999) calls *extended consciousness*. These developments lead to integrative ego-functioning (see Chapter 2, Section I), which gives the ability to reflect on current experience and allows the individual to balance that experience against broader experience and, thereby, to make it less intense, more manageable, and to contain it.

Rachel had disavowed her ego-functioning in order to achieve intense experience with me that, however, "required" me to contain her and that experience. It was a form of adhesive identification (Meltzer, 1975) or a claustrum (Meltzer, 1992). It was not that Rachel had insufficient ego *development*. Rather, it was that this was a form of experience to which she was well used from childhood, but which also, crucially, she found both extremely attractive *and* from which she found it difficult to extricate herself. Its attraction, as will be explored, was both in its defensive opportunities—a continued reliance on me which meant that she could avoid facing the struggles of a more independent life—and in the intense quality of experience that could be achieved. Rachel could suspend and disavow her ego-functioning through immersion in current, affective experience, relying on me to act as a self-regulating other.

Orientating the individual to the world

The affective appraisal mechanism is not neutral. It *prefers* sameness and *is averse to* difference (in relation to the set of developing preferences). This depends upon the degree of development; for example, Elizabeth Urban describes a six-month-old and an eight-month-old child reacting differently to a doll being taken away—the six-month-old reacting with puzzlement, the eight-month-old with distress (Urban, 1988). These characteristic reactions mirror the degree of cognitive–emotional development and, therefore, the significance that the doll might have to each infant.

The sensitivity to sameness and difference does not necessarily mean that the individual always acts crudely so as to achieve sameness and avoid difference, it is just that this will play an important part in *processing* their experience. The individual will "naturally" be related to the constantly-changing stream of reality and will feel in some way dull and lifeless if they become defended against or dissociated from that stream. The affective processing acts in relation to this stream of experience and can apply in a crude or a more mature manner. For example, an adult with developed, integrative ego-functioning will register that giving to charity makes them poorer (something, presumably, undesirable), but may nevertheless choose to give to charity because of their broader set of preferences. Without integrative ego-functioning, such preferencing of sameness and difference operates much more overtly and crudely, as in Rachel's case, at times. For example, Rachel reacted powerfully against separations from me, ignoring the broader perspective of the necessity of such separations (for both of us).

This reaction does *not* mean, therefore, that the individual is unrelated to reality, simply that the individual *appraises* experience more narrowly, according to the dictates of the present moment. Depending on their particular personality type, personal history, and the status of their ego-functioning, the individual may prefer, for example, a constant stream of heightened experience, disordered experience, or an experience of changelessness. Attachment patterns such as secure, anxious–avoidant, anxious–resistant, and disorganized–disorientated also reflect such choices (see Holmes, 2001).

This mechanism of appraisal underlies the operation of the pleasure principle and can account for the development of the reality principle (see Chapter Three). It is not the same, however, to prefer sameness and be averse to difference as to seek pleasure and avoid unpleasure. A child may become attuned to a set of circumstances and prefer those circumstances because they are *familiar* rather than being, strictly speaking, pleasurable, although there will be a certain sense of satisfaction (broadly defined) involved in achieving sameness between the situation and the individual's set of preferences.

Rachel's pattern of relating to me was certainly not always pleasurable for her, but it was a manner of relating to which she adhered resolutely. While it was certainly familiar to her, I also came to understand it to be due to her subjective experience of her identity and to a vicious circle of relating that ensued therefrom, as will be explored shortly.

Developing a picture of the relations between self and other

Being primarily object-related from the beginning, the affective appraisal mechanism operates in order to orientate the infant/individual to relational patterns with primary caregivers, rather than simply to represent static images of self and other. Sandler's *early* understanding of the "representational world" was just such a static model (Sandler & Rosenblatt, 1962). Stern, on the other hand, calls such relational structures *representations of interactions which are generalized* (RIGs), although he now prefers the phrase *ways-of-being-with-others* (Stern, 1998, p. xv). Attachment theory knows such structures as *internal working models* (Bowlby, 1969).

These internal working models remain in adult life, unless modified through experience. Being non-verbal structures (which develop before the left hemispheric, structured, integrated ego-functioning), they remain, in some respects, unconscious determinants of behaviour stored as *implicit memory* (Stern et al., 1998; Fonagy, 1999), often in conflict with more mature, conscious, integrated, ego-orientated behaviour. In this way they often become the significant subject matter of analysis. While they represent internalizations of early interactions, they also have their own internal structure and nature—the preferencing of similarity and aversion to difference—which must be taken into account in integrating them with the ego.

The reaction to separateness need not, therefore, be explained *wholly* in relation to particular childhood experiences, but relates significantly to the internal functioning and nature of the affective appraisal mechanism. Rachel's interactions with me could not be explained wholly by her personal history.

Generating a sense of being (core consciousness)

The mechanism of appraisal is never without content. The content is the individual's continual perception of, and reaction to, their inner and outer world. It is affectively toned, in the sense of being filtered and preferenced. That which draws our attention—what we notice—is a matter of *selection*, although an "emotion" is not always triggered. While there is always a preferencing and a selection of information, emotions and feelings usually only occur when something particularly significant is being flagged up to consciousness (see Chapter Three).

This stream of experience is the individual's basic subjectivity and perspective, and provides them with a *sense of being*. In addition, there are those sets of experiences with which the individual identifies and which he or she takes to be "me". In the absence of integrative ego-functioning, the individual's sense of self is completely encompassed by the particular experience he or she is having—there is a sense of being but no sense of "I". There is no continuity to the experience other than that which is provided by the background *proto-self* (Damasio, 1999), against which experience is, in part, "measured". Stern describes the development of this limited continuity in infants as the "sense of an emergent self", which he specifically relates to Damasio's proto-self (Stern, 1998).

This "sense of being" is what Damasio describes as *core consciousness*, which

> provides the organism with a sense of self about one moment—now—and about one place—here. The scope of core consciousness is here and now. Core consciousness does not illuminate the future, and the only past it vaguely lets us glimpse is that which occurred in the instant just before. There is no elsewhere, there is no before, there is no after. [Damasio, 1999, p. 16]

For much of the time Rachel was living entirely in the moment and was completely determined by her current experience. It amounted to her whole experience—there was no elsewhere, no before, and no after. There was, however, the rudimentary activity of identification and disavowal by which she accepted certain experiences as "me" and disavowed others as "not-me". In particular, she tended to identify with powerful experience and did not feel "herself" if her experiences were not intense. As Fairbairn (1943) and Klein (1946) hold, splitting occurs not only in regard to external experience, but also in respect to the individual themselves—which they called the splitting of the ego. In contrast to Fairbairn and Klein, this model holds that there is little intrinsic coherence between (subsequent) experiences in infants unless vouchsafed by the primary caregiver. Through these forms of primitive defences (see Chapter Two, Section I)—splitting and projective identification—Rachel exerted considerable pressure over her present moment to try to make it acceptable and bearable for her. In this sense it could be said that she was not truly "living in the moment", as Rachel herself pointed out to me, as she was trying to hang on to previous "moments" or to alter what would have been more "natural" to this "moment".

Experiences of infinite affect

Living in the moment—living without a sense of "I"—means that each experience is powerful and intense. Matte Blanco (1975, 1988) describes such experiences as infinite—limitless. For example, with no before and no after, each experience will feel as if it is going on forever. This could be endless pleasure/heaven or endless pain/hell. Neither will there be any particular "edges" to space, as one place is unrelated to any other. Experience can take on a sublime quality, although that may be tinged with beauty or horror. The individual's sense of being will feel full (Weil, 1956), rich, powerful, exciting, and energetic. Jung referred to certain of such powerful experiences in the adult as *numinous*, while Freud called them *oceanic*. Rachel's experiences were sometimes sublime, but often unbearably terrible.

The primary link to reality

The affective appraisal mechanism gives us our primary reaction to reality—it is our first gut-level response. Rachel was intensely tuned in to me and to what I was feeling and doing through her affective responses, her emotional core. Although these responses may have seemed warped, or even paranoid, at times, in contrast to the more considered, broader reaction, filtered through integrative ego-functioning, they represented her initial "take" on the situation. This is the "rapid, unconscious, pre-attentive analysis of an emotional stimulus" (Schore, 1994, p. 238) that Ohman (1986) describes. Matte Blanco (1975) points out how this first gut reaction may be very necessary when faced with danger—we may need a spontaneous reaction to get us out of trouble: too much "thinking" could be fatal.

While Rachel frequently experienced the current moment as determining her whole being, with the experience being nearly infinite in extent, yet it was, in a significant way, reality orientated in that it did concern my actual behaviour, comments, and attitude towards her. Being in touch with this emotional core of her personality made Rachel feel vitally alive and spontaneous and she valued it highly. With her integrative ego-functioning suspended or disavowed, however, she was flooded by these emotional experiences and her reactions were, in some significant sense, paranoid.

To sum up: with her ego-functioning suspended, Rachel experienced everything more intensely—it felt more powerful, more real, more significant, and more true to her because, without integrative ego-functioning to give the broader view and to frame and contain each particular experience, each experience came to constitute her whole being. Each new experience was vitally important. She was living intensely in the now, which was very attractive so long as I acted to vouchsafe a good experience of being for her. As a very significant part of her world, in the context of the intense, intimate, analytic relationship, I came to function very much as a *self-regulating other*. She became profoundly dependent on me for her sense of being, which felt to her like a dependence on me for her whole existence.

* * *

Further elements of the clinical picture

Annihilation

As well as trying to achieve states of identification and union with me, which she experienced as sublime in nature, Rachel wanted to avoid states of difference, which she experienced as painful and terrifying, and which led to states of disintegration and annihilation. This was not simply splitting between good/pleasant and bad/unpleasant experiences; rather these were experiences of affect that were experienced as infinite in nature and felt to threaten her whole existence and identity.

When I was separate from Rachel—in particular, when she did not experience me as regulating her self in the way that she wanted—she experienced me as abandoning, horribly cruel, uncaring, and even murderous (particularly as she knew I knew how she wanted me to behave). As described above, while such feelings might well be described as paranoid and seen as the result of an unconscious phantasy (see Chapter Four), I understood them to be the result of Rachel's *actual* experience of me and, for that reason, held with greater certainty, conviction, and vehemence. This context also, perhaps, gives a sense of why Rachel was splitting so powerfully—avoiding bad experience, and attacking the bad analyst-me, and trying to secure good experience, and adhering to the good analyst-me.

There is a further factor that makes such experiences of separation feel truly like annihilation. As described at the beginning of this chapter, Rachel said that she felt she would die, that she would not survive, or that she would kill herself: she had a constant, underlying sense that she could not cope. The loss of integrative ego-functioning means that the individual becomes alienated from his or her usual sense of self, and, in particular, from his or her body, that is held, in part, by the proto-self and in part by the later-developing ego. Freud (1923b, p. 26) called the ego a body ego (the ego eventually subsumes the earlier proto-self). The loss of ego-functioning, then, can be experienced as an unreal feeling, a dissociation from the body, and, commonly, as dying. The more that ego-functioning is disavowed, the more acute is the experience of dying. The individual also senses that, in relinquishing their integrative ego-functioning, they are relinquishing the broader awareness of self and that they are thus left exposed to the world, dependent on the vagaries of others—they recognize that they are living in dangerous waters. At the extreme, discordant experiences can even disrupt the sense of continuity that comes from the regular, background experience of the proto-self—an example of this is given in Chapter Three.

The vicious circle

This experience of annihilation is one of the factors that leads to a vicious circle of dependence that is a vital phenomenon clinically. The more the individual loses or disavows their ego-functioning, either to further the sublime experiences of union or to avoid the terrifying experiences of separation, the more they are affected and regulated by the other, for better and for worse. The good experiences feel increasingly good and the bad experiences feel increasingly bad. In alarm and desperation the individual turns to the other for help, protection, and regulation of his or her sense of being. In turning to the other and away from themselves, they further suspend their ego-functioning, weakening their sense of "I", their sense of solidity, and their sense of being a potent agent in the world.

Rachel felt that she had no substance in herself and that it would not be possible for her to extricate herself from her terrible predicament. She felt she needed me to provide good experience and fend off bad experience, and vouchsafe her very sense of existence. Her centre of gravity was, therefore, substantially based in me. The vicious circle had closed over her head so that it seemed to her inconceivable that she could do anything for herself. She was well and truly locked into this desperate cycle and it took much painful struggle and many years of analysis to begin to free her from it. As Fonagy comments: ". . . if the therapist's mentalizing capacity is used by the patient to support and maintain his identity, the patient's dependence upon the therapist for maintaining a relatively stable mental representation of himself will be absolute" (Fonagy, 1991, p. 651).

Disintegration

Subjectively, the loss of ego-functioning feels to the individual as if he or she loses all sense of continuity and "going on being" as each new experience defines his or her whole self. The individual feels that he or she has no stability, not knowing how they will react at the very next moment. There is no peace, calm, or security. They feel that, just because the last experience was all right, this does not mean that the next experience will not be terrible—like the general, they are only as good as their last battle. They experience themselves as a sieve that cannot hold any good experience. Recognizing the occasions when they have had good experience only exacerbates the feelings of guilt and shame that they feel about themselves and their inability to be satisfied with their lot.

When the shift from one state to the next becomes particularly sharp and intense, and ego-functioning is almost completely suspended, the individual feels as if he or she is disintegrating or has disintegrated. Even the continuity provided by the proto-self can, at the extreme, be disrupted (see the example in the discussion of the autistic–contiguous position in Chapter Four).

It is understandable that the individual turns to the analyst/other under these circumstances. In the end, however, they will always feel let down by the other, as did Rachel by me. The other cannot, in the long-term, operate adequately as a self-regulating other and may, indeed, make things worse if they try to do so, which would amount to colluding in a vicious circle that will lead nowhere.

*   *   *

Towards a resolution of the clinical situation

While the development of an understanding of Rachel's experience in terms of identity, annihilation, the vicious circle of dependence, and the regulation of the self by the other, helped me to orientate myself, and make sense of what was going on in the analysis, the practical working-through of this impasse put much more focus on the operation and understanding of affect, the struggle with my countertransference, and the development of a "properly" analytic attitude.

A change in attitude

Rachel and I had reached an impasse whereby we both realized, in our different ways, that something had to change. It was clear that Rachel was asking me to act so as to vouchsafe her existence, with each interaction between us feeling to her like a matter of life-and-death. She continually felt she was being threatened with intense and powerful states of annihilation. She could no longer bear living at this pitch of existence, being in a continual state of disintegration and terror. I had also understood that the way the analysis was proceeding was not helpful to Rachel, and it was becoming unbearable to me.

As an example of this perpetual state of crisis, on one occasion Rachel attacked me virulently, screaming her rage and hatred at me, telling me how appalling I was, how my attitude towards her was just wrong, and how she would complain about me to my training body (this was a threat that she had carried through to some extent previously). After the session I felt, for a period, that I was truly bad and that I wanted to die. In one way this was an example of my compliantly identifying with her wish to destroy me. In another frame I had been completely overcome by her projective identification and she had thus communicated to me how bad she felt.

I was not unduly concerned by this experience in itself as I was able to come to terms with it fairly quickly; however, it was an example of the sort of experience that was being generated in me on a fairly regular basis. I realized that it demonstrated the degree to which my own ego-functioning was being compromised, not only by Rachel's attacks on me but, I came to see, by my method and style of working.

As a result of such interactions between us Rachel determined to "take herself on board", and she backed off from me for a while, wanting to move on to a better way of functioning and genuinely, I felt, wanting to protect me. While this did give us a breathing space, the move was ultimately unsuccessful as, I believe, she still felt on some level that my identification with her was necessary for her very existence. Her desire for my identification would emerge in some other, more subtle form, for example, expressed as her increased anxiety if I did not behave in a certain way, rather than as an overt demand. I understood that as long as her integrative ego-functioning was suspended she would have an underlying sense that her life or death depended upon the occurrences in the next moment, and that she would feel, in a very real sense, in my hands.

While I had long realized that separateness was vitally important clinically, I began to see that I had come to over-identify with Rachel. I began to question whether the separateness that she feared and tried so desperately to avoid would not, in fact, be *helpful* in allowing her to establish her own separate identity, independent of me. This very much echoed what seemed like a rather "old-fashioned" view of identity; I say "old-fashioned" as I was more in tune with views of identity that stressed the effect of others in determining the individual's sense of self, for example, the social constructionist view (see Chapter Two, Section II).

Kernberg might describe my identification with Rachel as a "counteridentification", using Fliess's (1953) term, due to a reactivation of "early ego identifications and early defensive mechanisms in the analyst" (Kernberg, 1975, pp. 55, 65).

Regression

I thus began to challenge the idea of regression as a necessary stage in analysis which the analyst should foster in the spirit of the patient needing "to go back in order to better go forward" (*reculer pour mieux sauter*) (Jung, 1935, par. 19). In this regard Britton quotes Bion (1992, p. 166): "Winnicott says patients *need* to regress: Melanie Klein says they *must not*: I say they *are* regressed" (Bion in Britton, 1998, p. 71).

I came to agree with Bion, and realized how much Rachel had been regressed even at the beginning of the analysis. I came to see that my "kindly" identification, when it occurred, far from being helpful, was thoroughly unhelpful, as it fostered her further breakdown and fragmentation. I now understood that while such attitudes were well-meaning, they were misguided and had just the *opposite* effect to what I would have wanted.

I came to realize that what was necessary was the simple analysis of the clinical situation, that is to say, the analysis of exactly and only what Rachel brought, and the development of a properly analytic attitude. I call this a "properly" analytic attitude as prior to these insights I would certainly have thought that I was already adopting an analytic attitude, and would no doubt have fiercely defended my previous position.

Perhaps some of the fierceness of my defence might have been due to the fact that the depth of Rachel's experience had made it feel that we were engaged in a particularly deep and meaningful analysis. Britton describes the countertransference of the analyst with the hysteric patient as "of being regarded as an important person by an interesting patient . . . the risk is of an unconscious collusive partnership of mutual admiration" (2003, p. 83). I am not sure whether there was mutual admiration, but it certainly felt "overly" significant. These issues are further explored in Chapter Five and Part II.

In regard to Balint's concepts of benign and malignant regression, it can be understood that Rachel was in a malignant regression and, in particular, was not interested in re-establishing her own ego-functioning. This is, perhaps, a good way of distinguishing between a malignant and benign regression. In a malignant regression the patient attacks/suspends/disavows his/her own ego-functioning and relies on the analyst to contain him/her with the analyst's ego-functioning, while the patient remains intensely related to the analyst. In a benign regression the patient relates the new experiences of affect and self back to their *own* ego-functioning and thereby develops and restructures what had, perhaps, been previously an over-rigid ego structure. In other words, the individual develops a more inclusive, realistic, and flexible set of self-representations.

Countertransference

I also recognized that one of the main reasons I had not been able to achieve this "properly analytic attitude" previously was that I had been unable to deal with my countertransference feelings (neurotic and otherwise) of being "bad" for allowing, and/or causing, Rachel to experience what she was feeling. Coming to terms with these countertransference feelings of "badness", releasing myself from my over-identification with Rachel, and developing a different theoretical picture of what was going on, allowed me to change my attitude towards her and act differently in the analysis.

The change in practice

The first alteration I made as a result of these insights was the simple, inner change in attitude regarding separateness that has been described. I do not underestimate the difference that a change in the analyst's attitude alone can have, where nothing needs to be said—the magic that sometimes occurs in the session after supervision, or after the analyst's sudden insight. On this occasion, however, the attitude needed to be reflected in more overt, practical changes. One example of this was that I became more wary of any pleasantries that came at the weekend breaks or at holiday times: I no longer responded in like manner to Rachel's good wishes, although I did acknowledge them. This was partly because I was aware that she was looking for reassurance from me that I still felt warmly towards her, and partly because it felt patronizing, as responding like this seemed to reinforce the idea that I was the person on whom all depended.

Another alteration was in response to my recognition that the boundaries of the analysis had been eroded: for example, through the desperate phone calls to my home. There were also the times when Rachel would come back to the consulting room after she had been to the bathroom at the end of the session and tell me that she could not leave the house because she felt unable to physically manage it, as she could not support herself or walk. I now told her that if she could not maintain the boundaries I would not be able to continue the analysis.

Rachel experienced these changes as horribly cruel. She attacked me as heartless and resisted me in every way possible, although the intrusions stopped more or less immediately. On one occasion, however, soon after this shift, Rachel told me that she would certainly be dead in the morning and bade me a portentous "goodbye" as she left the room at the end of the session. While she had not told me this in an overtly blaming way, it was clear that she was laying responsibility for her imminent death at my door. It was a very powerful experience for us both, and I knew that she absolutely believed she would not survive to the next day.

Although I was well used to this sort of situation by now, it nevertheless had a considerable impact on me. I was left feeling shocked, concerned, frightened, and also very angry. She returned the next day, however, surprised to have survived, and the analysis continued. She *had* survived my separateness and, as she came to accept my generally more separate position, there was a gradual lessening of the crises and the periods of breakdown and fragmentation. For the first time it felt as if there were the beginnings of a genuine resolution of the underlying pattern.

I think that I was finally manifesting my separateness in a non-defensive way and it was this that was "containing". From this position I could help her understand her reaction to my separateness, name her fears, and help her to understand why she felt she would not survive. I was better able to embody and "live through" my side of the "interpretations".

Furthermore, while Rachel felt I was being cruel in insisting on these changes, *I* felt the opposite: I felt released from the burden of carrying her, a burden of which I had not been fully conscious. I was not so affected or distracted by feelings of anger and other difficult feelings inside me and, consequently, I was better able to think and make sense of what she was telling me. I was more able to understand her and to be "with her".

While it might be thought that I had simply become cold and unempathic, I would maintain that in fact I was, finally, being truly empathic in not defending myself or Rachel from her situation and the true nature and consequences of her early deprivation. It was now possible for that situation to be constellated in the analysis and I was able to show empathy toward that part of her that had not been properly addressed before.

While I believe the changes in attitude and the practical alterations that I made did constitute a shifting towards a more properly analytic attitude, I do not think that an analytic attitude consists in the application of these sorts of disposition toward patients *in general*. It was simply that, with Rachel, these were the kinds of attitudes that naturally emerged in constellating her early pattern of relationship, in her challenge of the analytic boundaries, and in the necessary response to this constellation and challenge.

In other words, these were the kinds of alterations that I needed to make, under these circumstances, in order to achieve what Symington (1983) calls an "act of freedom" or, as Caper (1999) might understand it, to dis-identify after having become identified. I must have unconsciously identified with Rachel's feeling that I was being cruel by allowing the erosion of the boundaries. The ability to identify sufficiently to understand the patient, and then to be able to dis-identify in order to think and interpret, can be understood to be the essence of the analytic attitude. What this will mean, in practice, will be different in each particular circumstance.

Kernberg (1975, p. 85) proposes that the analyst's technique needs to be modified in the case of borderline patients by setting limits so as to curtail the patient's acting out within the transference, for example, by proscribing prolonged insulting of the analyst or boundary breaking such as I have described with Rachel. He suggests that by gratifying the instinctual needs of the patient the acting out becomes the main resistance to further change. Kernberg acknowledges that such acting out sometimes represents the reproduction of "unconscious, pathogenic object relationships of the past" (*ibid.*, p. 89). With Rachel, my struggle centred on establishing my own boundaries and personhood and mirrored the way Rachel's own individuality had not been respected by a mother whose behaviour was unconsciously "justified" (by both Rachel and her mother) by her mother's "weakness" and need.

In relation to Kernberg's perspective of gratifying instinctual needs, the curtailing of the acting out can also be seen as a necessary stage in establishing the patient and analyst as separate individuals. This requires that the patient begin to establish or re-establish his or her own ego-functioning. The suspension of ego-functioning (which is the immediate cause of the loss of sense of "I" and loss of separateness) is effected precisely by the patient becoming immersed in one element of their affective experience. In other words, the gratification of instinctual needs is equivalent to immersion in affect, and brings about the suspension of ego-functioning; it is *this* that makes the gratification so significant. By establishing his or her own ego-functioning the patient can thus begin to relinquish the demand that the analyst act as a self-regulating other, which, in Rachel's case, was expressed partly by the demand that I take care of her even after sessions—a demand that was "necessitated" by the suspension of her ego-functioning.

Childhood experience

The final characteristic of this latter phase of the analysis was that it was now easier to relate any remaining difficulties to situations in Rachel's childhood. This warrants further comment.

Rachel's mother was extremely demanding and self-centred, little able to give her daughter any attention in her own right. Similarly, her mother dominated Rachel's father with her demands and moods. Her father had been strict, distant, and parsimonious. While he had formed an alliance with Rachel for a brief period when she was seven or eight years old, in her teenage years he had become somewhat obsessed with her sexual development, pacing up and down outside her room if she had boyfriends present, and scouring the town if she was late home. Rachel had been, to varying degrees, both good and compliant, and difficult and rebellious. When she was thirteen, she had instigated a dangerous sexual liaison as "one in the eye for her father" and to "get it out of the way". Her parents' marriage had been conflictual and difficult, and had broken down when Rachel was in her early twenties.

The main problem about working with Rachel's childhood in the analysis was that Rachel seemed to use the undoubtedly difficult relationships with her parents to support the idea of herself as a permanently damaged, unviable victim who required my ongoing (by which I mean undisturbed and unending) support, understanding, and sympathy. She felt she had little underlying hope of change, thinking herself too damaged. Rachel would have happily referred almost all of her current difficulties back to her past in a way that led to tired and clichéd analytic interpretations. Such interpretations were unhelpful, as they trapped us in a fixed form of relationship—the powerful, helpful analyst and the damaged, helpless patient.

Fordham (1974, p. 144), referring to a similar clinical picture, comments that "I cannot convince myself that a bad start in life will account for the syndrome"; while Britton writes, similarly, "I believe that adverse infantile and childhood circumstances do not always produce this result" (1998, p. 57). In my experience of working with Rachel, and others, the details of her childhood sometimes seemed to pale into insignificance compared to the way she was relating to me from what can be seen to be the dictates of her immediate nature—her desire for sameness and her aversion to difference.

While this preferencing of sameness and aversion to difference might be derived, theoretically, entirely from childhood experience, the Kleinian description of the paranoid–schizoid and depressive positions have moved the centre of gravity for these explanations somewhat more towards the individuals themselves in a way that seems to better fit with clinical experience. Rather than the paranoid–schizoid and depressive positions, however, the identity–affect model understands the crucial factors to be the nature of affect and the affective appraisal mechanism. It is also possible to describe the paranoid–schizoid and depressive positions in terms of the functioning of affect (see Chapter Four).

Childhood experience is the mould in which the individual is formed. However, the individual's own particular nature is *not only* significant in the way the individual reacts to, interacts with and, to some extent, alters his/her childhood environment, *but also itself defines* what is significant for the child in his/her development. In this way the nature of affect and the affective appraisal mechanism dictates which experiences are introjected in childhood in the first place. For example, experiences of separation can be traumatic precisely because the affective appraisal mechanism prefers sameness. This is a truism that it is important not to overlook.

In regard to the abandoning mother, Schore describes the significance of the shame reaction and the reaction to the necessary failure of the mother's empathic functioning. He writes,

> Winnicott (1958: 246) points out that the attuned, mirroring function . . . gives way to the maternal "graduated failure of adaptation", and that this is essential to the development of the child's capacity to separate and differentiate himself from the mother. [Schore, 1994, p. 209]

He also writes that Kohut (1971, 1977) proposes that "phase-appropriate, maternal shame-induced empathic failures and frustrations serve as a stimulus for the establishment of adaptive, internal self-regulatory structures" (Schore, 1994, pp. 210–211). Schore describes the work of Tronick (1989) who, he says, ". . . has demonstrated that the interactive stress of dyadic mismatches allow for the development of interaction and self regulatory [i.e. auto-regulatory] skills" (Schore, 1994, p. 209).

Rachel's infancy was marked *not* by "phase appropriate" maternal failures, where the infant can learn and manage to deal with frustration and exposure to shame, but rather by wholesale frustration by a mother preoccupied with herself. Rachel was not, then, able to work through these frustrations in infancy as they would have proved overwhelming and unmanageable for her as an infant. It was just these failures that were constellated and needed to be worked through in the analysis.

In Jungian terms it was as if, in the analysis, it was necessary for me to "incarnate" and "humanize" (Plaut, 1956) the most terrible archetypal figure of all—the abandoning mother. That is to say, I gave form to the previously unverbalized, unformed, and therefore uncontained, early experience (internal working models) in the analytic relationship. Withers (2003) sees this kind of interaction as the transference serving as a homoeopathic version of the original trauma.

Moving out of the malignant regression

Following the shift in my attitude, and Rachel's begrudging acceptance of my more separate position, Rachel began relating to me very differently. She began to have a very different sense of herself at times—adult, solid, and equal to others. She did not, so much, seek to be looked after and taken care of. She did not look for sympathy, concern, or to be important and special. These can be seen as examples of the development of a more solid sense of "I", as she gradually began to develop her integrative ego-functioning and was less immersed in affect.

Rachel began to talk about the difficulties of, and her resistance to, "getting better". In the analysis we talked about how attractive breakdown was, and I interpreted the sorts of phenomena I have described: the vicious circle, the states of union, and the *attraction* of fragmenting and not coping. We explored the losses involved in moving on, in particular the loss of the intensity and the highs, as well as looking at the difficulties in relating to me as one adult to another.

One final example: some six months later in a, by now, uncharacteristic outburst, Rachel demanded to know who it was she had seen leaving the house. When I, eventually, refused to tell her (after trying to explore the issue with her) she refused to leave the consulting room at the end of the session. With some difficulty we negotiated this situation and when, later, she was at home raging at me, she had an experience of "being born out of me"—a bloody and terrible experience that seemed like a significant symbol for what had been going on, and that marked the end of the phase of chaotic, relating-by-impact functioning.

As this forceful element, often associated with borderline functioning, began to resolve, the underlying hysterical element of her personality came to the fore. Here, fearful of taking the step of fully establishing herself, she more subtly "suspended her own idiom" (Bollas, 2000, p. 12) and would, resentfully, fit in with what she felt I wanted. This afforded her, again, a sense of sameness with me and she relied on me to continue to provide containing, ego-functioning. This hysterical functioning is discussed further in Chapter Nine.

Overall, however, Rachel's ego-functioning had become stronger. She related to me more as a separate individual, and it felt very different to be with her. She appreciated her newfound stability and sense of herself, as well as her ability to relate to others in a less conflictual and nerve-racking way. She reported that with me she felt in better, more ordinary, more human contact. She discovered, I believe, that I was present as a real, human, and separate individual. In due course we were able to set and work towards an ending.

Notes

1.   The functional differences between the left and right hemispheres should not be oversimplified and many functions, for example, language, depend on a complex interrelation of the hemispheres. See, for example, Solms and Turnbull (2002, Chapter Eight).

2.   Kohut (1971) describes the self-regulating other as the other being a *self-object*. Stern's term *self-regulating other* is used here in preference to Kohut's term self-object, as Stern's term preserves the notion that there is essentially an "other" who may act to regulate the individual's experience until the individual comes to auto-regulate their affect to a more substantial degree. Stern's term also describes the other's function as "regulator". Kohut's term is compacted and loses the sense of the underlying relationship, as well as carrying associations to the whole body of Kohut's work, which is not followed here, in particular his understanding of narcissism and the recommendations for analytic technique (Chapter Five).

affect

CHAPTER TWO

Identity

sense of myself

Introduction

A key perspective of this book is the degree to which our
current experience affects, and is affected by, our sense of
ourselves—affective experience and personal identity are
inextricably linked (hence the appellation of the identity–affect
model). This model proposes that the sense of self comprises two
different elements that are not usually distinguished—the *sense of
being* (literally the procession of affectively toned experience) and
the *sense of "I"* (a broader sense of self that overlies and frames
current experience). There are many forms of the sense of being and
many levels and degrees of the sense of "I", which are also, of
course, particular to each individual.

This division in the sense of self reflects a distinction that is
emerging clearly in the child development literature between the
non-verbal and the verbal sense of self. This distinction is most
clearly described by Daniel Stern (1985), but it is also reflected and
underpinned by the neuroscientist Antonio Damasio's (1999) work
on consciousness. This book explores the consequences of this
division between the non-verbal and verbal self, and the different
senses of self in adults. Stern's work with infants is described in the
second part of this chapter, which further elaborates the issue of
identity.

Damasio distinguishes *core consciousness*, which generates the *sense of being*, from *extended consciousness*, which generates the *sense of "I"*. This distinction is illuminating. Here is the full quote from Damasio that has been referred to, in part, above:

> Consciousness is not a monolith, at least not in humans: it can be separated into simple and complex kinds, and the neurological evidence makes the separation transparent. The simplest kind, which I call *core consciousness*, provides the organism with a sense of self about one moment—now—and about one place—here. The scope of core consciousness is here and now. Core consciousness does not illuminate the future, and the only past it vaguely lets us glimpse is that which occurred in the instant just before. There is no elsewhere, there is no before, there is no after. On the other hand, the complex kind of consciousness, which I call *extended consciousness* and of which there are many levels and grades, provides the organism with an elaborate sense of self—an identity and a person, you or me, no less—and places that person at a point in individual historical time, richly aware of the lived past and of the anticipated future, and keenly cognizant of the world beside it. [Damasio, 1999, p. 16]

At times as adults, under certain circumstances, we can experience a kind of "simple" consciousness when our current experience comes to constitute the whole of our sense of ourselves. At these times it is not as if, for example, we are "having" a feeling of anger that is separate from ourselves, but rather that we are *immersed* in anger and swallowed up by it. At these times we have a *sense of being* (angry) but little or no *sense of "I"* (nothing above and beyond the experience of the anger). Typically, these are times of heightened experience, for better and worse, with the *sense of being* felt more powerfully as the person is living intensely in the moment.

Examples of such moments of being engulfed in experience can range from experiences of rage, abandonment, or pain, to enjoyment, ecstasy, or quasi-mystical moments of oneness with others or the environment. The loss of sense of "I" is thus not always regretted or missed. This loss can be short-lived and is, at these times, a normal and often much sought after aspect of everyday experience, such as, for example, the absorption in a piece of music or in reading a book. Christopher Bollas (1992) calls such moments "simple self experience", and he contrasts them with "complex self experience". In the latter there are a broader set of experiences at play, as well as the individual having the ability to reflect upon the experience he/she is having. This ability is usually referred to as reflexive self-consciousness.

It might be argued that, even in the more prolonged experiences of immersion in experience, the sense of "I" is not really lost. For example, Louis Zinkin writes of his experience of watching some windsurfers:

> I looked up to watch some windsurfers on the water. Previously I had noticed them with a certain contempt, not only for the begin-ners who kept falling in the water ... but also for the experts whizzing backwards and forwards, rather pointlessly, as it seemed to me ... Now I suddenly saw them in a new way ... I marvelled at the effort and struggle, not simply to master nature but to become part of it in graceful harmony with the wind and the sea. Moreover, I too was in the scene, I was no longer a voyeur but a participant ... *I was at one with them and with everybody else ... I was simply aware of one harmonious world to which they and I both belonged. We did remain differentiated so I did not "fuse" with my objects.* [Zinkin, 1987, p. 126; my italics]

The change in consciousness is clear here, but, as Zinkin says, he remained "differentiated". This can be understood as the quality of *core consciousness*, the *sense of being*, where the individual retains a sense of their own subjective perspective and remains an individ-ual. The core of the individual, the affective appraisal mechanism, continues to register sameness and difference so that Zinkin could feel, at the same time, at one with his environment yet maintain his distinct core subjectivity and sense of being. Stern (1985) and Fordham (1969) both maintain that the infant is, in some real sense, an individual from the beginning of life, able to distinguish self from other. A sense of *fusion* occurs when, not only the individual's integrative ego-functioning is suspended, but the individual also crudely identifies with the other, perhaps even disowning their own experience.

The *quality* of the sense of being can vary a good deal, however, and an individual can have a sense of being (that is) completely empty, fragmented, terrified, disintegrated, or annihilated, or full, vibrant, ecstatic, fulfilled, or contented. While there can be some continuity in the sense of being, this continuity can be lost if the affective experiences are sufficiently powerful, irregular, and unpredictable. This continuity is provided, in part, through the background presence of the *proto-self* (Damasio, 1999).

Solms and Turnbull describe the feat of core consciousness (Damasio's concept) in coupling together the individual's inner and outer worlds:

> ... whereas the "content" of consciousness is attached to the posterior cortical channels that monitor the outside world, the "state" of consciousness is a product of the ascending activating system of the brainstem, which monitors the internal milieu of the body [Damasio's proto-self]. Thus, whereas the contents of consciousness represent changes in cortical zones derived from one's external perceptual modalities, the *state* of consciousness represents changes in the internal situation of one's body. [Solms & Turnbull, 2002, p. 90]

They also go on to describe the meaningful and evaluative elements of core consciousness:

> Far from being without quality, the background state of consciousness is therefore *replete* with meaning and feeling—indeed, it is the very bedrock of personal meaning and feeling. This aspect of consciousness therefore not only "represents" your self, it also tells you how you are doing ... [Core consciousness] is not only intrinsically introspective ... it is also intrinsically *evaluative*. It imparts *value*. It tells us whether something is "good" or "bad"; and it does that by making things *feel* good or bad (or somewhere in between). That is what consciousness, feeling, is *for*. [*Ibid.*, pp. 90–91, original italics]

This evaluative element is the essence of the affective appraisal mechanism, which is explored further in Chapter Three.

Also significant is the infant's/individual's sense of (rudimentary) *agency*: this can be weakened if the infant has been overwhelmed by experience in the absence of a good-enough caregiver who could help adequately regulate their sense of being; that is to say, the self-regulation by the other is inadequate. Under these circumstances the individual can come to feel a passive victim at the mercy of their environment.

The sense of self (comprising the sense of being and the sense of "I") is not, therefore, some edifice that is constructed and remains constant. Instead, it is a continually shifting phenomenon that acts like a vehicle in and through which we negotiate the world. These shifts in the sense of self profoundly alter the way we experience reality and, particularly when there is no sense of "I" due to the suspension of integrative ego-functioning, the sense of being is profoundly *determined* by reality. The sense of self plays a defining role in the range of psychic experience—from psychotic to every-day to spiritual experience—and enables us to explain a whole range of psychic phenomena and behaviour.

In some very real way, therefore, we do not simply *have* our feelings but we *are* our feelings, even when ego-functioning is working in a mature and flexible manner. This is despite the fact that, para-doxically, we can choose not to identify with experiences that are part of us. This results in parts of ourselves becoming split off, continuing their hidden life unconscious to us.

Overview of identity

There is a spectrum of views on the subject of identity. These range from a classical Freudian position, where a stable sense of self is understood to come as the result of developmental processes, to postmodern social constructionist views of the self where the self, if it can be found at all, is only understood in relation to the envi-ronment—the self as social construct.

Many others make important contributions to the debate: for example, from a clinical point of view, Klein's outline of the para-noid–schizoid position where there is a weakened sense of self due to the projection of parts of the self into the other (projective iden-tification); Winnicott's description of the achievement of unit status and the true self and false self; Lacan's understanding that the "I" is an illusion; and Jung's theory of the self, a term he uses very differently and which is central to his whole body of work.

The identity–affect model described here recognizes many different elements to a mature identity, an outline of which is as follows: the individual begins life with a simple sense of being, which is the subjective experience of core consciousness—the expe-rience of the outer world played against the inner sense of the body (the proto-self)—intrinsically influenced by the affective appraisal mechanism. The individual then comes to identify with and incorporate certain elements of their experience making sometimes crude identifications of what is "me" and what is "not-me". These primary/first-order representations embody the individual's *core identity*. Increasing emotional, cognitive, and neurological development bring the possibility of second-order representation and, therewith, stable representations of self and objects. These second-order representations provide a sense of "I"—Damasio's "autobiographical self"—and allow reflexive self-consciousness. The different elements of the personality and the self-representations are brought together through the ego's *integrative* powers to make the sense of "I" broad and inclusive—this is to be distinguished from the narrow, impermanent, and evanescent sense of "I" which is "merely" the self-referential element of subjectivity and the sense of being. In so far as ego-functioning is *flexible*, the individual can remain related to their affective core. Finally, the development of second-order representation, in parallel with the maturation of the prefrontal lobes and the left hemisphere of the brain, allows the individual to better regulate their own affective experience (affective auto-regulation) and therefore to be less reliant on the other to be a self-regulating other (that is, to regulate not just the individual's affects but also their whole sense of self).

These issues are explored further in this and the following chapters. This section of this chapter explores the different views of ego, self, sense of self, and identity. Although most practitioners still call on the concept of the ego in some form, the term is remarkably complex and the seat of much possible confusion. The chapter begins by analysing the term ego, distinguishing the different elements within it, in order to help clarify a number of conceptual difficulties.

Section II of the chapter looks at the views of Winnicott, Mahler, Stern, Weininger, Fonagy, Gergely, Jurist and Target, social constructionism, and Lacan, all in the light of the identity–affect model. Jung's concept of the self, and the question of spiritual experience, is explored later in Chapter Six.

* * *

I: The ego and identity

The ego—an introduction

Freud used the term ego very broadly and variously over the years. The ego is a translation of the term *Das Ich*—literally, "the I". Freud used the term, at first, to refer to the whole person, to the individual as subject and as active agent; after 1923 he expanded the term to cover the ego's functioning as the mechanism for adaptation and mediation between the individual's drives and the outside world, and the system of defensive mechanisms operating to deal with the conflicts between the drives and the world. Latterly, he drew out its operation as a coherent organization of mental processes that can integrate different aspects of the individual's experience and capacities (see Britton (2003), Laplanche & Pontalis (1973), Mangabeira (2000), Yorke (1991)).

This range of meanings does not always sit easily within the concept of the ego. There are three main, overlapping functions here: subjectivity and consciousness, the executive functions (being an active agent and the instigator of defences), and the integrative functions (of outer and inner worlds, of different parts of the personality, and adaptation to reality). These three functions are distinguished neurologically below. The fully functioning ego is, in fact, a complex system that combines early developing functions (subjectivity) with later developing functions (integration) and executive functions that can operate in a number of ways (for example, as primitive defences or ego defences) depending on the level of development and functioning.

A note on the ego and the self

Hartmann (1950), the founder of ego psychology, argued for the need for a specific and separate, broader term than the ego. He introduced the term "self" to refer to the whole person (both physical and psychic aspects), which included the ego. He came to this conclusion through an analysis of Freud's concept of narcissism, pointing out that the opposite of "object cathexis" was not "ego cathexis" but "self cathexis", and that building up a picture of the object (an object representation) can only happen in parallel to building up a picture of the subject/self (a self representation).

Hartmann (1939) was also interested to stress the non-defensive aspects of the ego, as he did not see the ego as simply the mediator of the conflicts between the superego, the id, and the outside world. The "conflict-free sphere of the ego" develops independently and, he postulated, also contains such functions as thinking, perception, language, learning, memory, and rational planning.

Many others follow Hartmann's usage of the term self to refer to the whole person, for example, Klein, Kohut, and Mollon. Kohut (1971), in particular, took up this broader categorization as it related to disturbances of the self in narcissism; Mollon (1993) also argues for the need for the concept of the self, related to narcissism (see Chapter Seven on narcissism). The model outlined here, however, is primarily interested in the *sense* of self and the self representation. This is understood to relate principally to the nature and functioning of the *ego*, as outlined below, the term self is therefore largely reserved for the Jungian usage.

Subjectivity, the ego, and primary narcissism

Originally Freud equated the ego with consciousness, although by *The Ego and the Id* (Freud, 1923b), his main thesis on the ego, he had shifted his position and asserted that the ego could also be substantially *unconscious*. This is evidenced, for example, by resistances to the process of analysis in which the individual is not only unconscious of the motives and mechanisms of the resistance, but presents compulsive, repetitive and unrealistic behaviour which is outside their conscious control (Laplanche & Pontalis, 1973).

The concept of the ego is fundamentally fraught with difficulty, particularly in relation to its early development. For Freud, the ego "proceed(s) from the *Pcpt* system [the perceptual system], this being its essential nucleus" (1923b, p. 23). If perception is the nucleus of the ego it would surely follow that the ego would be the centre of *subjectivity* (our sentient perspective on our environment) and *present from the beginning of life*. Things are not so simple, however, as Freud saw the ego as a function that develops over time, bringing more mature functioning in its wake.

Freud writes, "the ego is that part of the id which has been modified by the direct influence of the external world through the medium of the *Pcpt-Cs*" (the system of perception and consciousness) (*ibid.*, p. 25). The ego, then, is the *mediator* of perception and experience between the outer and inner worlds (part of its integrative function)—the inner world being largely associated with the drives and the id. Freud is taking the ego as the operative of the *reality principle,* as he goes on to make clear: ". . . the ego seeks to bring the influence of the external world to bear upon the id and its tendencies, and endeavours to substitute the reality principle for the pleasure principle which reigns unrestrictedly in the id" (Freud, 1923b, p. 25).

The ego is a more developed function, therefore, which allows a more "rational" perspective on the world. The ego is *both* that which experiences *and* an active agent.

Thus, for Freud, the ego cannot simply be *equated* with subjectivity as there are clearly experiences available to the individual that have not been "altered by the direct influence of the external world", specifically internal experience and primary process experience, for example, of the "hallucinated breast". So when, we can ask, does this subjectivity start?

Freud's understanding of primary narcissism offers a possible resolution of this conflict as it allows him to postulate a delay in the onset of perception of the outer world. In order to explain the narcissistic withdrawal of interest in others and an intense preoccupation with the individual's own self, Freud postulated that the infant is not, at first, object-related, but begins life in an auto-erotic state, obtaining satisfaction without recourse to an outside object through hallucination and wish fulfilment. The infant then moves to a state of primary narcissism, where the infant "cathects its own self with the whole of its libido"—a state of self-preoccupation and interest. Finally, the infant becomes properly object-related (Freud, 1914c).

Thus, Freud avoids the obvious contradiction of the nucleus of the ego being the perceptual system but *not* object-related by claiming that the perceptual system is turned *inward* at the beginning of life, and that the infant's interests and satisfactions are gained there. For Freud, the infant takes it that he/she has hallucinated the breast that actually satisfies him/her. For example, Freud writes that the *object* of the sexual instinct "is negligible in comparison with the organ which is their source, and as a rule coincides with that organ" (1915c, p. 132).

Klein did not share Freud's perspective on narcissism and thought the infant *was* object-related from the beginning of life.

Some later Freudians, for example, Fonagy, have also embraced this notion:

> ... it might be worthwhile to explore the consequences of abandoning the classical assumption concerning the presumed dominance of internal stimuli in the initial state of the infant. In fact, we hypothesize that at the beginning of life *the perceptual system is set with a bias to attend to and explore the external world and builds representations primarily on the basis of exteroceptive stimuli.* [Fonagy, Gergely, Jurist, & Target, 2002, p. 153, original italics]

The phenomena associated with primary narcissism are discussed further below.

Discussion

The identity–affect model understands, too, that the infant is object-related from the beginning of life. It distinguishes different elements in the functioning of the ego. Specifically, it differentiates two different centres of the personality. First, it differentiates the affective appraisal mechanism, bearing the sense of being/core consciousness, and located in the early-developing brain stem and right hemisphere of the brain. This core consciousness is inalienable and present from the beginning of life—it is our core subjectivity and amounts to our being sentient beings. Core consciousness develops in sophistication, relating to the amount of detail that the infant has experienced and registered. The affective appraisal mechanism is (powerfully) object-related and operates to preference certain experiences and orientate the individual to the world. Depending on how the lines of demarcation and definition are drawn, it might be thought of as either the primitive functioning of the ego or a precursor to, although constituent part of, the ego. In Jungian terms it can be understood to be the mechanism behind what Fordham (1969) called the primary self or, as is argued in Chapter Six, behind a revised understanding of the Jungian self.

This affective appraisal mechanism accounts for the functions that Klein observed in children and ascribed to the ego: that of distinguishing self from other, good from bad, registering sameness and difference (underlying the phantasies of incorporation and projection), and generating preconceptions that represent primitive yet abstract (amodal) expectations, and matching them with realizations (Hinshelwood, 1989, p. 284). Klein used the term *ego* as the subjective self (Britton, 2003, p. 93).

Second, the identity–affect model differentiates these primitive functions from the later-developing integrative functions, owing to the second centre of the personality located largely in the orbito-frontal cortex and left hemisphere of the brain. It is verbal–semantic in nature, generating second-order representation (Fonagy, Gergely, Jurist, & Target, 2002). It allows more sophisticated self-representation and self-reflection to occur, as well as affective auto-regulation, and accounts for the later-developing, integrative functions of the ego.

This differentiation allows us to reconcile Freud's apparent paradox of the ego being linked to subjectivity, but not object-related from the beginning of life, as well as being a developmental achievement that develops over time. There can be seen to be a subjectivity, through the affective appraisal mechanism and the sense of being, which is object-orientated from the beginning of life, which is later *supplemented* by integrative ego-functioning. The later-developing, integrative ego-functioning rests inextricably on the early developing right hemisphere, although the two are logically and developmentally dissociable.

For example, Britton (2003, p. 88) describes Miss A, whose ego-functioning, he says, is "disordered". Britton describes how she would flush the toilet repeatedly in order to get rid of her thoughts. Clearly, Miss A had a certain degree of subjectivity; however, it is the more mature ego-functioning that was "disordered". Her behaviour can be understood as being due to a suspension of integrative ego-functioning, owing to immersion in affective experience, and which required that she employ primitive defence mechanisms.

Freud is hamstrung by trying to offer a unified concept of the ego that accounts for both the development and the structure of the ego. His explanation of the *development* of the ego required him to argue, unsatisfactorily, for the delayed onset of proper subjectivity. At the same time as doing this he was *also* trying to account for the integrative and more sophisticated elements of ego-functioning, without distinguishing between the different elements of the ego and consciousness: a subjective sense of being and a sense of "I" consequent upon the development of integrative ego-functioning. Relinquishing a unified concept of the ego, and distinguishing between the different senses of self and the different functions that go to make up the concept, circumvents these difficulties.

The phenomena of primary narcissism—the infant's apparent lack of object-relatedness at the beginning of life—can be understood to be a consequence of the affective appraisal mechanism. The infant can be observed and understood to be highly attuned to the other but may not register those things that are too different (from their set of preferences) or that are not relevant to the individual, perhaps due to lack of development; thus it may *appear* that the infant is not object-related, while, in fact, they are relating intensely (see also Chapter Two, Section II and Chapter Three).

The executive functions: agency and defence

Freud's earliest understanding of the term ego was as subject and active agent (1895d). Britton's Miss A gives us a good example of the subject as agent. She was acting in order to affect her sense of security—to get rid of (presumably dangerous) "thoughts" (powerfully related to affects)—and thereby to alter her sense of herself.

Starting from the identity–affect model's understanding of the split sense of self (the sense of being and the sense of "I"), there is not seen to be one "locus" of "agency". The individual can be seen to act, react, or not react, related exactly to their ego-functioning and sense of self. This is reflected in the understanding of the different defences, which is another aspect of the executive functions of the ego as described by Freud.

Primitive and ego defences

The primitive defences are understood to be splitting, projection, projective identification, idealization, omnipotence, and denial. In the primitive state, where integrative ego-functioning has either not developed or has been suspended, and the individual's immediate experience (sense of being) constitutes their whole sense of self, the individual must powerfully manipulate their environment or their experience of their environment in order to achieve a tolerable self-experience.

In this state bad experience must either be *split off* or *denied*; others are experienced as having incredible power (of self-regulation) that can either be denied through the individual's assumption of *omnipotence* (which is, to some extent, the veridical experience of the other's power to regulate the self) or, alternatively, the other may be *idealized* or controlled through *projective identification*. Any elements of the personality not recognized as the individual's own may be *projected* on to the other.

Anna Freud (1936) lists the following more developed *ego* defences: regression, repression, reaction formation, isolation, undoing, introjection, turning against the self, reversal, sublimation and projection (some authorities consider projection as a primitive defence). Others have added displacement, rationalization, identification with the aggressor, passive to active, dramatization, reparation, manic defences, repetition-compulsion, and religiosity.

Reviewing this list of ego defences it is clear that each requires a greater development of the personality. They mostly require two centres of the personality. For example, turning against the self, reaction formation, and identification with the aggressor all require an *alternative perspective* so that one part of the self can *act upon* another. This alternative perspective is provided by the second-order representation of the self and the lexical-semantic, left-hemispheric functions as well as the growth of affective auto-regulation through the development of the prefrontal lobes. As Solms and Turnbull write,

> Freud considered this capacity (the capacity to inhibit drive energies) to be the basis of all the ego's rational, reality-constrained and executive functions. This inhibitory capacity was the basis of what Freud called "secondary-process" thinking, which he contrasted with the unconstrained mental activity that characterized the "primary process". It was this property (rather than consciousness) that gave Freud's ego—the "autobiographical self" of Damasio— executive control over the otherwise automatic, biologically determined functions of the mind. . . . "The repressed" is exempt from the inhibitory constraints imposed by the "secondary process", and it therefore functions according to the compulsive, stereotyped "primary process" mode of the id (or system *Ucs* . . .). The aim of the talking cure, then, is to bring to bear on the repressed the inhibitory constraints of the secondary process and, thereby, to

bring them under the flexible control of the ego. [Solms & Turnbull, 2002, pp. 286–287]

The developed, integrative ego-functions

Jacobson stated that "The system ego sets in with the discovery of the object world and the growing distinction between it and one's own physical and mental self" (Jacobson, 1965, p. 19), leading to the gradual development of "consistent and more or less realistic endopsychic representations of the object world and the self" (*ibid.*).

The affective appraisal mechanism, present from the beginning of life, leads to the development of representations of self and other due to its processing of sameness and difference. Such primary representations are, at the beginning, only fragmentary and relate very much to interactions between self and other, Stern's "ways-of-being-with-others" (1998). It is not until the more substantial development of the left hemisphere and the orbitofrontal cortex, which links to the left hemisphere, that begins at around twelve months of age, that proper "second-order (or secondary) representations" (Fonagy, Gergely, Jurist, & Target, 2002) can be built up. From this point complex self-representation, with its distinctive quality and nature, can come into being.

These second-order representations are examples of the left hemisphere's lexical–semantic, representation/naming of objects. This hemisphere is also responsible for Hartmann's rational functions listed earlier: thinking, language, learning, memory, rational planning, and perception. These second-order representations allow for a more unified representation of the individual, integrating and linking the different aspects of the individual. They offer the "alternate perspective" mentioned in regard to the more developed ego defences. They allow some "distance" from primary, core experience and thereby allow the individual *not* to be immersed in that experience. In this way they allow for symbolization, self-reflexive consciousness (self-consciousness), complex self-experience (Bollas), extended consciousness (Damasio) and, subjectively, the sense of "I". This captures the spirit of the naming of the ego *Das Ich*—the "I". While it could be argued that the "I" refers to the narrow, evanescent sense of "I"—the self-referential element of subjective experience—this would be limiting the definition of the ego to subjectivity alone. The broader, background sense of "I" following integration of the set of self-representations better reflects Freud's full definition.

Britton also emphasizes this integrative aspect of ego-functioning. Talking about his own use of the term ego, he writes,

> *The Ego and the Id* is so rich in ideas and varieties of description that those coming after have been able to take different aspects and develop their own version. Mine is as follows: in the individual, the ego is that part of the mental apparatus where integration takes place. Among the things to be integrated is the experiential-self with the self-observed—the subjective-self with the objective-self".
> [Britton, 2003, p. 91]

Note that Britton also distinguishes two types of self experience: the experiential-self/subjective-self and the self-observed/objective-self, which correspond to core consciousness/sense of being and extended consciousness/sense of "I".

While emphasizing the integrative aspects, overall Britton takes up a traditional view of the ego as *including* the subjective self, although he links it with Bion's notion of container–contained: "The ego enshrines the relationship described by Bion as that between the container and contained. It is at one and the same time the subject self (contained) and self-consciousness (its container)" (Britton, 2003, p. 100).

Britton is, therefore, describing the state where affect, and the second-order representation that contains affect, are integrated. This is understood, here, as the outcome of flexible ego-functioning.

The drives and affect

Freud also states that the ego is responsible for mediating between the drives and the outside world. There has been some debate over the usefulness of the notion of drives. For example, Stern comments that the actual observation of infants has shown that besides the regulation of sleep and hunger, what would have been called "ego-instincts", such as pre-emptive patterns of exploration, curiosity, perceptual preferences, the search for cognitive novelty, pleasure at mastery and attachment, play a very prominent part. He concludes that "the classical view of instinct has proven unoperationalizable and has not been of great heuristic value for the observed infant" (Stern, 1985, p. 238).

Sandler and Sandler also stress the role of affect over drive, writing,

> In the development of object relationships (that is, of structured role relationships), the part played by affective experience is central. *A subjective experience only has or retains meaning for the child if it is linked with feeling.* . . . This is in line with a view previously put forward on the role of feelings as psychic regulators—namely, that "the ultimate guiding or regulatory principle in adaptation from a psychological point of view relates to feeling states of one form or another and that to equate these with energic equilibrium and with drive equilibrium in particular may be misleading or incorrect". [Sandler & Sandler, 1998, pp. 69–70, original italics]

Recent studies of neuroscience, however, in particular those of Panksepp (1998), have brought the notion of drives back into the picture. Panksepp describes four "basic-emotion command systems" from a neurobiological point of view: the seeking, rage, fear, and panic systems. In mature functioning these systems then come under the brain's regulatory and inhibitory powers (see Solms & Turnbull, 2002, pp. 286–287, quoted above).

These basic-emotion command systems can be seen to be intimately relational in nature. They are the inherited "hardware" that steer the individual into relationship with their objects, under the auspices of the affective appraisal mechanism and, thereby, the individual's growing set of (*relational*) preferences. The "goal" of these affectively-based drives is essentially relational.

Summary of the ego and ego-functioning

The different elements of ego-functioning have now been explored: consciousness, subjectivity, the individual as active agent, reality orientation, the system of defensive mechanisms, and the organization and representational faculties integrating the different aspects of the individual's personality.

The ego is, therefore, a complex system that relies on more primitive elements, specifically core consciousness, intrinsically structured by the affective appraisal mechanism, and providing a basic subjectivity. There is a second, more developed, system that overlies these primitive elements. There are, therefore, two main systems at work.

The affective appraisal mechanism constitutes Ohman's first "pre-attentive analysis of an emotional stimulus" (Ohman, 1986). This is supplemented by the operation of the left hemisphere and the organization of second-order representations, which represent the "later conscious assessment of the relevance of the same stimulus". Schore writes,

> Krystal (1978) differentiates two lines of emotional development, an infantile nonverbal affect system and a verbal adult system, and Gazzaniga (1985) now proposes a basic primitive affect system and a verbal-conceptual system which are localized in different hemispheres. Research on the hemispheric lateralization of emotions reveals the existence of dual affective systems, a right hemisphere system dominant for the expression of nonverbal mood and affect, and a left hemisphere system involved in verbally mediated affective mood states (Silberman & Weingartner, 1986). [Schore, 1994, p. 238]

The identity–affect model distinguishes these different features of ego-functioning and understands that, when properly integrated, these functions operate together seamlessly. However, the primitive functions can be seen as an early form of ego-functioning, almost a precursor to ego-functioning. The identity–affect model concentrates on the status and functioning of the later, developed, integrative ego-functioning, echoing Freud's conception that ego-functioning is a developmental achievement. It is these developed, representational qualities, and the ability to regulate the individual's own affect, that comes with the development of the orbito-frontal cortex and the left hemisphere, that leads to the category shift in consciousness.

Freud did not distinguish these two systems in his outline of the concept of the ego. The two systems are, however, inextricably linked. Damasio, in his book *Descartes' Error* (1994), and Matte Blanco (1988), from a different perspective, both point out how emotions are constitutive of rationality itself, as is explored in Chapter Three. However, the later developing functions can be suspended, leaving the individual with simple, affectively toned experience.

With the development of the left hemisphere and the possibility for extended consciousness and second-order representation, the individual is afforded enormously enhanced organizational capacities, a broader perspective, and a freeing from immersion in immediate experience. This organization, the integration of different elements of the personality, and the "alternative perspective", allows the executive functions to operate in a way more fitting to the individual's broader needs and personality (to operate more as ego defences), rather than to act precipitately and narrowly in the manner of primitive defences. The executive agency does not, then, belong to the ego *per se* but operates according to the nature and degree of ego development, which includes a sense of personal agency (potency).

Two examples where disorders of the ego are seen to be central to pathological functioning are given by Kernberg and Erikson. In regard to ego organization, Kernberg describes the definitive element in borderline personality organization as a particular ego pathology. He cites the failure of the integrative capacities of the ego—the bringing together of self and object representations—as being due to splitting (Kernberg, 1975, p. 25), as well as the borderline individual's difficulty in achieving what he calls an "observing ego", without which the ego becomes flooded with affect (the absence of an alternative perspective) (*ibid.*, pp. 80–81). Erikson (1956) calls the lack of an integrated self concept and lack of integrated objects (for example, due to splitting and denial of "bad" self representations, and splitting of idealized "good" objects and denigrated "bad" objects) "identity diffusion".

When referring to the suspension of *integrative* ego-functioning, the identity–affect model is referring to the suspension of that function that integrates the different elements of the personality—different qualities and capacities and corresponding self representations. When referring to the suspension of ego-functioning, the model is referring to *both* the suspension of this integrative faculty and *also* the suspension of second-order representation itself, so that the individual is swamped with affect. Some of the attacks on thinking capacities that Bion (1959) refers to amount to the suspension and destruction of the second-order representational faculty. These different forms of "suspension of ego-functioning" are not necessarily always distinguished in this book.

Flexible ego-functioning

The identity–affect model lays bare, and underlines, the importance of the links between these two primary systems—the affective appraisal mechanism/non-verbal self and the integrative ego-functioning/verbal self. This is reflected in the notion of *flexible ego-functioning* developed herein. Flexible ego-functioning is a form of mature functioning that can allow access to the continued, new source of experience through the affectively-based appraisal/perceptive system *and* reference to the stable, ongoing, broader picture of the self held by the ego. The flexibility of the ego-functioning is demonstrated both in allowing new experience and also in the ego's ability to modify itself in the light of that new experience.

Fonagy, Gergely, Jurist, and Target understand this as "mentalized affectivity" which is "the adult capacity for affect regulation in which one is conscious of one's affect, while remaining within the affective state" (2002, p. 96). Their concept does not, however, specifically allow for the modification of the existing self-representation.

The ego's self-representation is, ideally, realistic, acknowledging the limitations and boundaries of the personality—in this way it represents the achievement of the depressive position. The affective appraisal mechanism, on the other hand, represents the sensitive, perceptive core and generates, if unintegrated with the more developed ego-functions, the paranoid element of experience. Flexible ego-functioning, then, allows an oscillation between the two states that Bion called Ps–D—the necessary breakdown of the existing, internal, containing theories (a shift to the paranoid–schizoid position) before a restructuring and movement back to the depressive position (Bion, 1963).

In a similar vein, Bollas (1992) suggests that we need to be able to shift between complex self states (characterized by a stable sense of "I") and simple self states (having a sense of being only). In simple self states he understands that the individual/subject is transformed into an object inside the other. As he puts it regarding falling in love,

> . . . the body of the other ceases simply to be an object of perception or internal representation and becomes the means of transformation—from the subject who seeks the erotic object to the subject who becomes an object "inside" the place of desire. [Bollas, 1992, p. 16]

Bollas thus recognizes the consequences for object relationship of these shifts in the sense of self. This shift to a simple self state represents the "use of the object" (Winnicott, 1969). The shift becomes addictive for borderline and hysteric individuals, who do not maintain integrative ego-functioning but wish to give it up to reside in the other; it is a real *achievement* for schizoid individuals to be able to "use" their objects, trusting them to provide good-enough experience, while narcissistic individuals wish to transform the *object* so that the object accommodates the narcissist without the narcissist themselves having to undergo transformation (see Part II).

The use of the object that Bollas describes—the shift to the simple self state—is only stably beneficial once flexible ego-functioning has been established, so that the individual can easily *return* to complex self states. Flexible ego-functioning describes precisely this ability to shift between simple and complex self states, although in mature, flexible ego-functioning the sense of "I" is maintained and is, indeed, enhanced, rather than eclipsed, by contact with affective experience. There are similarities between flexible ego-functioning and what Edinger (1972) called the ego-self axis in the Jungian frame, as is explored in Chapter Six.

For borderline and hysteric individuals, integrative ego-functioning needs to be achieved before flexible ego-functioning becomes substantiated. Schizoid and narcissistic individuals need to relinquish their rigid ego-functioning, transforming the self-representation, and allowing in new experience from the emotional core, before flexible ego-functioning can be established.

In his later years Freud put greater emphasis on *the development of the ego*, saying "Where id was, there ego shall be" (Freud, 1933a, p. 80), rather than seeing the aim of analysis as being solely to make conscious what was unconscious. The concept of flexible ego-functioning lays bare what such development entails and spells out the richness and difficulties inherent in its achievement.

Section II: Models of identity. From edifice to social construct

Object relationship

One of the main omissions of the classical Freudian position and that of Ego Psychology, which followed it closely, is the emphasis on the drives and Freud's structural theory (the ego, id, and super-ego) without recourse to a comprehensive object-relations theory. The understanding of the affective appraisal mechanism puts object relationship at the centre of the agenda.

This second section of the chapter addresses more directly relational models, such as those of Winnicott, Mahler, and Stern, and Fonagy, Gergely, Jurist and Target's social-biofeedback model. It also explores the concept of annihilation and the models of Weininger, Redfearn's subpersonality theory, social constructionism and Lacan. This part of the chapter focuses on these theorists' contributions to our understanding of identity, and particularly the development of the infant's identity, and critically examines the manner in which these models articulate with the identity–affect model, further developing themes already introduced.

Winnicott

Winnicott has a number of concepts which shed light on our understanding of identity—unit status, the true and the false self, and annihilation—and he was one of the first to thoroughly detail and emphasize the role of the caregiver and the provision of "good-enough" care in the healthy development of the individual. He was also true to Freud's conceptualization of primary narcissism, in line with Margaret Mahler.

Unit status

Winnicott's understanding of infant development traces "the infant's journey from absolute dependence, through relative dependence, to independence, and, in parallel, the infant's journey from the pleasure principle to the reality principle, and from auto-erotism to object relationship" (Winnicott, 1960a, p. 42).

Winnicott understands how, through ego development, the infant moves from an unintegrated state, characterized by primary process, primary identification, auto-erotism and primary narcissism, to a state of structured integration attaining what he called "unit status". The achievement of unit status amounts to the infant becoming "a person, an individual in their own right". It is related to the infant achieving a psychosomatic existence, with the psyche indwelling in the soma. At this point the infant is understood to have "an inside and an outside and a body-scheme" through the development of a limiting membrane, usually equated with the skin, which separates the infant's "me" from "not-me".

Winnicott thus emphasizes the differentiation of self from other in his concept of unit status. Jacobson's thoughts regarding the ego system beginning with the distinction between the individual and the object world are consonant with Winnicott's view (Jacobson, 1965, p. 19, quoted earlier). These views, however, raise the question of to which stage of development he is referring as, for example, Stern (1985), whose position is outlined below, holds that the differentiation of self from other takes place, in rudimentary form, from the beginning of life.

Davis and Wallbridge (1981, p. 34), exploring Winnicott's concept of unit status, suggest that the development of a unit self represents the attainment of "wholeness" and moments of "I AM". This would suggest that, while the growing differentiation of self from other are vital preconditions of the achievement of unit status, the onset of second-order representation could also be seen as a necessary condition, as it is this which brings a sense of "I". Furthermore, the notion of wholeness suggests that the experience of integrative ego-functioning, where the different elements of the personality can begin to be brought together, and which begins to occur at 15–18 months, is also a key feature of unit status. As was clear with Rachel, however, the achievement of unit status is not a once-and-for-all event, as the individual can later disavow ego-functioning, foregoing their unit status so as to subsist within the other.

Primary narcissism: Mahler, and Stern

The question of primary narcissism, however, and of whether there is an undifferentiated auto-erotic stage, remains. The concept of primary narcissism has been explored in the previous section of this chapter in regard to the development of the ego, perception, and, to some extent, object relatedness. This section explores these issues from the point of view of infant development.

In following Freud's understanding of primary narcissism and the lack of object relatedness at the start of life, Winnicott's views were predicated largely on the essential role he understood the caretaker to have in the provision of good-enough care for the infant, and the indistinct boundaries between self and other at this stage. Winnicott's views are perhaps best encapsulated by his emblematic and much quoted saying, "There is no such thing as an infant". He explained that he meant by this that "whenever one finds an infant one finds maternal care, and without maternal care there would be no infant" (Winnicott, 1960a, p. 39n).

Although Winnicott's support for the concept of an auto-erotic phase and of primary narcissism came from his object relational perspective, the view was still contentious, having been challenged by Balint in 1937 and, more contemporaneously to Winnicott by Melanie Klein, of whose views he was well aware. On the other hand, Winnicott's standpoint was consonant with the work of Mahler (Mahler, 1963; Mahler & Gosliner, 1955), whose theories were predominant at the time.

I shall address Balint's critique first. Balint writes that, in his experience, patients who were thought to be "turning away from object relationship" were, in fact, relating intensely—albeit to a phantasy object of their own creation. Balint proposes that in infants there is a state of "primary love", a form of intense related-ness to the environment. He claims that all narcissism is secondary to this primary love, and is caused by a disturbance between the infant and the environment, leading to frustration (Balint, 1937, 1960).

Klein also argues that there is no primary narcissism, i.e., turn-ing away from relationship, and holds that object relations coincide with narcissistic functioning (viz. Hinshelwood, 1989, p. 354, and see below). Instead, Klein analyses these phenomena in terms of the paranoid–schizoid "phase" (later "position"), which Segal (1983) referred to as the narcissistic phase. These views are in conflict with those of Margaret Mahler.

Mahler describes an early, undifferentiated phase in which the infant, living in an illusion of symbiotic unity with its mother, feels omnipotent (Mahler, Pine, & Bergman, 1975). Winnicott thought that it was important that the mother (implicitly) support this experience of omnipotence through her holding function. He saw the experience of omnipotence as an *actual experience* for the infant that comes when fantasy and reality correspond—the baby wants to feed and the mother provides the breast (Davis & Wallbridge, 1981).

Mahler designated the first few weeks of extra-uterine life as the stage of *normal autism*, an undifferentiated phase where there is no discernible distinction for the infant between inner and outer reality, and where the mother is not perceived as a "need-satisfying object". This indifference to external stimuli, Mahler held, protected the infant from extreme stimulation in order to facilitate psychological growth.

It was argued earlier in this chapter that, while the infant may *appear* to be indifferent to external stimuli, he or she may in fact be *relating intensely* to the object, although this is not recognized because he or she is relating to only a selective few elements. These elements correspond to those things that are similar to the infant's developing set of preferences, with everything else being ignored or not registered.

Following the phase of normal autism, Mahler details a phase of *normal symbiosis* in which the boundaries between self and mother are still more or less confluent and fused, although the boundaries may become more distinct, for a short time, when the infant is in an affective state of hunger, for example, and disappear again when the infant experiences gratification and satisfaction. In this phase the infant can be observed to be more clearly object related, but the boundaries between self and other are not drawn distinctly.

Mahler then details a number of phases and sub-phases of separation–individuation from the mother; from about five months onwards, when the bodily dependency begins to decrease, until about thirty-six months, when more stable mental representations of self and object have developed, leading to object constancy, where the continual presence of the mother is no longer so imperative (Mahler & La Perriere, 1965).

These dominant Freudian views of the 1960s and 1970s were profoundly challenged, however, by the work of Daniel Stern, who disputed both the notion of the autistic and symbiotic stages and the early state of undifferentiation. Stern proposed, in distinction from Mahler, and calling on the work of other researchers, that infants are able to distinguish self from other *from birth*. This is in line with Klein's view that the ego is present from birth. He cited, for instance, the fact that infants are able to distinguish the smell of their own mother's milk from that of a stranger (Stern, 1985, p. 39).

Stern formulated a model for the development of the *sense of self* in the infant, arguing that the sense of self acts as an "organising principle" for the infant (*ibid.*, p. 25), a view very much taken forward in this book in regard to the adult. He describes and distinguishes the *non-verbal self*, which has three subcategories or "domains" of self-experience—the sense of an emergent self, the sense of a core self, and the sense of an intersubjective self—from the *verbal self*, consisting of the sense of a verbal self and the sense of a narrative self.

Stern's model is a *layered* model that "assumes a progressive accumulation of senses of the self, socioaffective competencies, and ways-of-being-with-others. No emerging domain disappears; each remains active and interacts dynamically with all the others" (Stern, 1985, pp. xi–xii). All three non-verbal domains of self-experience are therefore present, in some form, from the beginning of life. (This is his updated model, as described in the introduction to the 1998 edition of *The Interpersonal World of the Infant* (Stern, 1985).)

The early-developing subcategories of the non-verbal self correspond to the different domains of the infant's self-experience. The *sense of an emergent self* describes the way in which the infant experiences the world against a background, relatively stable, sense of inner bodily self that Stern specifically identifies with Damasio's proto-self. This "yoking together" of the new stimulus and the background feelings gives the infant a primitive sense of self that Damasio suggests is the experience of consciousness itself (Damasio, 1999, p. 25).

The *sense of a core self* represents an outline distinction between self and others, including the establishment of *self-agency* (the recognition of authorship of one's own actions and non-authorship of the action of others), *self-coherence* (having the sense of being a non-fragmented, physical whole with boundaries and a locus of integrated action) and *self-continuity* (the infant feeling the "same" by virtue of the invariants created from the background proto-self).

Stern's and Mahler's positions here are, perhaps, not as far apart as they may at first appear, as Stern would recognize that self and object representations are "outline" and not finely detailed at this stage, although Stern would hold that the infant makes distinctions between self and object from the beginning.

Perhaps most significantly, Stern recognizes that the infant is intersubjectively related almost from the beginning of life, able to pick up, tune into, and even mimic the other's expressions and feelings. He cites the work of other researchers who have identified the activity of *mirror neurones* (Rizzolatti & Arbib, 1998), *adaptive oscillators* (McCauley, 1994; Port, Cummins, and McCauley, 1995; Torras, 1985), and the *contingency detection mechanism* (Watson, 1994) (see Chapter Three), which allow us to understand the functioning and development of the *sense of an intersubjective self*.

Stern talks of the significance of the *self-regulating other* at these early stages of life. The caregiver regulates, for example: the infant's arousal, the intensity of affect, the sense of security and attachment, the category of affect (for example, the infant looks to the caregiver to "discover" whether they should be afraid of something), and the infant's attention and somatic state (for example, hunger and sleep). He points out how many of the caregiver's functions are interpersonal rather than related to simply physical caregiving (Stern, 1985, pp. 244ff.).

Stern's view thus encompasses the vital and defining role of the caregiver for the infant's experience, in line with Winnicott, while offering a different view of early object relations, bringing into question the existence of an early auto-erotic phase and a phase of primary narcissism. This view that the infant is object-related from birth has become widely accepted, even by many of those whose roots are firmly within the Freudian tradition. As quoted above, Fonagy and colleagues suggest that the perceptual system is set with a bias to attend and explore the external world from the beginning of life (Fonagy, Gergely, Jurist, & Target, 2002, p. 153).

Stern goes on to delineate the verbal self, corresponding with the beginning of second-order representational functioning and coinciding with certain elements of unit status, as discussed above. This consists of a *sense of a verbal self*, where the use of language heralds a new domain of relatedness and a new medium of exchange with which to create shared meanings. Stern recognizes that language is a double-edged sword, as it drives a wedge between interpersonal experience as it is lived and as it is verbally represented; in other words, between the verbal and the non-verbal self. This division in the sense of self, reflected in the difference between the sense of being and sense of "I", has further important ramifications that will be explored in later chapters.

Stern dates the onset of the sense of a verbal self as being during the second year of life, gaining real momentum from about fifteen to eighteen months. It is followed by the development of a *sense of a narrative self* that builds on the infrastructure of language and allows the co-construction of narratives about the self with others, piecing together the story and placing the individual and their role(s) within it.

Continuity of experience and annihilation

The sense of a core self that Stern describes very much relates to Winnicott's understanding of annihilation. Rachel frequently experienced profound states of annihilation and, at times, a terrifying sense of disintegration. These states were usually triggered by a separation from me, due either to a weekend or holiday break or, more usually, following a crisis where she felt I was not seeing things in the way she wanted or needed me to.

My prime understanding of such experiences was that Rachel's ego was not functioning in an integrated manner, so that each moment's experience felt like it was the *totality* of her experience, where she was not linked to previous experience or to the other parts of her personality. A separation or disjunction from me therefore felt like a total loss. Implicit in this experience was the way the discontinuity reached down into her affective, non-verbal self, so that she felt she had no continuity of self and, sometimes, that she was disintegrating.

This is the level of Stern's "sense of a core self", where the individual experiences self-coherence and self-continuity. Kristeva (1974) describes this affective level as the *semiotic chora*—the rhythms, mobile energies, and subtle affects that precede the more stable identifications of self. Schore also writes, "The core of the self lies in patterns of affect regulation that integrate a sense of self across state transitions, thereby allowing for a continuity of inner experience" (Schore, 1994, p. 498). Emde (1983) also describes an "affective core" that guarantees a continuity of experience despite developmental changes.

The notion of an affective core echoes Winnicott's understanding of "the core of the personality", which he also calls "the central or true self". He writes,

> The central self could be said to be the inherited potential which is experiencing a continuity of being, and acquiring in its own way and at its own speed, a personal psychic reality and a personal body-scheme. It seems necessary to allow for the concept of isolation of this central self as a characteristic of health. Any threat to this isolation of the true self constitutes a major anxiety at this early stage, and defences of earliest infancy appear in relation to failures on the part of the mother (or in maternal care) to ward off impingements which might disturb this isolation. [Winnicott, 1960a, p. 46]

Winnicott understands annihilation as being due to the fact that the "inherited potential" becomes itself a "continuity of being", which is interrupted if the caregiver is not sufficiently holding and, as a result, the infant must "react", interrupting his or her state of being. This interruption is experienced as a state of annihilation.

For Winnicott, therefore, the infant's sense of continuity has to be guaranteed by the caregiver's holding. Stern would suggest that there can be a certain level of self-coherence and self-continuity offered by the proto-self. In my experience with Rachel, however, this self-coherence and self-continuity was easily disrupted when the affects were sufficiently powerful and disjointed, at which time one experience would be followed by another seemingly unconnected one in a terrifying manner. At these moments Rachel felt that she was disintegrating, being annihilated, and dying.

Winnicott writes that "it seems necessary to allow for the concept of isolation of this central self (true self) as a characteristic of health" (1960a, p. 46). This aptly describes the excruciating predicament in which Rachel found herself, as her emotional core was continually exposed without sufficient ego-functioning to filter and put her immediate experience into perspective.

Ogden (2004) compares Winnicott's notion of holding and Bion's concept of containment, and concludes that Winnicott's is a more fundamental concept, concerned with "safeguarding the continuity of the infant's or child's experience of being and becoming over time". Bion's conception of the container–contained is, in contrast, concerned with "the processing (dreaming) of thoughts derived from lived emotional experience" (Ogden, 2004, p. 1362). Containment is, therefore, to do with the formation of second-order representations (thoughts) relating to "coherent" experiences of affect. Similarly, Winnicott's notion of annihilation represents a more fundamental threat to the individual than Bion's "nameless dread". In the latter, the individual has an unformed, non-verbal presentiment (affect) of something wrong (dread) without being able to name, reflect on, or consciously understand it (it is nameless—there is no second-order representation).

These considerations suggest an objection to the identity–affect model that is briefly examined before continuing to explore annihilation, looking at Weininger's model.

Critique of the identity-affect model

Bollas argues that the borderline patient's "core object is to be found only through turbulent states of mind" and that the hysteric "suspends their own idiom" and seeks out who she/he is to the (m)other and then tries to identify with this object of desire and represent it to the (m)other (Bollas, 2000, pp. 9, 12). Was it, then, that Rachel was reacting because her continuity of being was being profoundly disrupted, or was this simply her manner of relating? Was this, in attachment theory terms, a disorganized or ambivalent pattern of attachment (Holmes, 2001), so that trying to solve the problem in terms of its own logic did nothing to address the underlying pattern of relating, but rather ensured the continuance of that pattern?

This critique has some validity, as Rachel's manner of relating does fit into these broader patterns. It can be argued, however, that the identity–affect and attachment models represent two different perspectives, and are complementary rather than mutually exclusive. The identity–affect framework stays closer to Rachel's own, subjective, perspective, describing the particular struggles, fears, and losses as she might see them. The attachment theory model offers more of a birds'-eye-view of the interaction. I needed to get alongside Rachel and understand what she was going through *and* see the broader perspective and consequences of her struggle (the attachment pattern). I believe that *both* perspectives were necessary to resolve the situation.

Annihilation: Weininger—the superego and the death instinct

Otto Weininger has developed an understanding of annihilation from a Kleinian perspective in terms of the superego and the death instinct. Weininger's closely observed clinical work with children reveals a wealth of detail about early interactions. He describes the infant's ability to "disown" their feelings, particularly those feelings that make them experience their world as a dangerous place. He writes,

> In these babies, any feeling like aggression, anger, satisfaction, plea-sure and even love is disowned; their reactions to their parents and others are only those reactions that are felt to be "safe ones"—that is, those emotions that will not result in being ignored, rejected, or abused. [Weininger, 1996, p. 6]

In his Kleinian frame, Weininger is at pains to point out that these reactions are not only due to the infants' experience of the parents but also related to their own aggressive feelings towards the parents. As Klein writes,

> . . . bad parts of the self are projected onto the mother . . . so that she is not felt to be a separate individual but is felt to be *the* bad self. Much of the hatred against parts of the self is now directed towards the mother. This leads to a particular form of identification which estab-lishes the prototype of an aggressive object-relation. I suggest for these processes the term "projective identification". [Klein, 1946, p. 8]

Like the projected parts of the self, the anger that Weininger discusses must be dissociated for, if it is expressed, the infant's own sense of badness is increased.

> The parents are seen as controlling people, and the baby must conform or be rejected. Conformity might mean "love", but expressing anger will result in dangerous rejection. In this way our fear of badness is our fear of being annihilated by the very people who are to care for us—our parents become our persecutors. [Weininger, 1996, p. 6]

In order to achieve the necessary degree of control, Weininger suggests that these babies develop severe superegos and that the superego becomes inextricably linked to the death instinct:

These babies experience parental anger and rejection, which can only be felt as punishment, as a disintegrating force, and as annihilation—the death instinct . . . the harsher and more punitive the superego, the stronger and more destructive the death instinct. [*ibid.*, pp. 11 & 13]

Freud modified his early theory to allow that it is the ego, as well as the superego, that orientates the individual towards reality, that is to say, largely, towards the caregivers' demands upon, and reactions to, the infant. It becomes an issue of a superego, rather than an ego, reaction, however, when the individual turns their aggressive behaviour towards *him/herself* in an apparently destructive manner. Weininger writes,

The resultant hostile behaviour toward the self is not, for the child, just at the service of destroying himself (i.e. the self-perception of one's own being in the world as the essence of what is wished destroyed). *The hostile behaviour is primarily, I think, at the service of destroying the needs and feelings that the child experiences which are causing the unbearable tension.* [*ibid.*, p. 13, my italics]

Discussion

Weininger emphasizes the hostile attack on the needs and feelings themselves, over and above the destruction of the "self-perception", the latter being a key position of the identity–affect model. A number of points can be made in response.

First, Weininger's observations do show up the very important phenomenon of the pre-verbal infant's ability to disavow feeling and mould him/herself to the caregiver. The infant has the ability, with increasing sophistication, to choose what to own and disown, to choose with what to identify and from what to dissociate or detach, and, ultimately, what to take as "me" and "not-me".

The disavowal that Weininger describes implicitly requires a mechanism that registers sameness and difference. As Watson (1994, 1995) has shown, the contingency-detection mechanism is tuned to near-perfect contingency at first, before it allows less-than-perfect contingency (Fonagy, Gergely, Jurist, & Target, 2002, p. 188). It may be that this is the mechanism by which the very early disavowal occurs, as anything less than perfect contingency with what the infant perceives as safe/preferred experience is not registered. With increasing development, however, the mechanisms for repression and more active disavowal and denial become possible.

Second, what Weininger describes as the "self-perception of one's own being in the world" is not, in fact, a simple image or perception but rather a more complex, integrative phenomenon that ties together various different, and sometimes conflicting, self-perceptions/self-representations (the angry elements, the good elements, the loving elements, the vulnerable elements, and so on). Suspending this integrative function means that the individual can continue to reside in simple identifications, feeling, for example, wholly good or wholly safe, until this precarious identification is threatened and the individual is pitched into feeling wholly bad or utterly in danger. Until these integrative capacities have developed in the infant, he/she will be dependent on the disavowal of affects or the self-regulation by the other.

It can be seen, therefore, that there are a number of defensive phenomena occurring: an early disowning and disavowal of affects, a later repression of affects, and a disavowal of integrative ego-functioning. The disavowal and repression of affects will mean that the later-developing, more complete, integrated picture of the self will also be compromised. These processes work alongside each other and, together, serve to undermine the personality. It is open to question in what way the hostile attacks would serve to destroy the needs and feelings. It would seem likely that the hostility is aimed at the destruction of second-order representational, thinking capacities of the individual—in so far as they have developed—and the integrative aspect of ego-functioning. Certainly that has been my clinical experience with adults.

Third, the relational element is absolutely key to these phenomena and can be understood in a different way to that outlined by Weininger. His book has a wealth of examples, one of which is that of a four-year-old boy, Sam, who was refusing to do anything that his parents asked of him. He would be aggressive and belligerent and would then, suddenly, talk obsessively about death. On one occasion he said that he wanted all the family to die at the same time, with his father and sister buried at the bottom while he was buried on top of his mother. Weininger comments,

Sam seems to have attempted to cope with his envy by becoming one with the good, desired, and satisfying object, his mother. By joining with her in death, he has the phantasy that he will never lose her . . . Death is the only solution Sam can arrive at. [Weininger, 1996, p. 57]

Weininger also commented on the Oedipal element in this vignette.

One can ask whether Sam's becoming one with his mother was an attempt to cope with his envy or, alternatively, whether his envy was the manifestation of his attempt to remain at one with his mother? *This suggests a different conception of envy as intimately related to separateness and thereby occurring, through the operation of the affective appraisal mechanism, from the beginning of life.* Sam's belligerence and attacks were towards anything that signalled that his parents were separate from him, and his obsessive talk of death related to his wish to kill off everything that was separate. He wanted, perhaps, to make death something that he could omnipotently administer rather than something that he experienced in opposition to himself, and which had the ability to separate him from others. At the age of four Sam had, potentially, achieved representational status and killing off his integrated self-representation would be a way of attempting to continue his adhesive identification to his mother.

Fourth, Weininger gives two other examples of four-year-old children who felt intensely and obsessively that they were "bad", and that they would, for example, pollute everything. It appeared, certainly in one of these cases, that the parents were good (enough), kind, and loving, although at their wits' end as to how to help their son's extreme distress. Weininger concludes:

I believe the child's anxieties were related to the object that he had created in his mind—*the phantasy object.* This object was not totally unlike the real object, the parent, but it was distorted. *The extent of the distortion was related to the child's sense of his own hostility towards the real objects.* [*ibid.*, p. 20, my italics]

As discussed in Chapter One in relation to paranoid experience, while the individual's own aggressive feelings are part of the phenomena, reinforcing the child's sense of badness, it is not necessarily the projection of these feelings, which then become persecutory, that is the key to these phenomena. The child feels intensely bad because they feel intensely *different* and *separate* and are bitterly opposed to that separateness (because it represents their whole experience of self). It is this intense reaction to difference that distorts the object. It is not so much a *phantasy object* then, just as it was not so much a *phantasy* of being united with his mother in the example of Sam, previously; rather it is the child's *real experience of separateness* that is appalling to him. As Alvarez (1992) has shown in her analysis of a boy with severe autistic features, it is the gentle and human introduction of difference that brings therapeutic progress.

Fifth, linked to the foregoing, it can be seen that it is the individual's reaction to sameness and difference that underlie both the ego-destructive superego and envy; and, furthermore, that the death instinct could be understood as the force that destroys the individual's own personality, or attacks the other, in an attempt to avert difference and achieve sameness. Envy demonstrates the sensitivity to sameness and difference between self and other (which requires, of course, the monitoring of sameness and difference), with envious attacks being an attempt to nullify the difference. The ego-destructive superego could be seen as that part of the personality that attacks the individual's ego-functioning in an attempt to achieve sameness with the other (see Sam, above). Carvalho's (2002) description of the individual's attempt to bind the object, rather than simply to eject affects by means of projective identification (see Chapter Four), also expresses the defensive aversion to difference and desire for sameness.

Finally, regarding annihilation, it is worth noting that experiences of annihilation are not confined to experiences of loss and abandonment. The experience can also occur when ego-functioning is lost or suspended in more apparently benevolent circumstances, for example, *le petit mort* (the "little death") of orgasm, or the feelings of dying, or of something dying within the individual, in a gentle and "benevolent" experience of regression. Allusions to death also litter the mystical and religious traditions—the New Testament quotes Jesus as saying that you must "die unto yourself", and the Koran says "die before you die". Although these experiences might be made more manageable by being framed by the particular religious tradition, they may also, of course, be alarming and terrifying (Chapter Six further discusses religious experience).

Fonagy, Gergely, Jurist and Target: the social biofeedback model of the development of the self

In their book *Affect Regulation, Mentalization and the Development of the Self* (2002), Fonagy, Gergely, Jurist, and Target have developed a detailed account of the development of the self and the subjective understanding of self and agency. Fonagy and his co-writers' theory is based on the notion of *mentalization*—the process by which we realize that we have a mind that mediates our experience of the world. The recognition that we have a mind amounts to the formation of "working", second-order representations of self and others; the operation of these second-order representations they call "reflective function". To (over)simplify the theory, we can say that in mature functioning (representational functioning/mentalization) the individual recognizes themselves and others as individuals and treats them with due respect and concern.

Fonagy, Gergely, Jurist, and Target present a *social biofeedback theory of parental affect mirroring* to explain how the child develops their representational model of self and others. Their model explores the way in which the infant's automatic expression of their emotion, and the caregiver's consequent emotionally-attuned facial and vocal responses, come to be linked in the infant's mind through a *contingency-detection mechanism*—a mechanism that recognizes sameness. The forging of this link leads, eventually, to *an experience of the self as a regulating agent*, and the establishment of second-order representation of affect states, which create the basis for affect regulation and impulse control.

Underlying these theories is an understanding of the intentionality of the psyche. They write,

> ... the currently dominant developmental view holds that even young children are so-called belief–desire psychologists who attribute intentional mental states—such as goals, emotions, desires and beliefs—to others as the causes of their actions. [Fonagy, Gergely, Jurist, & Target, 2002, p. 146]

"Intentionality" is, perhaps, a better and more neutral way of describing the "paranoid" nature of (particularly early) experience, as the word paranoid carries the notion of the individual experiencing themselves as being threatened; many of the intentional mental states attributed to others are not threatening in nature as, for example, in "She smiled at me . . . she likes me!"

Fonagy, Gergely, Jurist, and Target trace their model back to William James' (1890, 1892) distinction between "I" and "me". They understand James' "I" to be the *self as subject*, the *agentive* aspect of self, as in: "I want . . ." and "I will go . . .". The "I", they suggest, is also the active agent responsible for constructing the self-concept "me", which is the *mental representation* of self.

In contrast to James and Fonagy and his colleagues, the understanding developed in the identity–affect model is that the sense of "I" associated with *action and agency* is impermanent and evanescent. This is *not* the more stable, background, containing sense of "I", related to integrative ego-functioning, that the identity–affect model describes. Action can give the *illusion* of selfhood as it gathers together and "concentrates" the individual in action, often precisely to make up for the *absence* of a developed sense of "I". For example, it is possible to undertake *any* action—going to the shops or driving a car—without a sense of "I". Indeed, the more a person is immersed in action the *less* of a sense of "I" they have, although they may, in fact, be experiencing a *fullness of (the sense of) being* (Weil, 1956). The use of "I" in "I will go . . ." is the self-referential element of subjective experience, which accords only a limited sense of "I-ness".

The identity–affect model understands the sense of "I" to be the subjective experience of integrative ego-functioning that brings together the different parts of the individual self that have been recognized as "me". The identity–affect model understands both "me" and the sense of "I" to follow from the representational aspects of the self. Without integrative ego-functioning the individual has no proper sense of "I", although he or she can make crude identifications about what is "me" and what is "not-me" that can, eventually, be built up into a sense of "I". Activity can continue without a sense of "I", and with only a sense of being. This sense of being can be a sense of being effective, clever and so on, and does not require a proper sense of "I". It is this paradox that social constructionism and Lacan pick up on, as described in the following sections.

Basing their understanding of the sense of "I" on agency, Fonagy, Gergely, Jurist, and Target describe five types of self agency: *self as physical agent*—"I can move things"; *self as social agent*—"I can have an effect on others"; *self as teleological agent*—"If I gesture the other looks . . . I have the means to bring about ends" (starting from 8–9 months); *self as intentional agent*—"I do things because I have prior intentions (e.g., desires) and I act on those"; and finally *self as representational agent*—"I understand that what occurs in my mind is a representation—what appears to be the case may not be", e.g., you may wrongly think there is an object in the box but I know it has been removed. This requires that the individual can hold in mind multiple representations of the world simultaneously, viz. Stern's narrative self. Fonagy, Gergely, Jurist, and Target's model coincides with Freud's description of the ego, as that clearly includes executive/agentive elements, as discussed in Section I of this chapter.

Because Fonagy and his colleagues base their understanding of the sense of "I" on *agency,* their model differs fundamentally from the identity–affect model in regard to the understanding of the sense of self. The different forms of agency they describe could be understood, it is suggested here, to follow from the different levels of *ego development and ego-functioning:* "Intentional agency" follows from the development of an alternative perspective (second order representations) from which to view the affective core—"desires are inside me"; while "representational agency" is due to the further development of integrative ego-functioning—the holding of multiple representations.

The consequences of this are that, in the identity–affect model, the subjective experiences of the self are understood to be a lot more differentiated. The model embraces and details the subtle shifts in the sense of "I" and sense of being, with the sense of "I" altering and dipping out at times and, in pathological and spiritual states, for lengthy periods. The identity–affect model sees the self as a *vehicle* in and through which we navigate our environment, with the state of this vehicle significantly influencing and, at times, determining our actions. Fonagy, Gergely, Jurist, and Target, on the other hand, treat the self more as an *edifice* whose construction sometimes needs completion and sometimes becomes deconstructed.

Fonagy and his co-writers appear to recognize the self as vehicle, writing, for example, at this level, we are moving to deal with self-regulation as much as affect regulation. Affect regulation concerns the regulation of affect, but it has implications for the self since it helps to bring the self into existence. [Fonagy, Gergely, Jurist, & Target, 2002, p. 95]

and

the more familiar one is with one's subjective experience, the more effective regulation can be. Correspondingly, the more advanced one is with affect regulation, the closer it is to self-regulation. [*ibid.*, p. 436]

However, what they are describing as *self-regulation* occurs when the individual has developed to the level of self as representational agency, and is able to satisfactorily regulate their own experience. *The identity–affect model is interested in the way that, prior to the development of a functional second-order representation of the self, affective experience almost wholly constitutes "self" experience.*

Bennie

These differences and similarities are perhaps best illustrated with a case example. Fonagy, Gergely, Jurist, and Target describe Bennie, a Jewish man in his early fifties, who had been receiving good grades at an elite university before dropping out with "classic symptoms of schizophrenia". He spent almost a decade living on the streets and in single rooms, refusing medication, yet "relishing his choice to live within a delusional world . . . on a sacred quest for meaning" (p. 448). Bennie recalled this time as a "period when he was fully alive", becoming defensive when reminded of his suffering during this period: for example, the occasions when he was beaten up.

Bennie was hypersensitive to others, being, for example, profoundly affected by a friendly glance from a storekeeper. Fonagy, Gergely, Jurist, and Target comment, however, that he was not always acute in his understanding of others' intentions, being quite paranoid in the way he confused what appeared to be innocuous interactions. For example, when his two-year-old nephew fell asleep after a game of hide and seek, Bennie's interpretation was that the child was bored with Bennie's company, without any appreciation that his nephew's sleepiness might have had an independent cause. The therapist concludes:

> With some help Bennie has moments in which he exhibits the capacity to reflect upon his affects. Although it is perhaps idealistic to hope that he might attain mentalized affectivity more fully, the battle to seek it is surely worth fighting. [*ibid.*, p. 452]

I would agree with everything that the therapist has said about Bennie; however, I would add the following perspective and comments. We could understand Bennie's "relishing his choice to live in a delusional world", being "on a sacred quest for meaning", and "feeling really alive", by understanding that at this time he had suspended his integrative ego-functioning and was centred solely in the moment, experiencing everything intensely and powerfully. The fullness of his affect gave everything heightened meaning and significance. (Bennie continued to experience ideas of reference while seeing his therapist.) Such an understanding can help us understand why Bennie might make such an otherwise apparently irrational choice.

The account of the therapy makes a number of references to Bennie's poor relationship with his father and his feeling that he could not please his parents, comparing himself unfavourably to his more "successful" sister. One could speculate that he had not been able to integrate his feelings of hurt, envy, and, possibly, rage with his father as a child (Bennie did not attend his father's funeral as an adult). Bennie had, perhaps, formed an unsatisfying false self, which broke down in his university years following the "breakthrough" to these other forms of experience.

It could be understood that Bennie had become enthralled and entrapped by these new levels of experience and, as a consequence of this thrall, he became disempowered, overpowered by the intensity of affective experience, losing touch with his ego-functioning, his sense of "I", and his sense of agency. In addition to the particular *form* of agency—Bennie had lost his sense of self as intentional or representational agent—there is also the level of impact the individual feels they can have in the world, that is to say, agency on the potency–impotence spectrum. In Bennie's case, the affective experience was at times so extreme that he felt *acted upon* rather than an active agent—affective experience occurs spontaneously and can be experienced as coming from outside if the individual does not recognize the affect as their own. He became a willing traveller, a passenger, for a time, on a quest determined by these affective experiences.

Sometimes, latterly, the therapist reported that Bennie felt a "deep, deep sadness about the trajectory of his life"—his ego painfully reminded him of the broader reality of his situation. He had not found the means to redress the balance between his emotional core and his ego, although his progress in therapy had led him to making many improvements, for example, having stable relationships with his caregivers and becoming a useful reading tutor at the local library.

In adults, Fonagy, Gergely, Jurist, and Target understand the kinds of difficulties Bennie exhibits to follow from the *disavowal of reflective functioning*. On the face of it they are presented with a problem with those patients who, like Bennie, demonstrate a sensitivity to others. They recognize this as a problem, and suggest that this is due to the "fractionation" or "splitting of reflective function across tasks and domains", explaining that the integration and generalization of mentalization does not occur when there has been maltreatment (2002, p. 354). They understand that "patients with severe personality disorders do develop a certain level of nonconscious mindreading skills", and hypothesize that if a child's caregiver's reactions were *so* negative, they are forced to fall back on the strategy of influencing the other by action rather than words (*ibid.*, p. 367).

The identity–affect model, in contrast, understands the sensitivity to others to be an essential element in borderline, hysterical, and even schizoid behaviour, as has been described throughout this book so far. To paraphrase Britton (1998, p. 46): within every schizoid individual is a borderline individual waiting to get out, and vice versa. Even autistic defences are predicated upon extreme sensitivity to others; for a good example see Alvarez's (1992) description of her work with an autistic boy.

Loss of sense of "I" and the alien self

Fonagy and his colleagues do address the loss of sense of "I", and understand it as being due to the internalization of an alien self that is not congruent with the individual's "residual self" (see also Fonagy & Target, 1995). They understand the powerful projective identifications characteristic of such individuals to represent attempts to make the outer world congruent with their inner experience. While the externalization of internalized experience (inner working models) is an important factor in later experience, the identity–affect model shows how these patterns are reinforced and maintained by *current experience*, and the effect this has on the individual's identity.[1]

In other words, while Bennie's personality during his time at university was not adequately integrated to include affective experience (so that his sense of himself was not vital and full, due, perhaps, to experiences in childhood), his breakdown does not simply represent a repetition of an earlier split. It was, rather, a massive shift into affective life, partly, perhaps, as a compensation for the earlier lack of integrated affectivity. Thus, it represented a choice of a "full life" of meaning and experience over a meaningless, frustrating, false-self life. This shift becomes entrapping and seductive, however, with the individual wrecked by the siren call of such powerful experience. The loss of the sense of "I" is due to suspension of ego-functioning consequent upon immersion in affect.

There is a powerful force working to break up the ordered, integration of ego-functioning. This is the force that Freud described as the death instinct. In the identity–affect model this force is understandable in the narrow frame of reference of the immediate, subjective moment, though appallingly *destructive* from the perspective of the broader personality. The everyday manifestation of this force is the desire to "get out of your head" through drinking, drugs, vivid experience, or even, simply and more benevolently, relaxation—to move from a complex to a simple sense of self. At the extreme, the breakdown of integrative ego-functioning allows access to experiences of infinite affect, as well as experiences of fusion with the other and, perhaps, the (apparent) intimacy of adhesive relating.

In contrast to Fonagy, Gergely, Jurist, and Target, the suspension of ego-functioning in the identity–affect model is understood to be a broader category than mentalization, and inclusive of it. The suspension of ego-functioning has further phenomena related to it, particularly the loss of sense of "I", powerful affective experience of a characteristic, "infinite" nature, and the requirement that the other act as a self-regulating other in an intense, adhesive relationship.

Intrapsychic agency and childhood experience

Finally, the identity–affect model outlined here shifts the centre of gravity back towards the individual by proposing an intrapsychic agency that does not need to be *entirely* explained with recourse to childhood experience. Fonagy, Gergely, Jurist, and Target believe that they must "vigorously" defend the environmentalist position (the importance of parenting on child development), as arguments in favour of genetics might otherwise "remove the logical foundation of most psychodynamic or psychoanalytic approaches, rendering the present proposals, amongst others, untenable" (2002, p. 97).

A substantial portion of their book, consequently, is taken up by trying to derive certain phenomena from early childhood experience, almost as if from first principle. For example, they develop the concept of "markedness", which is the caregiver's exaggerated emotional response, such as intense surprise or delight, which flags up to the child the difference between "pretend" and real, self and other. They understand markedness to have a crucial role in decoupling inner from outer world experience, necessary for the moving on from a position of "psychic equivalence" (the notion that what exists in the mind must exist "out there", and that what exists "out there" must exist in the mind).

The identity–affect model, on the other hand, understands the child to be intrinsically able to distinguish self from other from the beginning of life. The degree and manner of this differentiation depends on the level of perceptual development. The adult exaggeratedly marking their response will *reinforce* the difference between pretend and real, self and other rather than *create* it. In addition, the marking behaviour, perhaps, signals to the child that it is "all right" to feel the particular experience they are having, that they are not alone, that the adult can pick up on the feeling empathically, and can or will act as a self-regulating other.

In summary therefore, the identity–affect model is congruent with, although somewhat different from, Fonagy, Gergely, Jurist, and Target's model. The former offers, additionally, an understanding of the self, and the subjective sense of self, as more fluid and more fully and intimately influencing experience. It allows us to better understand certain clinical phenomena from the *subject's* perspective. The delineation of the affective appraisal mechanism allows us to see the operation of an active mechanism *within* the psyche, and not to have to derive the whole of the adult's behaviour directly from its roots in childhood experience. The identity–affect model closely follows Fonagy and his colleagues, however, in their understanding of the significance of the formation of second-order representations, and parallels their understanding of the significance of the role of the caregiver in affect regulation and the significance of this on the child's development.

*   *   *

Subpersonality theory

The final section of this chapter moves from models that see the self as edifice to those that emphasize the *mobility* of the sense of self and see the self more as a vehicle for the individual.

As well as the psyche being split vertically between conscious/ ego and unconscious, the psyche can also be seen to be split horizontally, in the fashion of Dr Jekyll and Mr Hyde, generating different sub-personalities. Such splits need not be seen as rigid, pathological dissociations between different sub-personalities, but are a way of addressing different self-experience at different times. For example, in a low, anxious mood the individual may feel hopeless and helpless while, a few hours later, they may feel completely different, feeling positive, upbeat and energetic, making plans for the future and engaging actively with friends. The more powerful and discrete/dissociated the self-experience, however, the less integration there is between the different elements.

Joe Redfearn's (1985) book *My Self, My Many Selves*, uses the term "sub-personality" as a generic term to cover those phenomena that might be understood in terms of Kleinian part objects, internal objects, parts of the body-image, different brain functions, phenomena such as social values, and Jungian complex theory. Knox (2003) has also related complexes and archetypes to Bowlby's internal working models.

Redfearn describes how such sub-personalities at times come to be experienced as the whole of the individual, and also how the individual can come to identify with different parts as they "wander around" their personality. In these circumstances the individual's overarching, integrating ego-functioning is suspended as he or she becomes immersed in these different aspects of his/her personality which, at times, come to feel like his/her whole self. Flexible ego-functioning can, potentially, link up and make sense of these different self-experiences, integrating them into a linked set of self-representations that functions as a realistic model/picture of the self. A simple example of one way in which an individual can come to reconcile different self-experiences is to recognise that he or she has different feelings and moods that each have different meanings and purposes relating to and, potentially, informing the individual about the current circumstances.

Social constructionism

Social constructionism is the term for a broad grouping of theories applying to the realms of psychology, social psychology, sociology, philosophy, political theory, and linguistics. There is no one "social constructionism" and, indeed, the term underpins various sub-groupings such as social constructivism, discursive psychology, critical psychology, deconstruction, and post-structuralism. I am indebted to Burr's excellent overview of the field in what follows (Burr, 1995, revised 2003).

Social constructionism opens up a number of areas concerning identity and self-experience that are relevant to the clinical sphere. It takes a radical view of the self as being without a stable, essential core, intrinsic to the individual, but sees individuals, instead, as multiple, fragmented, and incoherent. Social constructionism eschews "essentialist" terms like "personality" and personality traits and attitudes representing qualities, skills, and temperaments within the individual. For example:

> ... the words "anger", "hatred" and "envy" and the concepts to which they refer pre-date any one person's entry into the world as an infant, and in the process of learning to talk we have no choice but to come to understand ourselves in terms of these concepts. [Burr, 1995, p. 48]

Social constructionism sees the self as thoroughly relational, with the individual understood to construct a self out of the discourses (frames of reference and ways of interpreting the world) derived from our cultural (including linguistic) and social world. Such an analysis explores the way individuals are constantly positioning themselves in a manner that is acceptable with respect to their culture's local rules for their own benefit and gain. It also elucidates the manner in which such positions are laden with judgement, value, purpose, and prejudice. For example, Jackson reports Davis's (1961) observation of a psychotherapist "[trying] to convert a person with a temporary physical handicap into a *patient*. The therapist emphasised the disabilities' seriousness, to persuade the person to relinquish 'normal' roles usually played in favour of total patienthood" (Jackson, 1988, pp. 124–125 in Burr, 1995).

Discussion

In its understanding of the multiple, fragmented and incoherent self, social constructionism draws our attention to a number of important elements and concerns relating to identity and the verbal and non-verbal self.

First, it demonstrates the, in some respects, *arbitrary* nature of the elements of the personality with which an individual identifies. To develop a full, inclusive, and congruent self-representation—to include those elements of the personality that the individual may wish to disown—is the result of much hard labour (and possibly analysis). Winnicott's concept of the false self recognizes some of the conditions under which a limited, false identification may occur. The fact that the choice of second-order representations that go to make up the self-representation is arbitrary, however, does not make it illusory or unsound, simply contingent.

Second, social constructionism draws our attention to the fact that the individual adapts themselves to their environment and is thoroughly relational—that the elements of the personality with which the individual identifies are powerfully related to how this will *position* the individual in respect to the other. Not believing that there is a stable core to the individual, some social constructionists argue that the individual is more or less wholly determined by his or her environment. At one end of the spectrum, social constructionism has proclaimed the "death of the subject" where, as Althusser argues, we are simply the bearers of social structures, little more than human puppets, who only *experience* themselves as agents. Kenneth Gergen (1999) argues that the current emphasis on being an individual is destructive and dangerous, and that recognizing our relational being would help us to manage conflict and difference less damagingly.

These considerations have important consequences clinically. If the individual has no stable core and is determined by their relationships, should the analyst perhaps accept that they need to take on the role of self-regulating other? This is akin to Little's (1981, p. 54) dictum that the analyst must take one hundred per cent responsibility for his/her response to the patient's need (this is discussed further in Chapter Five).

The identity–affect model offers an important vertex from which to explore this complex area. The individual's preferencing of sameness and aversion to difference helps explain the individual's adaptation to their environment—that, at the extreme, the individual would simply fit in with the other. The development of flexible, integrative ego-functioning, however, allows the individual to move away from the crude preferencing of sameness and aversion to difference, and to respond out of the broader dictates of their personality so that the individual is not so completely influenced, regulated, or determined by their environment.

Social constructionism sometimes takes the crude preferencing of sameness to be essential to human functioning, concretizing the equation of sameness with goodness, and difference with badness. For example, in relation to the power of language that Foucault (1973) explores, to say that someone has a learning difficulty, to distinguish and separate them from the group of those who do not have learning difficulties, is not *necessarily* to make a negative value judgement about them, nor to take power and control over them. The difficulty is that there are many occasions in ordinary life when "different" *is* equated with "bad", and "same" *is* equated with "good". The racist and nationalist, for example, make just such equations. The equation only applies, however, when the individual *making* the judgement is operating without integrative ego-functioning. In society this is, unfortunately, often the case.

The first chapter described Rachel's process of moving away from crude equations of sameness and goodness, difference and badness. Increased flexible and integrative ego-functioning alters the sense of self, making it less affected by, and less reliant upon, the other, and enabling a greater ability to regulate oneself. Regarding the recommendation that the analyst should take responsibility for regulating the patient's self, my experience with Rachel, described in Chapter One, would suggest that taking on such responsibility *disempowers* the patient, increases their dependency, and colludes with a paranoid view of separateness. While the analyst does have to be sensitively aware of the impact of their comments, it is not the case that the analyst should necessarily act to avoid the introduction of separateness. Indeed, helping the patient work through the experience of the analyst's difference is one of the key elements of the process of analysis. Lacan, for example, whose work is explored below, held that, at the extreme, the analyst ought to aim at "absolute difference" (Verhaeghe, 1998, p. 181).

In the social constructionist view, the self-representation is a *co-construction* with others—this is essentially a description of Stern's narrative self. The individual can, however, collapse into becoming *determined* by others when broader, integrative, ego-functioning collapses. Some social constructionist positions, such as Foucault's, do recognize that the individual can have agency, for example, that individuals are able to "critically analyse the discourses which frame their lives", and to claim or resist them according to the effects they wish to bring about. "The individual is simultaneously constructed by discourse, and uses it for their own purposes" (Burr, 1995, p. 122). The identity–affect model offers an architecture of the self in relation to which these phenomena can be understood.

Third, social constructionism addresses the individual's lack of a stable core. With ego-functioning suspended, the emotional core of the individual is a mechanism without a fixed content—the essential nature of core consciousness and the non-verbal self is transient, although it will lead the individual to expect, and fall in with, particular *patterns* of behaviour—the internal working models. This, however, focuses on just one element of the psyche. Since ego-functioning *can* be suspended, it does not mean that human beings are *essentially* unstable and have no solidity. The self consists of a number of parts and, while we can exist/survive

without the solid ones, to take the "unstable" (without fixed content) core of the individual as definitive is misleading.

Finally, to turn to the anti-essentialist argument that there are no
inherent elements to the personality: this argument relates to the
contingency of the *naming* of affective experience. What we call fear,
anger, love, and grief, for example, is arbitrary and could be considered, as some Maoris do, as visitations governed by the unseen
world of powers and forces (Potter & Wetherell, 1987, p. 105 in Burr,
1995, p. 139). As Burr says "in the process of learning to talk we
have no choice but to come to understand ourselves in terms of
these concepts" (of fear, anger, love and grief) (*ibid.*, p. 48).

This arbitrariness emphasizes the gap between the primary,
non-verbal self and the secondary, verbal self that gives the non-
verbal self some form and representation, through naming. This
division is demonstrated by the tale of the blind men and the
elephant (see Preface)—how we name and describe things can only
ever be a subjective, culturally influenced approximation. Few
social constructionists say that we do not have a "true self"; most
simply hold that we cannot know it (Burr, 1995, pp. 81–103). This is
in parallel to Bion's (1970) concept of O, the ultimate, unknowable
reality. The question of essentialism is, therefore, an epistemologi-
cal issue of how we can come to know things, not an ontological
issue about their existence.

Lacan[2]

Lacan takes the argument a stage further. For Lacan, there is no self
and, as Nobus says, "in Lacan's view ... the degree to which
human beings are convinced that they possess a strong identity is
more indicative of psychosis than anything else" (Nobus, 2000,
p. 196). For Lacan the sense of "I", or self, is an *illusion* representing
the false identification with an *image* of the self—something that
occurs first in what Lacan calls the *mirror stage* (Lacan, 1949), where
the child catches sight of him/herself in the mirror. Such an image,
Lacan holds, gives the individual a welcome, though neurotic,
sense of stability, security, and unity.

Existentialist philosophers from Kierkegaard to Sartre have
pointed out that we identify ourselves with our job, our family, our
history, and our roles *defensively*, in order to give ourselves some

sense of security and solidity—we try to hang on to a sense of "I" and become frightened lest we should lose it. Lacan was steeped in this philosophical tradition. Sartre (1943) suggests that we try to give ourselves the solidity of physical objects, to exist in the way that, for example, a table does. He argues that this limits our development and does not let in new experience or change, and that this is ultimately futile; he calls this kind of being "*en-soi*" (in-itself).

Interestingly, Sartre makes a distinction between conscious and self-conscious states of mind, and claims that self-conscious states allow a freedom to the individual, having the quality of what Sartre calls "*pour-soi*" (for-itself). Sartre is arguing for the ability to free ourselves from singular, defensive identifications by moving on to second-order representations, which allow imagination and reflection. He is describing the ability to be more fluidly inclusive of different self-representations. Such philosophical traditions much influenced Lacan's thinking (Borch-Jacobsen, 1991) and are implicit in his model. Perhaps significantly for Lacan's subsequent views, Sartre did not appear to discover the "mystical route" out of his dilemma with identity—that of giving up representational thinking entirely to become immersed in affect. Lacan's model is similarly rooted in words and representations.

Regarding the self behind the illusory identifications that Lacan describes, Nobus writes,

> Lacan contended that the me is a mental component that "is constructed like an onion, one could peel it and discover the successive identifications which have constituted it" (Lacan, 1988, p. 171). But behind all these identifications there is no essential core, no central nucleus, no anchored true identity. The me does not operate as part of a larger "self", nor does it shield a hidden self. It is but a surface or wall behind which there is nothing to be found. [Nobus, 2000, p. 197]

Lacan's view is sympathetic to many of the concerns of social constructionism. As the quote from Nobus indicates, Lacan was also sceptical about whether there is an essential core to the individual. Indeed, his theories rest, to a large degree, on a similar analysis of the role of language in defining the individual.

Lacan argues that the unconscious, which he sees as the ground of all being, is structured like a language. In the unconscious the signifiers of language—for example, words, simple (first-order) representations, or perceptions—are not used as signs, pointing to the things signified, but are constantly sliding and shifting, a continually circulating chain, having no fixed meaning and therefore offering no stability for the individual (Klages, 2001, p. 2). He derives this view from Freud's understanding of the unconscious as governed by condensation and displacement—concepts directly relating to the structure of language (where meanings can be displaced from one signifier to another, or condensed into one signifier from others).[3]

For Lacan, human development is the process of trying to fix and stabilize this sliding of the chain of signifiers, which is achieved through the association of signifiers with signifieds, that is to say, making the signifiers signs, pointing to fixed and agreed objects. This stabilization of the chain of signifiers also allows the identification of an "I", even though this is only, in fact, an illusion. The child in the mirror stage is able to anticipate being whole and grasps at this image in order to gain a specious sense of stability. For Lacan, what is taken to be self is always *other than* the individual. Furthermore, the individual's identity is rooted in the "Other"—the individual is a *social* being.

Lacan understands that there are different *realms* in which the child/individual can reside. In the *symbolic* realm signifiers are fixed and language is stable. Before this is achieved the child passes through the *imaginary* realm, typified by the struggles of the mirror stage where the child makes his/her first imaginative leaps of identification. Most basic is the *real* realm, Lacan held, where there is no distinction between him/herself and others, where there is original unity, fullness, and completeness, where there is no absence, loss or lack (Klages, 2001, p. 5; Verhaeghe, 1998, p. 166). This is not, strictly, a developmental model, as, like Stern's senses of being, these realms are available from the beginning of life.

The real realm would correspond, in the identity–affect model, to there being only a sense of (the fullness of) being, where the individual is full up with, and encompassed by, the particular experience. This is an actual experience. Lacan, on the other hand, would see the real as an original state of unity that is irredeemably lost as soon as there is symbolization. The real is unknowable and unconscious, that is, it cannot be reflected upon, as any reflection represents an alienation from the subject itself. The subject is, there-fore, a subject *of* the unconscious (Lacan, 1988, pp. 54–65). As soon as the individual makes any identification or representation, this constitutes a *misrecognition*. The ego is, therefore, an illusion and a falsehood. Man, for Lacan, is essentially alienated from himself.

In moving into the symbolic realm the individual must recognize loss and, in particular, the loss of the original unity. This is something that the individual does not wish to do, with the wish to return to the real realm being a continual feature of adulthood. But this desire—and Lacan uses the term desire in a very specific way following on from Kojève, Hegel and Heidegger—can never be satisfied (Borch-Jacobsen, 1991, pp. 16, 208). The truth of the individual's being is to be, precisely, nothing (*ibid.*, p. 110) and, in particular, to be open to the unknowable unconscious. The individual must accept this loss and nothingness to avoid falling into the lies, false identifica-tions, and misrecognitions of the ego. Lacan drew his thesis from Hegel, who proposed a stage of "natural life" which does not know itself, and knows no otherness, before it becomes conscious of itself through the experience of limitation and death (*ibid.*, p. 16).

Discussion

Lacan puts the unconscious, with its ineffable, unknowable nature, at the centre of his understanding of the psyche. At the same time he casts doubt on the constructions and self-representations of the verbal self, while also giving pre-eminence to the verbal sphere and down-grading the significance of the affective elements. For the identity–affect model developed here, as argued in relation to social constructionism, the fact that the self-representation held in the ego is not wholly "realistic" does not necessarily represent a fatal flaw of the ego.

The development of second-order representation brings with it the ability to experience a stable sense of "I", and affords a perspec-tive from which to think about, contain, and organize affective experience. This growth in ego-functioning allows a stability to the personality so that the individual is not immersed in immediate experience without a sense of "I", although this process does involve some loss. Lacan gives a great deal of significance to such loss, one example of which would be Rachel's resistance to the loss of intensity of experience as the analysis proceeded.

The lack of realism of the ego/second-order representations can be understood to be due to a number of factors: first, to defensive objectives, with the individual denying or repressing their feelings, for example, of hatred; second, to a lack of development, self-knowledge, or misrecognition—it can be difficult to know what we really think (see Chapter Three); and third, on a more philosophical level, it may be due to the fact that, like the blind men and the elephant, the "picture" of the elephant is a construction built from the other senses—we cannot really "know" what is there. This latter criticism has only limited application, however, as, while the "ultimate reality" may be unknowable, we can only work from what we have— we are not saying that there is not an elephant there—this is to take up a "realist" position.

Although Lacan's cynicism about representation—his claim that we are under an illusion about our identity—is beguiling (see Borch-Jacobsen, 1991, Chapter One), what he raises in its place is not ultimately convincing. Lacan holds that the sense of "I" is an illusion, that there is no core, and that the individual must accept the nothingness that lies beneath this illusion. It is argued here that Lacan's position represents taking the subjective experiences of nothingness (see following section), the sense of transcendence associated with it, and the alienability of the sense of "I", at face value. Lacan does not appreciate that these experiences are due to shifts in the individual's experience of identity and ego-functioning and are relative to that, rather than ultimate truths about human nature.

Lacan also takes the inalienable and essential, but shifting and undefined, nature of the sense of being to signify that there is "no essential core, no central nucleus, no anchored true identity" (Nobus, 2000). The identity–affect model, on the other hand, takes the perceptual system (with its intrinsic affective appraisal mechanism) to be the core of the individual, as Freud took the *system Pcp* to be the core of the ego. This provides the individual with a continually changing stream of experience. The fact that it is continually changing does not make it any the less real; in fact, this shows that it is orientated to the continually changing external reality. The individual's task is to be in touch and congruent with the stream of perception, even if the stream itself has been "doctored" through the operation of the affective appraisal mechanism. Hence, for example, an experience of the same dog will be different to its dog-loving owner and someone who has a fear of dogs.

Finally, in parallel with Lacan's argument about desire, without second-order representation we are left with only the affective experience of the non-verbal self. This affective experience is problematic, as the absence of ego-functioning brings immersion in affect, dissociation, and psychosis. Hence Lacan, echoing Balint's comments about the impossibility of satisfying the individual in a malignant regression, concludes that desire cannot be satisfied. Lacan is left, therefore, with a hiatus, and a self that has no essential core.

The identity–affect model offers a different resolution to this difficulty. While accepting that the sense of "I" is only ever an approximate self-representation, it recognizes that it is a necessary factor for the containment of affect. With flexible, integrated ego-functioning desire becomes satiable, as the individual does not become immersed in affective experience from which he or she cannot extricate themself.

Lacan, however, does not see that affect can constitute the core of the individual's (sense of) being as, for him, what is vital is *language*. As Borch-Jacobsen writes,

> ... what Freud had described in terms of affect (love, hatred, anxiety, guilt) is entirely transcribed in terms of "signifying intention" and "social expression" (Lacan, 1966, 83). This feature remains constant in Lacan's later descriptions of the transference, to the point of hardening into outright dogma; affect, as experienced "beyond language," is hardly important (1977a, 40/248, 57/267); what matters is affect only as "transmitted by language" (1966, 83)—that is as exteriorised in intersubjective dialogue. [Borch-Jacobsen, 1991, p. 76]

In contrast to Lacan, the identity–affect model takes the experience of affect to be central to the psyche, and the working through and integration of affect "beyond language" to be key to the process of analysis, even if the affects themselves are considered to be examples of signifiers which are seen as unfixed and unreliable.

The experience of being nothing

The fact that I can experience myself as not existing does not mean that I do not exist, or that I have no core. The experience of being nothing follows from the suspension of integrative ego-functioning and therewith the cessation of the sense of "I", a lack of identification with any self-representation, and with the individual being encompassed by the experience of the present moment. Here there is a *sense of being* that is, on this occasion, a sense of being empty. The *sense of being* is like a conduit determined exactly by what is flowing through it. Our *sense of being* can be one of dying, being annihilated, not existing, being full of joy, or love, being omniscient, being the most powerful person in the world, or being Napoleon Bonaparte.

The French Christian philosopher and mystic Simone Weil said, "We have to know that we are nothing, that the impression of being somebody is an illusion . . ." (Weil, 1956). She thought that being nothing was the highest state that we could attain. She described how, at these times, the individual experiences a "fullness of being"; indeed, it is from Simone Weil that I have, essentially, taken the notion of "being". Religious traditions offer many examples of being nothing—the Buddhist notion of the self being an illusion is one such example. Some Jungians also take the ego-less, "transcendent" state as the pinnacle of human experience and development (Field, 1996; Young-Eisendrath, 1997; and see also Chapter Six on Jung and spiritual experience).

The more deeply we feel something, the less of a sense of "I" we have, while feeling increasingly true to our "real selves". This is a paradox that lies at the heart of issues of identity. This fullness of being, which can feel sublime, can easily turn sour as the affect in which we are immersed changes. The individual who is out of touch with the leavening of the broader perspective, provided by integrative ego-functioning, can become "full of themselves". As Lacan says, the conviction of a strong identity is indicative of psychosis, with the individual overtaken by, immersed in, and identified with, a particular experience of being. The individual's identifications need to remain fluid, broad, and inclusive in order to avoid this. In Winnicott's terms, the true self must remain hidden, or, in Jung's terms, the ego must not identify with the self.

Only flexible ego-functioning can allow us to drink from the deadly but life-giving waters of life and contain us while we do so.

Notes

1. It would be wrong to portray Fonagy, Gergely, Jurist, and Target as holding a simplistic view of early experience. However, as they write,

    > We move away from the model where the early relationship is principally seen as the generator of a template for later relationships (e.g. Bowlby, 1980). Instead, we argue that early experience, no doubt via its impact on development at both psychological and neurophysiological levels, determines the "depth" to which the social environment may be processed. [2002, p. 7]

2. I am indebted to Bob Withers for the challenging dialogue over this section—any remaining misunderstandings of Lacan are my own.
3. Matte Blanco's analysis of the unconscious, similarly to Lacan's, also takes its starting point in Freud's analysis of the characteristics of the unconscious. Matte Blanco's analysis represents a critique of Lacan's view. Matte Blanco includes, in addition to condensation and displacement, analysed by Lacan, *timelessness, replacement of external by internal reality* and *absence of mutual contradiction*. Matte Blanco (1975) analysed all these functions as being due to the unconscious registering the *symmetry*, the sameness, between one thing and the next, so that, for example, a man in a dream could represent a father, a son, a husband, a lover, and so forth—it is the sameness, the "man-ness" that is common to each. In Matte Blanco's terms it is the recognition of sameness that allows the chain of signifiers to circulate and slide, and that this process has a very definite logic to it (symmetry).

CHAPTER THREE

Affect

Introduction

Rachel's experiences of affect—her overwhelming experiences of terror, hate, annihilation, disintegration, hopelessness, and powerlessness—were clearly central to her difficulties. In working with this part of her it felt as if we were working with the sensitive *emotional core* of her being. This chapter looks at the neurological underpinning of affect, and the division between the non-verbal and verbal self; it explores further the concept of the affective appraisal mechanism and relates the identity–affect model to the psychoanalytic view of affect, in particular, the difference between primary and secondary functioning. It also introduces Matte Blanco's views on symmetry, and his understanding of the subjective experience of affect, and explores how this relates to sameness and difference. The chapter relates the split between the non-verbal and verbal self to the autonomy of affect, knowing and not-knowing, potency, and humility; and, finally, it provides an overview of the very important phenomenon of affect regulation.

Fonagy, Gergely, Jurist, and Target (2002, pp. 67ff.) outline what they describe as an Aristotelian and a Stoic attitude towards affect.

These attitudes could be seen to be mirrored in different attitudes to Rachel's feelings—to what extent were they helpful or to what extent were they problematic? Aristotle held that affects are fundamental to a happy life and are only harmful in so far as our characters are too weak to counteract and moderate them. He saw affects as beliefs that provide judgements about the world which can be justified or not. The Stoic philosophers, on the other hand, saw affects as false judgements and corrupting forces that lead us astray and, as a result, we must distance ourselves from them and act on the dictates of reason alone. For the Stoics, affects were beyond our control, things that happen to us and that we must resist. While it might have been tempting to see Rachel's affects as purely problematic, delusional, and without foundation, I felt strongly that there was an important truth at the heart of her experiences to be respected—that there was a baby in there with the bathwater.

Fonagy, Gergely, Jurist, and Target argue that the Aristotelian and Stoic attitudes can be reconciled in the two different systems of emotional response outlined by neuroscience, as in the model presented by LeDoux (1996). LeDoux describes the two emotional response systems in the brain: a primary, quick, affective, gut-level response, and a secondary cognitive response that refines the first response. LeDoux gives the example of a walker in the woods catching sight of a curved shape out of the corner of her eye. The curvature and slenderness are processed quickly by the thalamus, rapidly followed by the amygdala, which, says LeDoux, is the brain structure central to emotional response. This system operates unconsciously, triggering a warning signal to the individual, readying him or her for action: "there-is-a-curved-slender-shape-which-could-be-a-snake". This is followed by a second system, involving the more advanced, cognitive cortex, which distinguishes whether the object is a coiled up snake or a curved stick (*ibid.*, p. 165).

The Stoic attitude to affect reflects the more primitive, thalamus–amygdala system—an affect is something that happens to us; whereas the Aristotelian attitude reflects the measured, secondary, cognitive processing, which allows the individual to take some control over their feeling.

The two systems outlined by LeDoux correspond to Ohman's (1986) two dissociable modes of processing affective information: a pre-attentive analysis of the emotional stimulus followed by a later, conscious assessment of the significance of that stimulus. These two main, separate, systems operating within the brain (with many different sub-systems) are the infantile, non-verbal, affect system and the adult, verbal–conceptual system, which are localized in different hemispheres (Gazzaniga, 1985; Krystal, 1978). The right hemisphere bears the non-verbal sense of self (the sense of being) and the left hemisphere, the verbal sense of self (the sense of "I").

The early-developing right hemisphere is responsible for affect, the unconscious, attachment, empathy, a sense of corporeal and emotional self, and an organ of perception giving an orientation to reality (Schore, 2001). It operates in an affective, visual–configurational manner, consisting, in part, of non-verbal internal working models. The later-developing left hemisphere operates in a lexical–semantic manner, containing verbal internal working models, and is responsible for the conscious processing of emotional material (Schore, 1994, p. 238).

LeDoux is, in fact, interested to distinguish the emotional from the rational system in the brain. He characterizes emotion as a "full-blown emotional reaction" (the thalamus–amygdala system), for which he gives the example of Davy Crockett, who said that his love for his wife was "so hot that it mighty nigh burst his boilers" (LeDoux, 1996, p. 284). The identity–affect model takes a different line, and a definition of affect, emotion, feeling, and instinct is called for in order to clarify the field.

Definition of affect

In line with André Green (1999), the term affect is used here as a generic term to cover the terms affect, emotion, mood, feeling, impulse, and instinct. As will be explained below, affect is understood to pervade the whole psyche, with the different terms reflecting a spectrum of meaning along the axis of physical/somatic at one end of the spectrum, to psychic at the other. The terms "impulse" and "instinct" are taken to be more somatically toned (strictly speaking triggers or constituents of emotion (Damasio, 1999, p. 341)), while the terms "emotion", "mood" and "affect" contain both psychic and somatic components. "Feeling" is the most psychologically differentiated term, largely confined to the psychic sphere (Mizen, 2003, p. 286n). Affects, then, are elements of experience, with more or less feeling tone, and more or less emotional in nature. They may originate from within the body—a drive, instinct, impulse, desire, or aversion—or may be in response to an event outside the body.

Affect in the identity–affect model

This book uses a broader and deeper understanding of affect than LeDoux, who is interested primarily in the more differentiated and bodily innervated reaction of "emotion". The view developed here does not see affect as distinct from rationality, but as an essential part of the perceptual system (Damasio), sometimes functioning itself as a rational function (Aristotle, Jung (1921)), with the experience of affect intimately related to identity (the identity–affect model), and determining the nature of subjective experience (Matte Blanco).

Damasio discovered that individuals whose affective capacities were impaired also experienced cognitive impairment and he argued, consequently, that rationality cannot be properly distinguished from emotion. He writes,

> The apparatus of rationality, traditionally assumed to be *neo*cortical, does not seem to work without that of biological regulation, traditionally assumed to be *sub*cortical. Nature appears to have built the apparatus of rationality not just on top of the apparatus of biological regulation, but also *from* it and *with* it. [Damasio, 1994, p. 128]

A further radical intuition of Damasio's, which underpins the pervasiveness of affect in his understanding, is that *consciousness itself is a form of feeling*. As described in the previous chapter, Damasio proposes that consciousness arises from the linking of the new event/perception to the background proto-self (1999, pp. 19–25)—consciousness, then, is *"the feeling of what happens"*—the title of Damasio's book. The rational system is, therefore, built *out of* the affective system.

There is one further stage that underpins the understanding of the operation of affect in the psyche, one that takes Damasio's picture a step further: this is linking affect to an understanding of *appraisal,* and to the work of Matte Blanco on *symmetry.*

The affective appraisal mechanism

The term "appraisal" derives from the work of the psychologist Magda Arnold (1960) on emotion. Arnold wanted to characterize and define what distinguished emotion from other states of mind and proposed the notion of appraisal. She defined this as the mental assessment of the potential harm or potential benefit of a situation and argued that emotion is the "felt tendency" towards anything appraised as good and away from anything appraised as bad. Arnold proposed that emotions differ from non-emotional states of mind by the presence of appraisal in their causal sequence (LeDoux, 1996, p. 50).

All experience is filtered and appraised, however, not only "emotions". The appraisal system operates continuously, monitoring our situation, even though not every event triggers an emotional reaction; for example, LeDoux's illustration of the curved snake/stick—if it is recognized as a stick there is no emotional reaction, if as a snake then the individual is galvanized into a response. Bowlby, who also made much use of the concept of appraisal, writes,

> Sensory inflow goes through many stages of selection, interpretation and appraisal before it can have any influence on behaviour, either immediately or later. This processing occurs in a succession of stages, all but the preliminary of which require that the inflow be related to matching information already stored in long-term memory. [Bowlby, 1980, p. 45]

Regarding the matching of the sensory inflow to information stored in the long-term memory, Damasio argues that primary (core) consciousness itself is predicated on the sensing of what is *new*, and that the psyche is therefore constantly alert for change, and is essentially an organ for sensing *change* (1999, pp. 19ff.) This change is noted in respect to the proto-self—the background state of the individual. Knox (2005) also describes an integrative, intrapsychic "compare and contrast" faculty, "the means by which one part of the mind can find out what another part is experiencing" (*ibid.*, p. 626), which she understands as due to the transcendent function, a mechanism inherent in the Jungian concept of the self.

It is in relation to sameness, difference, and change that the work of Matte Blanco is of relevance. According to Matte Blanco, the unconscious operates according to the principle of *symmetry*— registering and preferencing the sameness between things and implicitly precluding differences—while the ego operates by the principle of *asymmetry*, recognizing the differences between things and not averse to those differences. *It is clear that the mechanism for registering change requires, and amounts to, a mechanism for registering sameness and difference*—a recognition of *change* is a recognition that something is *the same as or different from* the situation before.

Matte Blanco's analysis of the functioning of the psyche, and in particular rationality, mirrors Damasio's in that Matte Blanco (1975) points out that rational functions rely completely upon the more primitive recognition of symmetry/sameness. For example, the apparently complex, rational process of classification rests on the ability to recognize the sameness between the items to be categorized—to recognize whether a dog is a bearded collie or a border collie requires that we register the sameness between the particular dog and bearded collies in general. Sameness also underlies abstraction—note the recognition of the relatively *abstract* curvature and slenderness of the shape-that-might-be-a-snake in LeDoux's primitive thalamus–amygdala system.

It takes only a limited imaginative leap to suppose that, rather than the psyche being populated with different mechanisms, the mechanism outlined by Damasio for unconsciously registering change and generating primitive consciousness from a *neurological* point of view is the same as the primitive mechanism in the psyche that registers sameness and difference and that profoundly influences our sense of self and emotional experience, as outlined by Matte Blanco and expanded upon in the identity–affect model from a *psychoanalytic* point of view.

This primitive mechanism for registering sameness, difference, and change is understood to be the basis of the *affective appraisal mechanism* and is the core of the functions outlined in Chapter One of this book: generating core consciousness and, subjectively, the sense of being; subjectively experiencing affect as infinite; perception and classification; the primary, gut-level, link with reality; relating; and distinguishing self from other and developing representations of self and other (cf. Schore's (2001) list of the functions of the right hemisphere given above). These functions all represent different facets of the same system. They all represent the individual's *primary* reaction to reality/their environment. This reaction is, then, usually, supplemented by a *secondary cognitive* dimension, depending on the development, functioning, and purposes of the individual, which will determine, or at least strongly influence, the way that things are experienced, felt, and contained.

Sometimes these primary assessments will trigger a full-blown, emotional reaction of attraction towards, or aversion from, the object in question—strictly speaking it is this level that corresponds to Arnold's (1960) version of appraisal. Such an emotional reaction can be accompanied by bodily responses and emotional feelings. For example, if we have once been bitten by a dog this will leave an impression that will last for some time, unless ameliorated by other factors.

Even when there is no overt emotional reaction, affective processing will still have taken place. For example, on a walk through the woods we are continually assessing shapes and forms that might be sticks, rabbits, or snakes. We are always alert for a situation that would require a "full-blown emotional reaction" and our basic process of perception is continually sorting our experience accordingly. LeDoux holds that "the core of the emotional system is [thus] a mechanism for computing the affective significance of stimuli" (1989, p. 271). As Solms and Turnbull put it: "consciousness . . . consists of feelings (evaluations) projected onto what is happening around us" (Solms & Turnbull, 2002, p. 92).

It is worth noting that LeDoux argues that there is no such thing as an "emotion faculty" and there is no single brain system dedicated to "emotion". The various classes of emotions are mediated by separate neural systems that have evolved for different reasons (LeDoux, 1996, p. 16). As already stated, Panksepp (1998) delineates four "basic-emotion command systems" in the brain: the seeking, rage, fear, and panic systems. What links each separate emotion is their presence in consciousness; in this way emotions are similar to thoughts, although there will be characteristic differences depending on the system that supplies the elements that are to become conscious.

This affective appraisal mechanism is somewhat different from that which Fonagy, Gergely, Jurist, and Target call the Interpersonal Interpretive Mechanism (IIM) (2002, Chapter Three), as they are describing a more developed mechanism. Indeed they distinguish two types: IIM-a, early affect based mechanisms, and IIM-c, later cognitive mechanisms, which, they argue, are related to early interpersonal relationship and affect regulation. The affective appraisal mechanism described here can be understood to be the underlying principle behind their mechanism(s), which operates in the infant in various forms according to the degree to which ego-functioning has developed.

As Knox (2003), p. 164) points out, Jung's concept of the feeling function, describing a function of "subjective valuation" (Jung, 1921, par. 899)—evaluating "good" or "bad", "nice" or "nasty", "beautiful" or "ugly"—is also a form of appraisal.

Coming from the perspective of infant developmental research, Gergely and Watson (1999) have proposed the existence of an innate *contingency-detection module*. This follows from Watson's observations of the contingency-detection *mechanism*, which showed the infant's increasing (after 2–3 months) preferencing of high but imperfect degrees of contingency (Fonagy, Gergely, Jurist, & Target, 2002, p. 167) and a preference for imitation over exact sameness, and "nearly, but clearly not, like me" experiences (Magyar & Gergely, 1998). Gergely and Watson's contingency-detection *module* demonstrates that infants rate and predict contingencies forward and backward in time. For example, this module shows how the child investigates whether he/she is responsible for moving a mobile attached to his/her leg, slowing the movements of the leg to check the effect on the mobile (Fonagy, Gergely, Jurist, & Target, 2002, pp. 162ff.). They are, then, proposing a neurobiological function that reacts to and registers sameness and difference.

Knox (2001, 2003, 2004) suggests that the ability to recognize samenesses follows from *image schemas*. This is Johnson's (1987) term for the earliest form of mental organization, which structures and organizes experience while themselves remaining without content, outside of conscious awareness. Knox, following Ramachandran (2003, p. 58), links the operation of image schemas to the operation of the *angular gyrus*, the part of the brain where occipital, parietal, and temporal lobes meet, which may be responsible for *amodal perception*. Owing to this function we may feel that sounds might have a colour, or words might have a shape, and so on. Knox writes,

> This capacity to reflect deep links between superficially dissimilar things is exactly the function performed by image schemas, which could therefore be the earliest representations formed as a result of the function of the angular gyrus in cross-modal synthesis. [Knox, 2004, p. 71]

Similarly, research has demonstrated the existence of *mirror neurones*, which mimic the brain activity in an observer to the brain activity of the person being observed (Rizzolatti & Arbib, 1998). Other experiments have found *adaptive oscillators* that permit the individual to synch their movements to those of others who are moving (McCauley, 1994; Port, Cummins, & McCauley, 1995; Torras, 1985).

There is, then, much discussion of, and research into, the neurobiological underpinning for this important psychological function of the recognition of sameness and difference, vital for intersubjectivity and relatedness. It may be that it is a complex function with many different brain structures contributing to the different facets of its functioning. An alternate view is that these functions might represent different stages in development, for example, image schemas may be the first "formed outcomes" of the neurological ability to recognize sameness.

In summary, therefore, the identity–affect model understands that there is a preliminary affective appraisal of sameness and difference which sorts experiences into preferenced categories. This is already an affectively toned process, and the preferencing is intrinsic to the process. *In the infant*, the degree of overt emotional reaction depends partly on the brain system involved; for example, whether it is fear or pleasure but, also, significantly upon the mode and manner of regulation of the affect by the other. Such interactions are incorporated into the individual's experience as internal working models. What this means, in practice, is that the level of distress or pleasure an infant experiences and expresses will be related to the reaction of the caregiver, and whether the experience is managed by the caregiver within tolerable limits to the infant.

Whether a tolerable level of sameness (to the preferred criteria) is achieved will be a crucial factor in allowing the formation of a relatively stable background proto-self and a stable base of benevolent internal working models. These represent a secure base from which to experience new experience.

In the older child and adult, stability is lent, both by the broader base of experience, and a potentially stable and more formed proto-self, as well as the possibility of calling upon the rational, verbal system with which to reason, frame, and make manageable the current experience. The growing accommodation of difference, as described by Watson, demonstrates evolving developmental goals. For example, having established the proto-self the infant can begin exploring the further ramifications of their activity and relationships to caregivers. In a psychoanalytic frame this represents the development of rudimentary ego-functioning and the establishment of asymmetrical functioning consequent on ego development (see Matte Blanco, below). The shift to accommodate difference is not a once-and-for-all process, however, and an individual will often return to a position of preferencing sameness and resisting change, for example, at times of stress. The degree of sameness required by infants is of a different order to that required by adults.

As has already been noted in regard to primary narcissism, the initial preference for near perfect contingency may give the impression of an undifferentiated, auto-erotic state of symbiotic union with mother. Such a preferencing may help establish an initial sense of security and stability for the infant, from which the experience of self and other can be explored and elaborated; it does not imply that the individual is not object-related.

The pleasure principle, the reality principle, and the identity–affect model

The identity–affect model understands the psyche's primary categorization of experience to be in terms of sameness and difference (to the evolving set of preferences), while Freud (1900a) understood the primary categorization to be according to the pleasure principle. Sandler (1960), Sandler and Rosenblatt (1962), and Sandler and Joffe (1969), talk in terms of the infant building up a set of (primary) representations constituting a "representational world",[1] which bears out the significance of sameness and difference to preferences. For example, they describe how

> Representations function to "inform" the mental apparatus as to the state of the organism. *Discrepancies* between wished-for and perceived states (representations) lead to pain, and *congruence* between them lead to feelings of pleasure and of safety and well-being. [Perlow, 1995, p. 92, my italics]

According to the identity–affect model, sameness is experienced as good and difference as bad, although clearly there is some sort of correspondence to what is pleasurable and unpleasurable: for example, inherent to the fear mechanism is an aversion. That the link is not absolute is demonstrated by the fact that an individual may come to masochistically prefer unpleasure, although we are then talking about an altogether higher level of sophistication.

With sameness primary over pleasure, although linked, an infant or an adult will regularly prefer what is *familiar* over what is *pleasurable*—the "pleasurability" is held in the set of preferences against which the individual judges the sameness or difference (viz. Bowlby (1980, p. 45) quoted above). For example, Zajonc (1980) performed an experiment where individuals were presented with novel visual patterns, like Chinese ideograms, subliminally—so briefly that the subjects were unable to accurately state whether or not they had seen the stimulus before. The subjects judged the previously exposed items as preferable over the new (previously unseen) ones (in LeDoux, 1996, p. 53). Young children can be observed to prefer what is familiar, at times, over what is, strictly speaking, pleasurable. Thus, the internal working models (representational worlds) that are built up are not necessarily structured by pleasure, but rather by the patterns of relating to the caregivers, that is to say, what is set up is a familiar *pattern*. Such patterns will be structured by the infant's desire for sameness with, and aversion to difference from, their caregiver.

This understanding of the affective appraisal mechanism as *underlying* the pleasure principle allows us to understand the move from the pleasure principle to the reality principle. The widening field of consciousness accompanying integrative ego-functioning means that a wider set of preferences, reflecting more elements of the personality, can be taken into account, rather than what is simply pleasurable. For example, a child will come to see that, while he might want the sweet that is in his brother's hand, it might not be in his overall best interests to snatch it—this could also be out of self-interest, or out of concern for his brother. It is the attractiveness of "infinite" experience and its effect on the sense of identity (for example, feeling omnipotent) that will militate *against* moving toward the reality principle. We can note that both the "pleasure principle" and the "reality principle", as they have been outlined above, are "reality orientated", with the difference being the limited field of reference of the pleasure principle (the limited field of reference before integrative ego-functioning is established). In regard to the example of the sweet-snatching, the short-term goal of getting the sweet satisfies one narrow part of the personality, but ignores the broader, longer-term view of the consequences.

Psychoanalytic views of affect

While Freud (1915e) writes that "every piece of work comes down to affect", psychoanalytic views of affect have often been in the Stoic mould, seeing it simply as the problematic aspect of the psyche, disturbing the gold standard of rationality. For such a vital element it is surprising how little has been written on affect, although Sandler, Green, and Matte Blanco are notable exceptions.

Sandler, for example, over time came to regard affect, as Henry Smith reports, as "the basic organiser and motivator of the psyche and viewed representations as, variously, made up of affect, shaped by affect and, in a sense, the source of affect" (Caper, 2001, p. 597).

Classical psychoanalysis focuses on the discharge of instinctual tensions in some form of satisfaction. Freud gave two definitions of affect, not entirely compatible with each other. His early view is rather mechanistic, seeing affect as a *quantum*, a quantity or sum, of excitation: "capable of increase, diminution, displacements and discharge, and which is spread over the memory-traces of ideas somewhat as an electric charge is spread over the surface of a body" (Freud, 1894a, p. 60).

The free or bound state of this energy specifies very different kinds of functioning (primary and secondary process—see below) (viz. Green, 1999, p. 161). This would correspond to the Stoic attitude to affect as problematic, and Green points out that Freud initially stressed the detrimental consequences of affect on the function of thinking (Green, 1977, p. 177).

Freud's second, *qualitative*, view begins to engage with affect's role in perception. This definition states that affect is a corporeal and psychic experience constituted of a number of elements. First, affect is a discharge orientated towards the inside of the body—a corporeal, visceral side (the discharge may be orientated externally but this is secondary to the internal discharge). Second, affect is constituted of feelings of two types: a perception of corporeal movement (a form of self-observation), and sensations of pleasure and unpleasure (Green, 1999, p. 163). In this second definition, *affect is seen as a "signal"*, which gives affect a function analogous to that of thought in signalling something to the individual—Aristotle's sense of affect providing a judgement of the world.

The idea of the *quality* of affect also explains certain phenomena. As Green says,

> Up to a certain threshold, the affect wakens the consciousness, widening its field, whether in the direction of pleasure or unpleasure. Beyond a certain threshold, the affect disturbs consciousness; one is "blinded by passion". Below a certain threshold, the discharge is deprived of affect, the affect is not registered. Beyond a certain threshold, the affect submerges the activity of consciousness to such an extent that the subject falls into dissolution, even loss of consciousness. [Green, 1999, p. 165]

This is a good description of the different configurations of ego-functioning; that is to say, whether there is an enlivening contact with affect (flexible ego-functioning), too little contact with affect (inflexible ego-functioning), or a flooding by affect for a short or long period (integrative ego-functioning suspended).

Green's own distinctive contribution to the analysis of affect borrows from some of the ideas of Lacan and language outlined in the previous chapter, and builds on Freud's two definitions of affect. Green (1977) suggests that in the second, qualitative, definition of affect—signal affect—affect operates with a semantic, meaning-giving function in the chain of signifiers (*chaine significante*), whereas in the first quantitative definition, affect overflows the "concatena-tion" and breaks the links of signification in the chain, disorganizing communications and destroying sense-making structures.

What this means clinically is that, at times, affect serves as "a reactive defence against an internal void" in which the intense affect

> is the only proof of his own existence that the analysand can give himself, and where affect, rather than serve to carry the meaning, takes care of the function of externalising the self, within the limits of internal space, to all the parts of the psychic apparatus in which the object threatens to intervene inopportunely. [Green, 1977, p. 208]

We can note that Green is registering the link between affect and identity (the individual's threatened loss of existence).

Primary and secondary process

Overall, Green is introducing the notion of unfettered affect being the instrument that keeps the chain of signifiers shifting, as in Lacan's understanding of the unconscious. This is the key to the distinction between primary and secondary process. Laplanche and Pontalis define the two as follows:

> [In primary process] psychical energy flows freely, passing unhin-dered, by means of the mechanisms of condensation and displace-ment, from one idea to another and tending to completely recathect the ideas attached to those satisfying experiences which are at the root of unconscious wishes (primitive hallucination); in the case of the secondary process, the energy is bound at first and then it flows in a controlled manner: ideas are cathected in a more stable fashion while satisfaction is postponed, so allowing for mental experiments which test out the various paths leading to satisfaction. [Laplanche & Pontalis, 1973, p. 339]

This understanding of affect is in line with Freud's replacement of the concept of the *system Ucs*, in his first topographical model of the psyche, with the id (the "seat" of affect), in his second topo-graphical model. It is one of the ego's prime roles to inhibit primary process.

Matte Blanco

Matte Blanco's views are central to the identity–affect model. He takes Freud's concept of the id and its relation to the unconscious an enormous, category leap forward. He understands the operation of affect to coincide with the operation of the unconscious or, in his own words: "in its more preponderantly symmetrical aspects emotion coincides with the system unconscious" (Matte Blanco, 1975, p. 305).

Matte Blanco (1975) started by analysing the five characteristics of the unconscious that Freud outlined: timelessness, displacement, condensation, replacement of external by internal reality, and absence of mutual contradiction. He concluded that these characteristics could be explained if one understood that the property of "unconsciousness" is a consequence of what he called *symmetry*, where there is a preferencing of sameness and concomitantly an implicit aversion to difference, while the quality of ego-functioning is the registering and bearing of difference, which he called *asymmetry*.[2] He understood that in everyday consciousness we are dealing with things which have a *bi-logical* structure, an admixture of symmetrical *and* asymmetrical logic—feeling *and* thinking. The more symmetrical functioning that is taking place the more the experience has the quality of "unconsciousness".

In this way Matte Blanco was producing an understanding of the logic of the unconscious, which he also came to see as the logic of emotion. Using Matte Blanco's understanding of symmetry and asymmetry, phenomena that might have previously seemed mysterious and inexplicable can be seen in a new light and make perfect sense in terms of their own logic. For example, a dream figure who is helpful or hurtful comes to embody the *quality* of the analyst that the patient is struggling with—the dream figure and the analyst are seen by the patient as the same/symmetrical in regard to the quality of helpfulness or hurtfulness—the symmetry also means that any differences between the analyst and the dream figure are ignored. Furthermore, Matte Blanco's understanding of the *subjective* experience of affect and its infinite nature is illuminating. Eric Rayner's (1995) book on Matte Blanco offers a very good introduction to his work.

This understanding of symmetry and asymmetry cohere with the understanding of the affective appraisal mechanism and ego-functioning as described in the identity–affect model. The affective appraisal mechanism operates symmetrically—preferring sameness and averse to difference in respect to the individual's evolving set of preferences, while the development of ego-functioning means that affect is contained and the individual can bear difference, separation, and frustration of their preferences (a detailed example of symmetrical and asymmetrical functioning is given below).

A note on the unconscious

Matte Blanco writes, "When Freud discovered the laws governing the unconscious, he actually discovered the intimate nature of emotion, even though he did not express it in this way" (Matte Blanco, 1975, p. 307).

It would be an enormous task, beyond the scope of this book, to unpack and explore the concept of the unconscious and delineate its relation to affect. A few comments, however, can perhaps serve to indicate the direction that such an exploration might take.

The concept of the unconscious is usually called upon to explain the clinical observation that individuals are sometimes strongly affected in a way that cannot easily be explained by their conscious aims and desires. Or, as Laplanche and Pontalis put it, that mental life is "full of active yet unconscious ideas" and that "symptoms proceed from such ideas" (Laplanche & Pontalis, 1973, p. 475). The mysterious quality and influence that "the unconscious" has on the individual can be explained in terms of the nature and behaviour of *affect* and, in particular, the affective/instinctual elements that have not been processed and integrated with the ego. Freud was proposing something similar with his introduction of the concept of the id to replace his understanding of the *system Ucs*. This affect can be experienced as powerful, infinite, terrible, sublime, or monstrous in nature. Freud also held that the unconscious was structured by the Oedipus complex. The Oedipus complex could be understood in terms of the preferencing of sameness, representing a symbolic expression of the desire for union with the mother, and the aversion to difference, representing a symbolic repudiation of the father.

The *reified* "unconscious" is not the only use of the term, however, and a number of neuroscientists have been quoted above as saying that, for example, affective processing goes on *uncon-sciously*. In this case, the term "unconsciously" is being used as an *adjective* and should be distinguished from "the unconscious" used as a *noun*. As Laplanche and Pontalis (*ibid.*) suggest, the term "unconscious" is best understood as an adjective describing "those contents that are not present in the field of consciousness at a given moment". It is important to differentiate in which of the two ways the term is being used: whether someone is "unconscious" of their anger—it is not in their field of consciousness—(here the term is used as an adjective), or whether their behaviour is said to be affected by "the unconscious" (here it is used as a noun). In the latter case the particular alteration of behaviour can be understood in terms of the nature of affect and the individual's relation to it. For example, someone "unconsciously wanting to marry his mother and kill his father", could be understood in terms of the individual's desire for sameness and union (with his mother) and their aversion to difference and separation (his father's denying him this union).

To quote the neuroscientist Winson:

> Rather than being a cauldron of untamed passions and destructive wishes, I propose that the unconscious is a cohesive, continually active, mental structure that takes note of life's experiences and reacts according to its scheme of interpretation. [Winson, 1990, p. 96]

The unconscious as noun can be seen as a mental system—the non-verbal system of the right hemisphere—processing and affect-ing our experience and the "rational order of things".

Affect experienced as infinite

A very significant aspect of affect is the different ways that it can be experienced subjectively. There are circumstances when experiences are felt to be timeless, endless, eternal, powerful, numinous, imbued with beauty, archetypal, oceanic, and perhaps, also, infinite, to name a few adjectives. Such experiences have been referred to here, generically, as *infinite*. The experiences themselves are not of infinity but have a particular subjective form ("infinite-like") and follow the logic of symmetry and infinite sets.[3] In these circumstances symmetry predominates and an element of sameness and abstraction is experienced.

Ego-functioning and asymmetry

Matte Blanco, as has been described, shows that while unconsciousness is a consequence of symmetrical relations, the ego introduces *asymmetrical* relations, recognizing and allowing difference. The following example demonstrates both Matte Blanco's ideas in practice, and introduces the concepts of asymmetry and bi-logical structure.

If someone fails an exam, they might respond in various ways. Starting at the furthest end of the emotional spectrum, they may feel overwhelmed and totally swallowed up by feelings of inchoate badness and uselessness. They may feel that they will pollute the whole world with their uselessness and stupidity—their sense of "I" has been more or less completely lost and they have become overwhelmed by a sense of global or "infinite" badness. This is a psychotic state.

Slightly further up the emotional spectrum the individual might still feel intensely bad, feeling that they are useless at exams (note how the person feels that they are bad at *all* exams, and that this is an *eternal* truth about them). Perhaps, however, they retain something of a sense of "I" about themselves—the feeling of badness may be largely limited to exams.

Further up the emotional spectrum still, the individual may feel useless for a while, but recognize that the feeling may pass after a time. Their whole being is not swallowed up in the feeling.

Finally, as we rise to the more rational levels, where ego-functioning is taking place (and containing and integrating the affect), the individual is able to differentiate the particular elements in the situation: they might feel bad about having failed, but also wonder which questions they got wrong, and how that happened. They might also analyse their weak spots to see how they could do better next time. They do not have a global, affective response to their mistakes, but narrow the failure down to the manageable particulars.

While all individuals described here register the fact of the failure in the exam, the individual where ego-functioning predominates, says Matte Blanco, uses asymmetrical logic, that is to say, he or she can differentiate and recognize that failing *one* exam is not the same as failing *all* exams. Matte Blanco would say that the individual has formulated a *bi-logical* structure that is both rational (differentiating just one event) *and* emotional (feeling bad)—a bilogical structure that is both asymmetrical *and* symmetrical. The process of analysis, for Matte Blanco, is the process of helping the individual to move from predominantly symmetrical formulations to bi-logical ones; a process he calls *unfolding*.

The same spectrum of experience would be true of any feeling, from rage, hatred, envy, or fear to happiness, security, excitement, or love. At one end of the spectrum the individual is swallowed up by affect, at the other he or she can apply rationality to it. It is worth noting that too much asymmetry and rationality robs the experience of its passion, so that rage can hardly be described as rage if it does not penetrate someone to their guts. Likewise, love is hardly very attractive if it is severely limited, as is highlighted by the cartoon in the *New Yorker* which said: "Mr Peabody, I'd like to marry your daughter . . . For a while!" (Rayner, 1995).

While the affective appraisal mechanism and the ego are psychological mechanisms based in neurobiology, Matte Blanco describes the logical principles by which they function. This concludes the exploration of Matte Blanco's theories.

*   *   *

There are a number of further important vertices regarding affect that need to be explored: the autonomy of affect; the issue of passivity, omnipotence and humility; the question of agency and flexible ego-functioning; the issue of identification and core identity; questions regarding knowing and not-knowing, particularly in regard to Bion; and, finally, the concept of affect regulation.

The autonomy of affect

LeDoux's example of the stick and the snake does not do justice to the subjective aspect of the relationship between the verbal and non-verbal hemispheres. Subjectively, things are far more complex than: "Is it a snake?! ... oh, no, it's only a stick." A *whole world* opens up between the rational and the affective, between the verbal and non-verbal selves.

One vital aspect of this is that affects are essentially autonomous. LeDoux writes,

> Emotions are things that happen to us rather than things we will to occur. Although people set up situations to modulate their emotions all the time—going to movies and amusement parks, having a tasty meal, consuming alcohol and other recreational drugs—in these situations, external events are simply arranged so that the stimuli that automatically trigger emotions will be present. We have little direct control over our emotional reactions. [LeDoux, 1996, p. 19]

This is firmly in the Stoic model of affect as coming from outside. Jung sees affects in a similar frame. He writes,

> The autonomy of the unconscious ... begins where emotions are generated. Emotions are instinctive, involuntary reactions which upset the rational order of consciousness by their elemental outbursts. Affects are not "made" or wilfully produced; they simply happen. [Jung, 1934/1954, par. 497]

This insight is one of the cornerstones of Jung's whole theory. Indeed, Jung takes a radical approach to the non-verbal self as a whole and elevates it to a very special status in the psyche, as will be explored in Chapter Six.

This autonomy—the spontaneous generation of affect through interaction with the world—is something that we must all come to terms with in some way or other. A significant element of the first few years of analysis with Rachel was in helping her to see that the experiences that "hit" her and took her over, as if from outside, were, in fact, her *own* feelings. To register that they were her own is not to say that she could necessarily control their generation. However, through the analysis she was able to develop a different attitude and reaction to her affects, and thereby contain them.

There may be an element of choice involved in regard to submitting oneself to the autonomy of the non-verbal self. It can be, for example, a choice of taking up an essentially spiritual or religious attitude. Sometimes such experience can be sublime, "grace" being a good example, as Simone Weil (1956) describes so well. Bennie, who was described in the previous chapter, was happy to submit, more or less completely, to the "affective world" and its perspective. He "relished" this choice, feeling that he was "on a sacred quest for meaning" and feeling "fully alive". The immersion in affect brings with it a sense of heightened meaning and significance, as affect's "symmetrizing" function makes links between normally uncon-nected events. Similarly Gunderson and Singer (1975, p. 465) describe the borderline individual as someone who adds "too much and too specific affective material to simple perceptions".

Passivity, omnipotence, and humility

Such attitudes to the autonomous nature of affect can embed feel-ings of powerlessness and lack of efficacy and agency in the indi-vidual. Rachel certainly felt that she was powerless to affect, change, or control the world. For her this necessitated and required that I should vouchsafe change on her behalf, cementing the vicious circle of dependence further. This powerlessness and need, felt with such conviction, is, perhaps, one basis of the sense of "entitlement" to care that is sometimes described (Gunderson & Singer, 1975).

Such feelings of impotence will alternate with omnipotent and grandiose feelings as the individual becomes immersed in, *and comes to identify with*, the particular feelings. Rachel, having recog-nized her feelings as her own, struggled to cease to identify with them, giving up the specious sense of self/identity (a "fullness of being") and power that came with the identification, for example, sometimes feeling luminous and special.

The grandiose feelings she experienced were inextricably linked with her sense of identity, but also with the relational issue of adhe-sion to the other. Her feelings of being hopelessly needy and reliant on me, for example, became a powerful certainty that she accepted as part of her identity and that required and justified her adherence to me. Giving up such a view of herself also meant that she would have to "risk" becoming more independent of me. In the case of the narcissistic personality type, the grandiosity is more overt and related to domination of the other, rather than dependence on the other (see Chapter Seven).

Ultimately, an attitude of humility in respect to our powerful affective nature is important, recognizing that, in some respects, we are subject to it (as we are subject to the world). Such considerations apply particularly in the case of addictions where the individual has lost their sense of "I", and has become subject to the effects of alcohol, a drug, or an activity, and the feelings associated with it. As well as affording a heightened sense of being, the immersion in the affect associated with the addiction can provide the means through which other, less welcome, aspects of reality, such as vulnerability, anxiety, fear, and need, may be repressed and kept out of consciousness for a while.

The first three steps of the Alcoholics Anonymous "Twelve Step" programme come to mind in this regard:

> We admit that we are powerless over alcohol and that our lives have become unmanageable.
>
> We have come to believe that a power greater than ourselves could restore us to sanity.
>
> We have made a decision to turn our will and our lives over to the care of God *as we understand him*. [Alcoholics Anonymous, 1939, Chapter 5]

This is essentially a declaration that the individual will cease to identify with the feelings that have so overpowered him or her, and in which they were entirely immersed. The declaration represents a returning of the power to "God", giving up the specious omnipotence and identification.

Flexible ego-functioning and agency

Broucek (1979), Mollon (1993), and Fonagy, Gergely, Jurist, and Target (2002) take the experience of efficacy and agency to be the basis of the sense of self. The experiences described above indicate that the sense of agency can be disavowed, with the individual taking up a passive position in relation to their affective reactions.

While it is, perhaps, the case that whenever an individual has a lowered sense of agency this is accompanied by a weakened sense of "I", the identity–affect model would suggest that this is due to the fact that both the sense of agency and the sense of "I" depend on flexible ego-functioning and that, therefore, the sense of agency is not definitive of the sense of self.

The differentiated understanding of the sense of self in the identity–affect model helps to explain the sense of the fullness of being that accompanies grandiose states—with the sense of "I" suspended, the individual can still experience a powerful *sense of being* due to the identification with, and immersion in, one aspect of the personality only. This gives a specious certainty and force to the individual while, overall, the individual still has a sense of powerlessness and dependency on the other for self-regulation.

Flexible integrative ego-functioning allows contact with the affective flow *without* the individual being immersed in their affects. This is due to the individual being more broadly identified with all aspects of their personality. Owning feelings and acting on them in a harnessed way (under the auspices of flexible ego-functioning) gives a feeling of potency and agency. This is in contrast to feelings of passivity and impotence, which alternate with feelings of omnipotence, when flexible ego-functioning is suspended.

Good, bad, love, and depression— identification and core identity

It is also important to note that, with the crude identifications of what is "me" and "not-me", the individual can come to feel that they are *essentially* "bad" or *essentially* "good". While such experiences do not necessarily come to constitute the individual's *whole* experience of themselves, it can feel to the individual as if this is what is "most true" about them. These non-verbal affective states, representing the subjective experience of internal working models, come to constitute the foundation stone of the individual's personality, pervading and dominating the individual's sense of themself.

These identifications represent ill-starred foundations that can compromise the construction of an effective and integrated self-representation, as more "positive" parts of the personality are overlooked or disavowed. Such identifications often emerge powerfully in analysis and can be particularly difficult to shift. An example is given, in Chapter Eight, of a borderline individual's powerful identification with depressive and nihilistic states (Dorothy).

Stoller (1968, 1975) describes what he calls *core gender identity*, the feeling that one is male or female, which becomes established between the second and third year of life. Chiland, calling on Stoller's views, suggests that the individual identifying with the other-gendered elements of themselves, disavowing their own gender characteristics, is at the root of transsexualism (Chiland, 2005, pp. 57ff.). It makes sense, therefore, in line with Stern's understanding of the sense of a core self, to talk in terms of the early identifications with certain aspects of the personality representing an individual's *core identity*.

Revisiting LeDoux's comments about emotions being "things that happen to us", Bollas puts this in psychoanalytic terms in relation to the object:

> Each provision of an object is a transformational act: for better or worse. Our successes and failures in this respect have a direct bearing on our ability to set up objects that evoke particular self states and those that do not ... I constantly engage objects crucial to my own self experiencing. Such management is part of a complex relation each of us has to ourself, and in some ways, through self care, we inherit the tasks of our mothers and fathers. The quality of any person's self experiencing will reflect the individual's skill in meeting idiom needs by securing evocatively nourishing objects. [Bollas, 1992, p. 25]

Transient experiences of being in love, "good", excited, interested, or aroused, sometimes lasting months or even years, can often be sought in a similar way by individuals attempting to "inhabit" particular parts of their personality and self-experience. Such experiences are powerfully influenced by the individual's core identifications/core identity, so that certain states, for example, depressive ones, can come to feel like the true core of the individual.

Knowing and not-knowing

The autonomy of our affective response—the fact that we do not consciously create it—means that we have to "come to know" our feelings. This is not as easy as it may sound. As Fonagy and his co-writers put it, "We are often deceived about our affects, believing that we feel one thing, when in fact it turns out that we feel something else. Moreover we can and often do feel different things at the same time" (Fonagy, Gergely, Jurist, & Target, 2002, p. 87).

The different perspectives outlined in this book are testimony to the different perspectives we can have on something that might appear to be obvious, and which is immediately before us—our mind. Ultimately, as suggested in the preface, we are blind men who can only approximate to the truth. Bion called this O—"the ultimate reality, absolute truth, the godhead, the infinite, the thing-in-itself" (Bion, 1970, p. 26). We can make formulations but, if these formulations are in regard to inner experience, these second-order representations can only ever be approximations. If they are in relation to the outer experience, there is a further sense in which that reality is unknowable, as it is filtered through the mechanism of perception where we cannot be sure what influences are at play.

Human beings have a natural story-making faculty, a tendency to confabulation, in order to make sense of our immediate, non-verbal experience. Bergoyne (public lecture, 1998) described how someone who has been hypnotized to believe a table is in the middle of the room will, after detouring "around" this non-existent table, make up all kinds of stories to account for their erratic transit across the room—anything from "I thought I'd take a look out of the window then decided against it" to "It was a bit warmer on this side of the room and I was feeling chilly". This is one of the reasons that the Lacanian school so mistrusts the representations of the ego. Freud described a parallel situation in his *Introductory Lectures* (Freud, 1916–1917, Lecture 6).

Analysts are certainly not immune from this natural tendency and are constantly formulating explanations for the occurrences within the consulting room. Bion (1970) describes the ability to leave a space between experience and knowing as "negative capability", using Keats's phrase. This ability to "not-know" for a time is vital to the analytic endeavour. Bion recommends that the analyst focus his attention on O, the unknown and unknowable, suspending or suppressing his knowledge (K)—through suppression of memory, desire, and understanding—as transformations of the patient in O (which is real) have greater value than transformations in knowledge K alone (Bion, 1970).

Bion recommends that the analyst attempt to *become* O, rather than merely *knowing* it, as knowledge can only ever approximate to O. This suspension of knowing (the suspension of ego-functioning and second order representation) allows the analyst to fully experience and become O, the infinite—an experience that Bion clearly understands as mystical in nature. The analyst's suspension of ego-functioning is only possible through an act of faith (F) by the analyst. Bion makes the link between knowledge and ego-functioning clear: "The disciplined increase of F by suppression of K, or subordination of transformations in K to transformations in O, is therefore felt as a very serious attack on the ego until F has become established" (Bion, 1970, p. 48). Bion's formulations of O and K can be understood, then, in terms of the non-verbal and the verbal self.

From another perspective, the difference between non-verbal and verbal experience corresponds to Bollas's (1987) notion of the *unthought known:* we can know something non-verbally, but we have not thought it, so that when we come to know it verbally it has a particular feeling of "rightness", as if we are coming to know what we have known all along.

Affect regulation

To turn finally to the issue of affect regulation, there are two vital elements here: first, the question of the effect of the caregivers' affect regulation on the infant and their subsequent development; second, the degree to which an individual is able to come to regulate their own affects.

It is in the work of object relations theorists such as Fairbairn, Klein, Bion, and Winnicott, and their precursor Brierley (1937), that affect is put firmly in the context of the relationship in which it occurs. This work has taken giant leaps forward in the past two decades following Stern, Schore, and Fonagy, Gergely, Jurist, and Target, in particular, and referring back to Bowlby's work on attachment. It will only be possible to give the briefest outline of a few of their findings.

Schore's (1994) monumental work of integration brings together the findings of numerous researchers across the fields of developmental neurochemistry and neurobiology, developmental psychology, developmental psychoanalysis, and infant psychiatry. It establishes convincingly the manner in which early maternal care directly affects the development of the brain and the infant's socioemotional development, largely through the mother's regulation or dysregulation of the infant's affect. The concept of the regulation of affect by the other, which was so evident in my experience with Rachel, is thus demonstrated to operate from the beginning of life and to have a crucial effect on the individual's neurological, social, and emotional development. Schore writes,

> Development essentially represents a number of sequential mutually driven infant–caregiver processes that occur in a continuing dialectic between the maturing organism and the changing environment. It now appears that affect is what is actually transacted within the mother–infant dyad, and this highly efficient system of emotional communication is essentially non-verbal. Human development, including its internal neurochemical and neurobiological mechanisms, cannot be understood apart from this affect-transacting relationship. [Schore, 1994, p. 7]

Schore also describes how changes in the child's behaviour, or in the child's internal world, can only be understood in terms of the development of internal structures which can support those changes. That is to say, we need a neurobiological model to supplement our psychoanalytic one. As Stern describes it, the infant's early environment is fundamentally a *social* environment. The mother's role as psychobiological regulator of the child's immature psychophysiological systems directly influences the child's biochemical growth processes which support the genesis of new structures (*ibid.*). Schore concludes:

> ... there is general agreement that the maturation of the capacity for regulating emotion and social interactions (Campos, Barrett, Lamb, Goldsmith, & Stenberg, 1983) and the ontogenetic attainment of the capacity for the "self-regulation of affect" (Krystal, 1988) are critical to the adaptive functioning of the individual throughout the lifespan. [*ibid.*, p. 9]

(Note that Krystal here uses the term "self-regulation of affect" to refer to the individual's regulation of their own affect, which elsewhere Schore calls affective *auto*-regulation.)

By mediating and modulating environmental input the mother facilitates the growth of connections between cortical limbic and subcortical limbic structures that neurobiologically mediate auto-regulatory functions (Schore, 1994, p. 33). That is to say, through her appropriate regulation of the infant's state, the mother actively contributes to the development of brain structures that will allow the individual to better regulate his or her own self-states as they develop.

There are a wealth of examples and detail on the different ways in which the caregiver's regulation affects the infant. They concern, in general, such things as gaze, facial recognition, stimulation, socioaffective environmental changes, the transaction of shame, joy, rage, conscience, and self-esteem. Schore relates these interactions to developmental, neurochemical, and neurobiological changes. As Stern comments, the mother's caregiving activity is predominantly interactional rather than functional (interacting and dealing with the infant's feeling states rather than, for example, simply feeding and changing nappies). This is in contrast to what might be understood from early psychoanalytic texts (see also Stern, 1985, p. 238).

To take just one example, as outlined by Gerhardt (2004, pp. 41–42): the caregiver's gaze and smile signals to the infant that the mother is experiencing pleasurable arousal. In response, the infant's own nervous system becomes pleasurably aroused, setting off a biochemical response, releasing beta-endorphin into the circulation and, specifically, the orbitofrontal region of the brain. Such endorphins help neurons grow by regulating glucose and insulin as well as making the individual feel good. Dopamine is also released and enhances the uptake of glucose in the prefrontal cortex. This is a benevolent cycle that not only feels good but helps the social brain to grow.

Fonagy, Gergely, Jurist, and Target argue, in concordance with their project to set affect and affect regulation in terms of intentionality and mentalization, that the particular kind of self-regulating activity carried out by the caregiver may strongly influence the developing infant's sense of agency and efficacy. They contend that if the infant detects a high degree of contingent control over the parent (the parent is responsive to the infant's affective expressions, for example) the infant is positively aroused (Watson, 1994) and may experience further self-regulation by the parent as being due to their own agency. They conclude that successful emotion-regulative interactions involving parental affect-mirroring may provide an experiential basis for the establishment of a sense of self as a self-regulating (auto-regulating) agent (Fonagy, Gergely, Jurist, & Target, 2002, pp. 173–174). That is to say, responsive parenting and effective regulation of the infant may lead to an enhanced sense of effectiveness and potency in the infant.

Fonagy, Gergely, Jurist, and Target contrast "disruption-soothing" modes of regulating the child's distress, for example, throwing the child up in the air or tickling the child in order to distract him/her, with "soothing-by-mirroring" modes, as described above—where the mother empathically picks up and mirrors the same affect and soothes and comforts the infant (*ibid.*, p. 174n). They suggest that in soothing-by-mirroring modes the infant experiences active causal efficacy, while in disruption-soothing modes the infant's experience is likely to be a passive one of externally induced affect-modulation. Whether one experiences affects as autonomous or under one's own control may, therefore, be related, to some extent, to early parental styles of affect regulation.

Schore also details the effects that the caregiver's *dysregulation* has on the infant and their subsequent development. He describes the relation of dysregulation to the neurobiology of insecure attachment patterns, borderline and narcissistic personality disorders, and psychosomatic illness. To give one example, he proposes that borderline personality disorder follows from the child not having been able to successfully negotiate the stage of healthy narcissism at about one year, due to the fact that the parent is not able to positively respond to the infant's enthusiasm. Instead, the parent reacts to the exuberant child by withdrawing, overwhelmed, and emotionally abandoning him/her, thereby inflicting a severe narcissistic blow from which the child never recovers. The individual is subsequently not able to regulate their own feelings of shame and lack of self-worth and consequently relates desperately, by impact, on the other (Schore, 1994, pp. 416ff.).

Such neurobiological explanations, however, do not necessarily account for the phenomena completely. While the development of experience-dependent structures in the brain might explain *part* of the clinical picture, such deficits and underdevelopments need to be supplemented by an understanding of current interactional patterns. The historical *under*development of, for example, the structures that auto-regulate shame are often reinforced and held in place by subjective and relational considerations. For example, the borderline individual's continuing disavowal of integrative ego-functioning maintains an adhesive relatedness to the other, and thus continues to preclude the possibility of "space" between self and other in which shame might be experienced and thereby gradually integrated.

The understanding within the identity–affect model reflects a shifting between subjective (intentional) and objective (neurobiological) modes of explanation. This is similar, perhaps, to the difference between a manual on how to drive a car, and a manual on how a car works. The identity–affect model maintains the subjective perspective, as it is from there that the individual and analyst must work. These two perspectives are understood, here, to be complementary rather than mutually exclusive.

Notes

1.   Later theorists stress the relational nature of these representations— Bowlby's "internal working models" and Stern's "ways-of-being-with-others".

2.   To detail Matte Blanco's analysis of the five characteristics of the unconscious: an event is experienced at *timeless* if only the similarity between one event and the other is registered and the difference ignored, so that "before" is the same as "after" (timelessness). *Replacement of external by internal reality* is achieved, along similar lines, where only the fact that "an event has occurred" is registered, and the fact that one event was due to sense perception while the other was generated by an inner feeling is ignored; i.e., the event is "placeless". *Displacement* and *condensation* both follow from recognizing only the similarities between one person and another; e.g., my father and my brother are both male and intimately related to me (their differences, e.g., their age, are ignored). Displacement occurs when one characteristic is transferred (displaced) from one individual on to the other—if I start treating my brother as if he were my father; condensation occurs

if characteristics are condensed into one person due to their similarity, so that it is as if my analyst also has all the characteristics of my father. The *absence of mutual contradiction* can occur, for example, in a dream where someone is both alive and dead—only the "personality" is registered and other "incidental" characteristics (whether they are alive or dead) are ignored.

3.   Matte Blanco renders his concept of symmetry in the strictly mathematical language of infinite sets. This can be off-putting for some, but the ideas are basically simple. If only the symmetry, the sameness, is registered, he argued, then logic of an interaction follows the logic of an infinite set. In this way my father, a single individual, can be seen as equivalent to all other men who have ever lived and who might ever live, which is an infinite number of men, purely by the nature of his maleness.

An infinite set acts in a strange way so that two groups can be seen as the same when they might seem, commonsensically, to be different. For example, it would seem that there would be more odd *and* even numbers than there are simply *even* numbers, but this is not the case as there are an infinite number of *even* numbers and there are an infinite number of odd *and* even numbers (the list of such numbers could go on forever), so they are equivalent. This occurs whenever we focus on a sameness between one thing and another, essentially an infinity is generated—my hand is, *in some way or other*, the same as all other hands, past present and future; a curved stick found in the woods is like a snake as anything curved is, in this respect, snakelike— all curved things are like all snakes. This is essentially a feature of abstraction and generalization.

CHAPTER FOUR

Klein, Bion, projective identification, and the paranoid–schizoid position

Introduction

As James Grotstein writes, "questions about the concept of projective identification still persist" (2005, p. 1051). This chapter offers a reframing of the concepts of projective identification and the paranoid–schizoid position. It challenges Klein's classical framing of these phenomena yet is largely, though not wholly, consonant with Bion's later model. Klein's original formulation was in terms of projective identification being the prototype of an aggressive object relationship, and was set firmly within the context and understanding of the paranoid–schizoid position. Bion's developments distinguished normal from excessive projective identification, understanding the former as a mode of communication. Bion developed therefrom the notion of containment, the container–contained, and a theory of thinking. Meltzer took the notion of the container–contained and further described the concept of the claustrum, while Steiner elaborated the notion of psychic retreats. While these later developments have made substantial reference to Bion's frame, they remain superimposed on Klein's classical frame, often without directly addressing the underlying structure.

The identity–affect model developed herein offers an alternate framework that, in this chapter, is elaborated in respect to projective identification and the paranoid–schizoid position.

Meissner (1980) held that "the use of the term projective identification implies a set of unexpressed assumptions", although other authors have suggested that it is not necessary to subscribe to a Kleinian meta-psychology in order to recognize and use the concept of projective identification (Ogden, 1982, p. 75, Sandler, 1987, p. 19). Even if it is agreed that the concept does not "imply" or even require those assumptions, they stand behind the concept and are made more or less use of, depending on the theoretician.

Klein's original formulation brilliantly gathers together, defines, and addresses key phenomena that now represent the heartland of analytic work with many patients. Klein helped bring these phenomena into the light, addressing a particular kind of object relationship characterized by a loss of sense of self, the impoverishment and fragmentation of the ego, the heightened significance of the other, the significance of separateness, paranoid thought forms, and the attempt to harm, possess, and control the other. This chapter first describes Klein's original formulations before setting them against the identity–affect model, then introducing later modifications and other critiques, notably those of Alvarez (1992).

The classical Kleinian framework

First, here is the definition of projective identification as given by the *Dictionary of Kleinian Thought*:

> Projective identification was defined by Klein in 1946 as the prototype of the aggressive object-relationship, representing an anal attack on an object by means of forcing parts of the ego into it in order to take over its contents or to control it and occurring in the paranoid–schizoid position from birth. It is a "phantasy remote from consciousness" that entails a belief in certain aspects of the self being located elsewhere, with a consequent depletion and weakened sense of self and identity, to the extent of depersonalisation; profound feelings of being lost or a sense of imprisonment may result.

Without a concomitant introjection by the object projected into, increasingly forceful attempts to intrude result in extreme forms of projective identification. These excessive processes lead to severe distortions of identity and the disturbed experiences of schizophrenia. [Hinshelwood, 1989, p. 179]

There is also the more succinct definition that projective identification is "a mechanism revealed in phantasies in which the subject inserts his self—in whole or in part—into the object in order to harm, possess or control it".[1]

In the classical Kleinian model, projective identification is directly related to the functioning of the paranoid–schizoid position. The *Dictionary of Kleinian Thought* gives the following definition of the paranoid–schizoid position:

In the earliest state of mind, persecutory anxiety is met by processes which threaten to (and do) fragment the mind. Its severity affects the move onwards into the depressive position because the integrity of the mind is severely disrupted. The splitting processes typically lead to a projection of parts of the self or ego (projective identification) into objects, with a depleting effect on the self. The depleted self then has difficulties with introjection and with introjective identification . . . [Hinshelwood, 1989, p. 156]

Klein's framework puts emphasis on the function of the ego in warding off anxiety through a splitting of the *ego* (rather than simply a splitting of the *object* into good and bad), an idea she derived from Fairbairn (1944). These split-off parts of the ego are projected into the object. It is due to these projected parts, now located elsewhere, in phantasy, that the individual tries to possess, harm, and control the object, who is not distinguished from the self. The projection of these parts has a depleting effect on the sense of self. As Klein writes,

. . . the early ego largely lacks cohesion, and a tendency towards integration alternates with a tendency towards disintegration, a falling to bits. . . . Prominent amongst (the functions of the ego) is that of dealing with anxiety. I hold that anxiety arises from the operation of the death instinct within the organism, is felt as a fear of annihilation (death) and takes the form of fear of persecution. The fear of the destructive impulse seems to attach itself at once to an object—or rather it is experienced as the fear of an uncontrollable overpowering object. Other important sources of primary anxiety are the trauma of birth (separation anxiety) and frustration of bodily needs; and these experiences too are from the beginning felt as being caused by objects. [Klein, 1946, pp. 4–5]

Klein writes further that bad parts of the self are projected into the mother so that

... she is not felt to be a separate individual but is felt to be *the* bad self ... Much of the hatred against parts of the self is now directed towards the mother. This leads to a particular form of identification which establishes the prototype of an aggressive object-relation. I suggest for these processes the term "projective identification". [*ibid.*, p. 8]

She continues,

It is, however, not only bad parts of the self which are expelled and projected, but also good parts of the self ... if this process (of the projection of good feelings) is carried out excessively, good parts of the personality are felt to be lost, and in this way the mother becomes the ego-ideal; this process too results in weakening and impoverishment of the ego. Very soon such processes extend to other people, and the result may be an over-strong dependence on these external representatives of one's own good parts. [*ibid.*, p. 9]

Grotstein points out that Klein distinguishes two modes of operation in regard to what is projected:

In the first mode, *parts* of the self are split off and projected into the object (Klein, 1946). In the second mode, the self *qua* self enters into a state of identification with the object to *become* the object and, through unconscious *imitation*, either passively disappears to a degree (Klein, 1955) and/or at the other extreme may seek aggressively to take over the identity of the object altogether ... [Grotstein, 2005, p. 1054]

Discussion

In outline, in contrast to Klein, these phenomena can be understood to derive from the use that the individual wishes to make of the (m)other in order to regulate the self (Stern, 1985)—the individual being acutely sensitive to the environment following the suspension or underdevelopment of ego-functioning. The different elements of these processes are addressed below: the loss of sense of self; the weakness and impoverishment of the ego; the lack of cohesion of the early ego; the heightened significance of the other; the paranoid experience of the other; the significance of separateness; and the attempt to harm, possess and control the other. It is, however, somewhat artificial to separate these different elements.

The loss of sense of self and the early ego: The *sense of "I"* is lost, due not to the projection of parts of the self on to the other but to the suspension of developed, integrative ego-functioning in adults, or due to the lack of development of integrative ego-functioning in infants, as already described extensively in this book. Klein saw the ego as the subjective self (Britton, 2003, p. 93) operating from the beginning of life, responsible for separating me from not me, discriminating good from bad, responsible for phantasies of incorporation and expelling, and phantasies of mating of preconceptions and realizations (Hinshelwood, 1989, p. 284). The subjective self— the sense of being—and these different functions, can be understood to be due to the operation of core consciousness and the affective appraisal mechanism. This "early ego" does not carry a sense of "I"; thus, it is not that the early ego has split, it is that there is intrinsically little *cohesion* in this state, as the sense of being is dominated by the latest experience to enter consciousness. The only cohesion is that provided by the background proto-self and, vitally, as guaranteed by the regulation of the self by the other.

With little cohesion, the infant, and the adult whose ego-functioning is suspended, lives intensely in the present moment. *Introjection* of good experience leading to a sense of stability is problematic, as this can only be guaranteed by integrative ego-functioning that holds together the broader elements of the personality (giving the sense of "I") beyond that which is being experienced in the present moment (the sense of being).

The heightened importance of the other: As a self-regulating other, the other is of vital importance, as what they do is crucial to the individual's experience and sense of self. In so far as the other is experienced as carrying parts of the individual's self, this is due to the fact that the individual's centre of gravity is located in the other.

What the other does, therefore, powerfully affects the individual's self—it can sometimes determine their sense of being, which amounts to their whole self. In addition, without their own second-order representations, the individual has no proper self-representation and relies on the picture of themselves presented by the other.

The impoverishment of the ego: Klein understands the weakness and impoverishment of the ego to be due to the projection of parts of the self on to the other. In the identity–affect model the individual is impoverished and weakened for a number of reasons. First, the subjective self is not seen as a coherent entity that is then split and impoverished, due to projection, but rather it is not intrinsically coherent in the first place, being dominated by the latest experience to enter consciousness. Klein, on the other hand, posits an ego from birth that she sees as alternately coherent or disintegrating. Second, the individual is dependent on the other for his or her own self-regulation, and the more powerfully they are affected by the other, the more they come to rely upon the other (the vicious circle of dependence described in Chapter One). Third, individuals become "impoverished" due to being either out of touch with their own affects and/or full up and identified with certain affects with the consequent loss of integration with other aspects of their personality.

Separation, the death instinct, and paranoid experience: Klein understands the fear of annihilation to originate in the individual him or herself as a result of the death instinct, where the individual's destructive impulses are projected into the object. The experience of annihilation is understood here to follow, *in addition to projection of such impulses into the object*, from the experience of separation from the object which is adhered to and is operating as a self-regulating other. As Joseph writes, ". . . the infant, or adult who goes on using such mechanisms (of projective identification) powerfully, can avoid any awareness of separateness, dependence, or admiration or of the concomitant sense of loss, anger, envy etc." (Joseph, 1984, pp. 65–66).

The destructive impulses refer to attacks on anything that may separate the individual from the other, such as first, the other's difference and independence; second, parts of the infant/individual's own developing ego, for example, thinking capacities, which may serve to separate them from the other; or third, aggressive feelings towards the other, which, as Weininger (1996) says, the infant/ individual disavows. The attack on parts of the developing ego is also described by Bion (1957, p. 51) as characteristic of the psychotic part of the personality, although he sees these parts as expelled into the other through projective identification. The identity–affect model would see the "death instinct" as being in the service of removing the separating ego-functioning (of both the individual and the other) in order to achieve sameness. It is not strictly about destruction, then, although it is very destructive to the personality.

The object is felt to be threatening and persecutory both when the individual anticipates a response from their own attack on the other and also, significantly, when they experience something of the other's power as self-regulating other, so that the other may bring on experiences of, for example, annihilation, pain, loss, and fear. This is a *veridical* experience of the other's power, under these circumstances. Later delinquent, sadistic, or perverse behaviour may be an attempt to "pay back" this kind of experience and make the other subject to the individual's power.

If the other operates as a good-enough (m)other (Winnicott, 1960b), adequately regulating the individual's affective experience and sense of self, then such interactions need not be persecutory in nature but may be experienced as mutually enjoyable interactions. In these circumstances the intentions of the other may be felt to be life-enhancing and benevolent.

The attempt to harm, possess, and control. The infant/individual is affected by the other and is interested in how they can affect the other. In this way the self is developed, and the limits and structure of the individual as a physical, social, teleological, intentional, and representational agent/self (Fonagy, Gergely, Jurist, & Target, 2002) are formed. If all goes well-enough, with the infant being supported and engaged with, and introduced to manageable levels of separateness at appropriate times, then the infant develops confidence in its ability to effect others and trust that others will regulate their experience acceptably—there is, therefore, no reason to attempt to harm, possess, or control them. When the other does not adequately regulate the self-experience, then the individual tries to harm, possess, or control them, either as a punishing, vengeful, ejection of bad feeling (the harming), or in an attempt to achieve good experience (possession and control). The non-regulating other is experienced as bad and is hated, feared, and controlled. This brings us exactly to the work of Bion.

Bion: communication and the container–contained

Bion has done most to develop the concept of projective identification. He differentiated normal from excessive projective identification (1959), he extended the understanding of projective identification, showing it to be essentially a form of communication (1962a), he derived from it his model of the container-contained (1962a) and he related it to his model of thinking (1962b).

Bion recognized that the process of projective identification is normal,

> constituting one of the main factors in symbol formation and human communication, and determining a relationship of empathy with the object by providing the possibility of putting oneself in somebody else's place and, in doing so, understanding his feelings better. [Grinberg, Sor, & Tabak de Bianchedi, 1971, p. 26]

He distinguished normal from pathological or excessive projective identification by the latter's violent and forceful evacuation of affect and parts of the ego into the other where, in phantasy, it is believed they may be controlled.

From his view of projective identification Bion abstracted his model of the relationship of "container-contained" whereby, "according to this model, the infant projects part of his psyche, especially his uncontrollable emotions (the contained), into the good-breast container, only to receive them back 'detoxified' and in a more tolerable form" (*ibid.*, p. 28).

Bion (1962a) further hypothesized that this sojourn in the container was *necessary* for these contained elements, *beta elements* (which, in this form, cannot be thought about), in order to modify them into *alpha elements* (which are able to be thought about). This is understood to occur through the activity of the mother's/ analyst's/other's reverie, which is an example of what Bion calls their alpha functioning. He is offering here a model of thinking that embraces the function of the (m)other in the development of thinking, sheds light on those situations where thinking is impaired, and coheres with the clinical experience of projective identification.

Discussion

What Bion understands as the infant projecting "part of his psyche, especially his uncontrollable emotions", into the (m)other to be contained, amounts to *one aspect* of the infant being with a mother who acts as a self-regulating (m)other, reacting to the infant's communications and distress. This is simply the affect regulation. This describes projective identification as a form of communication.

For example, the (m)other's regulation of the affect that is troubling the infant may be through her ability to think about it, engaging her second-order reflective capacities, which Bion calls *reverie*; she may even name what is wrong to the infant—"It's your tooth coming through!"—and she may take action, for example, administering some teething gel. The regulation could also amount to being alongside the infant in his/her distress, nursing and comforting him/her, which includes the (m)other showing the infant she knows he/she is in pain (the soothing-by-mirroring function), or distracting the infant (the disruption-soothing function that Fonagy, Gergely, Jurist, and Target describe (2002, p. 174n)).

This affect regulation maintains the affect within bearable limits. It keeps the infant's inner world manageable and on course towards a time when they may be able to regulate their affect by themselves to a greater extent. As Schore suggests, this can only begin when the mechanisms for such auto-regulation have sufficiently developed. This requires the development of object constancy and, ultimately, the ability for the individual's own second-order representation, that is, the ability to think about the experience—alpha functioning. An illness, for example, is so much more bearable, for adults and children, when the diagnosis is known and the consequences can be thought about—even if they are bad ones. The verbal self can then reflect upon and contain the non-verbal experience, in this case, of illness (viz. also nameless dread).

The identity–affect model holds, however, in addition to Bion, that when ego-functioning is suspended or not yet developed, the (m)other's affect regulation amounts to the (m)other's regulation of the individual's *self*. The fact that the affect is intimately bound up with the individual's identity, because it amounts to their whole sense of self at that time, makes an enormous difference to the experience. It is *this* that gives the interchange the qualities of an "excessive projective identification", with the loss of sense of self and other qualities, although it is understood in the different frame of the identity–affect model.

The difficulty for the analyst in dealing with, digesting, and returning these "affects" to the patient is that these affects are set in a particular object relationship (to the self-regulatory other) and carry and define the individual's *whole sense of self*. It is for this reason that the clinical situation is so much more fraught. (The issue of the analyst taking on this role of regulator, that is the analyst's projective counter-identification (Grinberg, 1962), is discussed in the next chapter.)

When the individual is not interested in integrating the affect within themselves and taking up ego-functioning, the anxieties and resistances involved are so much more profound. The individual here is concerned, ultimately, with not wanting to be an individual in their own right. This is a form of malignant regression. The individual fears that they will not survive if they cannot remain adhesively identified to the analyst. It is this that the analyst has to struggle with in dealing with an "affect" projected into them.

This understanding sets the immediate interaction (the particular projective identification) against a broader kind of object relationship and helps us to understand the clinical difficulties involved. When Bion says that parts of the ego are projected into the other, this can be understood, in the identity–affect frame, to be due to the attack and suspension of ego-functioning (precisely by the immersion in affect) and the *"requirement"* that the other act as a self-regulating other.

If the individual is interested or prepared to integrate the affect under the auspices of their *own* ego-functioning, then the clinical situation is that of a benign regression and feels very different. This describes "normal projective identification" as a form of communication.

The claustrum and psychic retreats

Meltzer also emphasized the wider context in which projective identification is taking place, further developing Bion's concept of the container–contained and proposing the concept of the *claustrum* (Meltzer, 1992).

In the claustrum the individual is not simply trying to evacuate their affect but trying *to come themselves to reside* in the other. This is one particular example of the kind of wider object relationship being described here, where the affect is intimately bound up with the individual's sense of him/herself as insubstantial and unviable, very much related to their identity. Meltzer sees the claustrum as a form of container with different "compartments", which he characterizes as "life in the maternal head/breast", "life in the genital department" or "life in the maternal rectum", each compartment having somewhat different characteristics. Relations to the other, under the auspices of the claustrum, are characterized by the process of intrusive projective identification. Meltzer, however, also characterizes a form of *narcissistic identification* with the object, which he calls simply "intrusive identification" because, as he writes, . . . [he] is not at all sure that [projective identification] is the only means of achieving [the shift to more pathological forms, e.g. "inspiration" being confused with the "delusion of clarity of insight" etc.] and he adds that

> [his] material points only to a specific aspect of projective identification, one which is bound up closely with the epistemophilic instinct . . . [which] seeks . . . the immediate emotional satisfaction of omniscience and this it accomplishes by intruding inside the sensory apparatus and mental equipment of its internal object. [Meltzer, 1992, pp. 75–76]

The term *narcissistic identification* adequately reflects many of the phenomena under discussion here. Caper (1999, pp. 100, 107, 124) also develops this term, referring particularly to the omnipotent element of the phantasies involved and to the one-person element of relating, for example, the phantasy of omnipotently taking over and possessing the other.

Steiner (1993) has also developed the concept of the container with his understanding of "psychic retreats" and their organization as they exist in the patient, and between analyst and patient. He understands these phenomena as a retreat into a third position between the paranoid–schizoid and depressive positions and immune from the anxieties particular to them. The anxiety of the paranoid–schizoid position is fear of annihilation by projected deadly products of the death instinct (*ibid.*, p. 26), while that of the depressive position is fear of the destruction of the good object by the infant's newly acknowledged destructiveness through the acceptance of his ambivalence (*ibid.*, p. 27).

Carvalho (2002) argues for an alternate reading of the phenomena associated with Steiner's psychic retreats—an understanding in addition to Steiner's, rather than in place of it. He writes,

> ... some patients at least were not driven primarily by destructive impulses or by the need to escape from anxieties consequent upon such impulses. They seemed more driven by the need to cohere and survive in relation to the lack of secure attachment in the past ... such organisations serve to bind the *object* rather than the *instinct*, and to avert the overwhelming affect associated with the object in circumstances where the subject's experience of them is a failure of attunement, if not of absence, neglect or abuse. [Carvalho, 2002, pp. 153–154]

Carvalho is, therefore, emphasizing the role of identification of subject and object, and referring to the role of affect in these organizations, in contrast to a picture based primarily on the ejection of affects.

In line with these particular formulations by Meltzer and Carvalho, it can be stressed that these processes (projective identifications) can helpfully be set in the context of the desired form of object relationship. I found with Rachel that understanding our interactions in terms of the projective identification of affects and the parts of herself that she was ejecting was often too narrow a framework. The broader understanding of her desire for me to take up a permanent role as a self-regulating other, with her adhesively identified with me or residing inside me in the manner of a claustrum, fitted the situation much better. I am suggesting this broader perspective operates *in addition to, not instead of*, the narrower perspective and focus of the particular affect being transacted.

Related critiques of projective identification—are parts of the self projected?

There are a number of critiques of projective identification that reflect on the picture drawn above. Alvarez, working firmly within the Kleinian tradition, makes a number of telling points derived from her work with children, in particular questioning whether it is parts of the self that are projected. She writes, calling on the work of Spillius and Joseph,

> The concept of projection, even the more subtle Kleinian one of projective identification, tended in the past to carry the implication that, although the experience is taking place outside the self, *it must have originated within the self*. However, Spillius and Joseph have drawn attention to the fact that the term projective identification is often used to cover situations where what is being projected is not a part of the patient's self, but an aspect or part of his internal object which needs exploring. So a part of his internal world is being projected outside, but not necessarily a part of his self (Spillius, 1988, p. 82; Joseph, 1978, p. 112). Both Grotstein (1981) and Sandler (1987) prefer the term externalization, and I do not know whether it is useful to extend the meaning of projective identification this far, except for situations where the patient is really forcing the analyst to play the part of the earlier object. [Alvarez, 1992, p. 81]

Alvarez writes of a further phenomenon,

> Work with very young psychotic children, however, often makes one suspect that this "projected" part may never have belonged to the personality in the first place, at least not in a solid way. It may need to grow . . . [*ibid.*, p. 86]

In response to these kinds of experience Alvarez proposes the concept of "reclamation", where the analyst may need to act to *reclaim* aspects of the patient that are *not yet formed*, in the way one may reclaim land that has never been used and is at present unusable.

Alvarez makes a further criticism of the concept of projective identification in regard, specifically, to Bion's notion of communication. She asks,

... do the powerful feelings of alarm aroused in the mind of the therapist arise as a result of being sent there by the patient? At the very least, are they evoked by the projective identification processes described by Klein and Bion? Bion stressed that one type of projective identification, normal to infancy, involved a very primitive, perhaps the most primitive form of communication (Bion, 1962a, p. 36). [Alvarez, 1992, p. 57]

Alvarez's answer is that sometimes "... the alarm [in the analyst] may also be a response to something even iller in the patient, something which has given up, and become incapable of sending out any communications at all" (*ibid.*, p. 58).

It therefore seems that Alvarez is arguing for what comes from the analyst *him/herself*, out of his or her own separateness, rather than the feeling having been projected there by the child (in the case that she is describing). Perhaps the analyst, empathically identifying with the patient, senses what is "missing" through comparison with their *own* person and takes up a more active role in order to reclaim what has not yet been formed. This would accord with the understanding of the caregiver acting as a self-regulating other, who not only reacts to the child's distress, but also reacts from the breadth of their own experience, introducing new opportunities and experiences to the child.

Joseph also points out, simply, that communication might not necessarily be the *aim* of a particular projective identification although it may be the *result*. She writes,

Since projective identification by its very nature means the putting of parts of the self into the object, in the transference we are of necessity on the receiving end of projections and, therefore, providing we can tune into them, we have an opportunity *par excellence* to understand them and what is going on. In this sense, it acts as a communication, whatever its motivation, and is the basis for the positive use of countertransference. [Joseph, 1984, pp. 174–175]

All these considerations cast doubt on the traditional understanding of parts of the self, or even the whole self (Klein, 1955), being projected. It is the characteristic feeling that the other is determining the individual's experience (is a self-regulating other) and, specifically, that their *sense of being* which amounts to their *whole self* is being regulated, when ego-functioning is suspended, which is understood to correspend with what Klein calls a *part of the self being projected*.

This model adjusts, slightly, the understanding of the type of object relationship that is taking place, in regard to Bion's model. The identity–affect model holds that the relationship is broader than the transaction of a particular affect, and is about *self*-regulation. The model reframes the way the particular elements may be understood in regard to Klein's model. *Experientially* this model is, perhaps, close to Sandler's understanding of these phenomena relating to omnipotent expectations and obligations of role-responsiveness imposed upon the object to meet the infant's needs (Sandler, 1976).

The foregoing has not specifically addressed the *content* of what is being projected or externalized (other than its status). The individual is frequently attempting to constellate his or her early experience, held non-verbally in implicit memory as internal working models, in the transference–countertransference where they may be borne, thought about and, finally, integrated—very much as Bion would say. Understanding these processes, not just in terms of evacuations or communications, but also as forms of object relationship concerned, crucially, with the individual's identity and affect, puts the clinical picture in a somewhat different light.

A note on phantasy

The element of phantasy in projective identification has not yet been discussed here. Klein was very aware of the difficulty in understanding these phenomena in terms of phantasy. She wrote, "The description of such primitive processes suffers from a great handicap, for these phantasies arise at a time when the infant has not yet begun to think in words" (Klein, 1946). Klein understood phantasy as the psychic representation of instinct, writing, "I believe that phantasies operate from the outset, as do the instincts, and are the mental expression of the activity of both the life and death instincts" (Klein, 1952, p. 58). While Klein's concept of phantasy has been much questioned when applied to such early object relations, and much defended, notably by Isaacs (1952), ultimately Ogden's clarification of phantasy "not as inherited thoughts, but as a biological code that is part of instinct" (Ogden, 1986, p. 15) is persuasive.

However, these considerations aside, phantasy can be understood to be an aspect of our confabulating faculty—the intentionality of the psyche—and to *follow from*, and *to be secondary to*, the patient's *veridical* experience of the other, for example, as powerfully affecting him/her. In other words, the phantasy is not primary or causative in the situation, it is based on the experience of the other, originating, primarily, from our experience of the outer world, rather than as a consequence of an inner phantasy. Bion states this, in part, when he writes: "the patient does something to the analyst and the analyst does something to the patient; it is not *just* an omnipotent phantasy" (Bion, 1980, p. 15).

Sandler describes an intermediate position by suggesting that the individual builds up a "representational world" that is an admixture of outer world and inner experience (Sandler & Rosenblatt, 1962). This does not fully account for the phenomena, however, as the individual's experience of the world can vary considerably from moment to moment. The identity–affect model's understanding of the individual's varying sense of being, in the absence of a stabilizing, overarching sense of "I", explains such variations. The individual's phantasy, which *follows from* experience, is their attempt at understanding their affective experience. If the understanding that is reached is skewed, it is because of the status of the individual's identity, and the importance that the other wields as a self-regulating other. (Caper (1994) gives an example of the phantasy of the analyst's omnipotence, which is discussed in the following chapter on technique). Those "understandings" that are not skewed are not generally thought of as phantasies or delusions.

The paranoid–schizoid and depressive positions and ego-functioning

The descriptions above, particularly regarding the loss of sense of self and the early ego, amount to a description of the state of affairs in the paranoid–schizoid position. This remains an ongoing *position*, not just a developmental *phase* prior to the development of ego-functioning proper, as it represents the continuance of the non-verbal, affect-based system in the right hemisphere of the brain. As has been described, this is an essential part of our whole psyche, underlying and constituting an element of rational functioning. It also represents a continual, essential, core resource and part of our being, relating us to others. It only becomes problematic when ego-functioning is inflexible or is suspended in some way.

This inflexibility represents the co-existence of hypersensitive, affective experience (paranoid elements) and inflexible, unfeeling (schizoid) elements, where access to the emotional core is cut off for defensive purposes, perhaps because the affective experience has been overwhelming. The co-existence of these two elements leads to the position's accurate appellation as paranoid–schizoid.

The achievement of integrative ego-functioning, holding the broader perspective of the personality and relinquishing intense forms of experience (which come about through the *suspension* of ego-functioning and through adhesive relating) amounts to the achievement of the depressive position. This is an intrapsychic and interpersonal achievement as the individual is able to "hold together" the different representations of self (integrating the elements of the personality) and other (for example, the "good mother" and the "bad mother"). Such a broader perspective is always evolving, of course, as new elements of the personality can be integrated with the older part—the "depressive position" represents holding the broader perspective.

If ego-functioning is inflexible, the holding of the broader perspective can be literally "depressive" as it is used to exclude new material by denying life-giving contact with the emotional core. The appellation of the depressive position could be understood to relate to the giving up of the intense experience and omnipotent, unrealistic self-representations. Klein (1935, 1940) understands the depressive position to follow from experiences of guilt due to ambivalent feelings toward the object, consequent upon the object being seen as a whole object by the individual, who has managed to unite both the object's "good" and "bad" aspects. While this description encompasses the integrative element of ego-functioning, Klein emphasizes the key role of the feelings of guilt and depressive anxiety. While this may be one factor responsible for bringing about this shift, it is by no means the only factor.

Bion (1963) charts shifts into affective experience, followed by the return to integrate this experience with the ego, as Ps–D. This would be another way of describing flexible ego-functioning.

A note on the autistic–contiguous position

Ogden, building on the work of Meltzer, Tustin and others, proposes a position or mode of functioning that is more primitive than the functioning of the paranoid–schizoid position, which he called the autistic–contiguous position. He understands this as "a way of conceiving of the most primitive psychological organization through which the sensory 'floor' of the experience of self is generated" (Ogden, 1989, p. 4). Ogden's concept reflects Damasio's idea of the proto-self as the sensory floor against which consciousness is generated and which serves as the background self. Ogden writes,

> The autistic–contiguous position is understood as a sensory-dominated, presymbolic area of experience in which the most primitive form of meaning is generated on the basis of the organization of sensory impressions, particularly at the skin surface. A unique form of anxiety arises in this psychological realm: terror over the prospect that the boundedness of one's sensory surface might be dissolved, with a resultant feeling of falling, leaking, dropping, into an endless and shapeless space. [Ogden, 1989, p. 4]

This primitive form of experience relates to the period when developing the proto-self is one of the primary tasks of development. In terms of the autistic–contiguous position it represents the ongoing significance of the proto-self as a background sensory-affective floor. This area is *pre-symbolic* as there is no second-order representation.

The fear of the loss of physical boundedness is indeed a truly terrifying experience. On one occasion with Rachel, discussing setting a date to end the analysis triggered an experience of having no body at all. She lost the framework by which she could comprehend all experience: she was truly petrified and felt that she had gone mad. Rachel quickly recovered and, following this experience, she unexpectedly felt that she was able to be much more "in her body". We speculated whether the fear of this totally unembodied state had meant that she had previously kept herself somewhat removed from her body, as if it was something that could let her down, and which she had had to keep constantly stimulated in order to ensure that it was truly there. Clearly the prospect of the loss of the analysis was also significant (having "nobody"), which perhaps demonstrates once again the profound importance of the self-regulating other in the development of psychic structures like the proto-self. Having negotiated this threat to the sensory floor of her experience, a couple of weeks later we set a date on which to end the analysis.

Final thoughts

The phenomena of projective identification are, perhaps, so difficult to grasp because, as adults, we are always affecting others and regulating them, and being affected and regulated by them. Personality traits such as "kindly", "considerate", "compassionate", or "aloof", "cold", and "uncaring", express, in part, our judgement of the individual's preparedness to engage in such regulation of the other. This is, therefore, a cultural phenomenon as well as an interpersonal one, with the cultural influences subtly pervading our expectations. For example, the expectation of regulation by the other, and the lessening of the sense of responsibility for ourselves, lie behind the growing "blame culture", and represent a widespread passivity and lowering of integrative ego-functioning. The normalness of such expectations and practices muddies the clinical water, for both patient and analyst and is, as well, reflected in different analytic styles, for example, more or less "empathic", "warm", or "aloof". This brings us, seamlessly, to the question of technique.

Notes

1. I have been unable to trace the reference for this quotation ... with apologies to the author.

CHAPTER FIVE

Technique and analytic attitude

Introduction

Chapter One described my development of a "properly" analytic attitude and the struggle with my countertransference. It also looked at the significance of identification—in particular, of the pressure Rachel put on me to identify with her, and of the analyst's identification with the patient in general. My challenging of my views on regression was also discussed and related to an understanding of the need for the analyst to remain their natural self, separate from the patient. This was related to what Caper describes as the analyst's natural tendency to identify, and the analyst's struggle not to identify or, having identified, to come to dis-identify with the patient, thereby achieving, perhaps, what Symington describes as an "act of freedom". This chapter returns to Caper's example of the patient's phantasy of the analyst's omnipotence, cited in Chapter Four, and explores the difficulties for the analyst in achieving an analytic attitude in view of the patient's struggle with their identity. It begins by looking at the transference in the light of the identity–affect model.

The transference and interpretation

The transference "works" because both patient and analyst are always monitoring the situation through the medium of their affective appraisal mechanism. *On some level* the patient and analyst register the symmetry/sameness between the present situation and other significant situations. These samenesses mean that the analyst may be felt to be like, or sometimes simply to *be*, mother, father, brother, sister, lover, bully, or saviour, and the ending of the session may be experienced like, or *as*, the end of a relationship, a death, a loss, an abandonment, a release, or an escape, depending on what is going on for the individual.

Just as the patient is tuned into the analyst, so the analyst can use their affective appraisal mechanism as a "precise instrument for probing the patient", as Heimann (1950, 1960) put it. The analyst is monitoring the analytic situation and registers samenesses and patterns between what is going on and significances of which the analyst is aware. It is hoped that the analyst is able to use such information from the non-verbal self constructively. This may mean the analyst holding off from interpreting immediately, allowing him or herself to not-know, integrating the feelings and intuitions from the non-verbal self with his or her thinking function and past experience and, finally, making an interpretation that is apposite and that addresses the analytic situation. This is not always the case, of course, and Bion (1970) talks of the analyst interpreting too soon, being unable to not-know.

One manifestation of the equivalence of the analyst's and patient's use of the affective appraisal mechanism is when the patient, usually the narcissistic patient and usually for defensive reasons, interprets the analyst's actions and interpretations back to him or her—for example, saying that the analyst is trying to protect him or herself from the truth of what the patient is saying. This can become a serious obstacle to the analysis (this issue is further explored in Chapter Seven).

At the other end of the spectrum is the, usually schizoid, patient who is extremely deferential towards the analyst and who never allows him/herself to interpret the analyst's activity. In this case the analyst never becomes a real person for the patient; the patient is missing an important dimension from their own personality—not integrating their emotional core and affective appraisal mechanism. This has significant consequences for both the individual and the kinds of object relationship they form.

The analyst's interpretation of the transference in the here-and-now amounts to putting patients in touch with their emotional core, as it draws patients' attention to their immediate feelings about the analyst. The difficulty for the analyst is in knowing when to make such interpretations. This is partly an issue of when to emphasize the current affective situation over the broader situation that the analyst's wider perspective may, one hopes, be holding. To some extent this is also a question of which of the many "samenesses" to interpret. If, for example, the patient talks vaguely about wanting to change their job, the analyst might interpret that perhaps the patient wants to change their analyst. Such an interpretation can sound, and may actually be, simply paranoid. These are the stereotyped, so-called, "you-mean-me" interpretations. Other "samenesses" that might be explored would be, for example, other situations that the patient may want to change, or other dissatisfactions that they may be experiencing. Such intuitions need to be set against the analyst's broader experience with the patient, that is to say, they must be integrated with the perspective of the analyst's broader ego-functioning. It is this that may, one hopes, set the analyst's interpretations apart from the patient's relationship with their own affective experience.

There were periods with Rachel when I did not make many interpretations relating her experience back to the transference as she would, it seemed, happily reduce her whole experience to what was going on in the analysis. Such interpretations only appeared to increase the intensity of her affective experience. She did not need to make more links and associations as she was already flooded by them and by her affects—there was too much meaning. The transference had become what O'Shaughnessy (1993) describes as an "enclave" from which to avoid the more challenging aspects of reality. I recognized that Rachel's struggle was to develop her integrative ego-functioning, her separate identity, and her sense of viability in the world. At these times I concentrated on interpretations of the *process*, for example, the fact that Rachel was relating in this way to me. This brought her back to the broader perspective of her integrative ego-functioning.

As has been emphasized, experiences relating directly to the emotional core, when ego-functioning is suspended, feel more true to the patient. This is parallel to Caper's point (1994, p. 27) that the patient will sometimes accuse the analyst of being artificial, precisely because the analyst is insisting on being real, that is, reality-orientated, rather than colluding with the patient's expectations of him as a "desired external phantasy object". In terms of the identity–affect model, this is because the analyst is maintaining an analytic attitude and is not supporting the patient's wish to suspend (the patient's and the analyst's) ego-functioning. For example, Rachel reported that she felt most real with me precisely at the times when I had lost my bearings and was affording her access to infinite experience through my over-identification with her.

The analyst, too, must beware of preferencing types of interpretation that have a powerful, subjective experience of truth, believing that these are more meaningful and true than other types of interpretation, as in, for example, the Lacanian practice of ending sessions when a particularly deep and resonant note has been struck. This seems to emphasize powerful moments of emotional truth over the equally important issues of overall understanding, containment, integration, and more ordinary ego-functioning.

The difficulty in achieving and maintaining an analytic attitude

The title of this section is inspired by Caper's paper "On the difficulty of making a mutative interpretation" (1995). It is partly a dialogue with that paper but mostly serves to get to the heart of issues of technique.

In a previous paper, "Does psychoanalysis heal?", Caper (1994) described what he saw as one factor relating to the analyst's acceptance of (identification with) the patient's projective identification. He writes,

> . . . in forming the transference, the patient projects a part of himself (in phantasy) into the analyst and subsequently feels that the analyst has become identified with this part . . . When the patient elevates the analyst to the status of a healer, he does so by projecting his omnipotence into the analyst, leading himself to believe that

the analyst possesses magical curative powers, and that the analytic process is somehow a longed-for realization of his belief in the particular external phantasy object called a personal god. . . . The patient actually provokes (through verbal and non-verbal communication) a state of mind in the analyst that corresponds to what the patient is projecting into him in phantasy (Heimann, 1950). This state of mind is a type of countertransference that Grinberg (1962) has called projective counteridentification. [Caper, 1994, pp. 20–21]

Caper goes on to recommend an attitude of humility in the analyst. He recognizes the limits of the analyst's effectiveness and that they cannot heal, echoing Freud's (1912e, p. 115) quotation from the seventeenth-century surgeon who said, "I dress the wound, God heals it". Caper suggests that this humility can only be achieved if the analyst has come to terms with their own omnipotently destructive impulses. If the analyst has not done this they will try to defend against those impulses by trying to "cure". It is this that edges the analyst toward counter-identifying with the projective identifications that Caper describes.

Grotstein understands the counter-identification to be an intrinsic part of the projective identification. He therefore proposes the term "projective *trans*identification" precisely to illustrate the two-person nature of projective identification. He describes a two-part process: first the projecting subject "gestures, prompts and/or primes" their object (Caper says the patient "provokes" the analyst); this is followed by a "spontaneous empathic simulation" within the "optimally receptive object"—in other words, the analyst spontaneously identifies. Grotstein sees subject and object as constituting "two independent self-activating systems" (2005, p. 1053).

While Caper's points about attitude and Grotstein's analysis of the form of the interaction are well made, there are two other issues that are relevant here, one regarding phantasy and the other regarding the difficulty in dealing with such projective identifications. As already discussed, my experience with Rachel showed me that such interactions rest not primarily upon phantasy, but upon the real experience of the other as a self-regulating other who has, at times, almost unlimited power over the other—to the patient it can certainly *feel* as if the analyst is omnipotent if the patient's ego-functioning is suspended. This experience is normal and universal

in infancy, although it is perhaps experienced particularly powerfully in those individuals whose caregivers did not give them the
illusion that they themselves were responsible for creating their own
satisfaction, as Fonagy, Gergely, Jurist, and Target describe (2002,
pp. 173–174), that is to say, they were unable to give them a trust in
others. Essentially, as infants, we have all been subject to self-regulating others—to emphasize, once again, not just those who regulated our *affects* but also those who regulated our whole sense of *self*.

It is, therefore, this *self*-regulation by the other that is characteristic of projective identification and which makes projective identification so ubiquitous and normal. As described in the last chapter,
projective identification becomes excessive when the individual
powerfully resists becoming responsible for their own affects and
self. That is, they resist, for a variety of reasons, taking up affective,
and self, *auto*-regulation. Owing to the universality of regulation by
the other it is no coincidence that Caper has chosen the phantasy of
healing as his example of projective identification. The experience of
self-regulation by an other is deeply ingrained within us, and
continues to be a fact, indeed a truism, of adult life (others can affect
us and sometimes profoundly so). We are not just dealing with a
phantasy, although phantasies will arise from the experience of it.

Importantly, the analyst has to struggle with this issue on a very
personal level. This is an issue that relates to how the analyst
constellates *their own* identity: that is, how much they rely on others
to make them feel good, how much they have developed and rely
upon their own integrative ego-functioning, how open they are to
their own emotional core, how they handle the affects that arise
therefrom—thus, in summary, how much and in what way they
require others to regulate their own self. These considerations will
powerfully affect how the analyst operates and will influence their
analytic style. As the French naturalist, Comte de Buffon said,
"*Style, c'est l'homme*" (Style is the man)[1]—the analyst's analytic style
is intimately interwoven with their personality.

If the analyst is not to projectively counter-identify with the
patient who approaches with their sense of self in tatters, asking for
help, as I did with Rachel at times, the analyst has to be clear on a
whole host of issues relating to their own identity. This is not just a
matter of "technique", but relates personally to the analyst and the
manner in which they relate to, and constellate, their own affects

and identity. To put this another way, interactions become projective identifications when the individual attempts to force the other to act as a self-regulating other and the analyst accepts that role. Obviously, however, *whatever* the analyst does will in some way affect the patient so that, for example, if the analyst does *not* identify with the patient, this will also have profound consequences. Caper writes,

> ... the analyst ... must accept the fact that, by withholding immediate solace, he is in a way "causing" real suffering in the short run for the sake of the greater long-term relief that comes from psychological integration. [1994, p. 26]

Responsibility

In terms of consequences, Margaret Little writes that "for the whole of his response to his patient's need, the analyst's responsibility is 100 percent" (1981, p. 54). While the analyst must certainly recognize and take responsibility for the effect they have on the patient, Little's conclusion is questionable. She writes,

> There may have to be times—moments or split seconds even—when, psychically, for the analyst nothing exists but the patient, and, nothing exists of himself apart from the patient. He allows the patient to enter his own inner world and become part of it. His whole psyche becomes liable to be subjected to sudden unheralded inroads, often of vast extent and long duration. He is taken possession of, his emotions are exploited. He has to be able to make all kinds of identification with his patient, accepting a fusion with him which often involves the taking into himself of something really mad; at the same time he has to be able to remain whole and separate. Unless the analyst is willing to commit himself and makes that commitment clear it is often quite impossible for a patient to commit himself to his analysis. [*ibid.*, pp. 57–58]

I practised exactly this kind of commitment to my patients and found that, instead of being helpful, it was subtly but profoundly unhelpful, as has been described. There are deep, powerfully-held, personal issues at stake here. Little's description is contradictory in that the psyche remaining "whole and separate" is incompatible with the psyche becoming liable to be subjected to "sudden unheralded inroads, often of vast extent and long duration". The "wholeness" and "separateness" she describes can be understood to be that of the core *sense of being*, whereby the individual can still feel that he has remained separate, as with Zinkin's example of the windsurfers quoted in Chapter 2, Section I. The analyst under these circumstances is not, however, operating with integrative ego-functioning and is not presenting themselves as a separate object to the patient.

At the time when Little's recommendation characterized my style of practice I would certainly have said that I remained a separate individual. Yet I can now see that this was not the case, and that I was not able to adequately deal with Rachel's affects because I was so completely open to them and, therefore, my own identity was compromised. "Remaining a whole and separate person" refers, in the framework outlined here, to a subjective experience that is consequent upon the operation of integrative ego-functioning. It amounts to an achievement of the depressive position *in the analyst*. The intense focus on the immediate experience presented by the patient continually pulls the analyst *away* from the broader perspective and *into* intense forms of relating, particularly if the interactions are highly charged.

Passivity, regression, and identification

Little recommends the analyst make "all kinds of identification" with the patient and comments that unless he is able to do this "it is often quite impossible for a patient to commit himself to his analysis". It is often argued that a period of union is necessary before the patient can "emerge". In the Jungian frame Strauss writes,

> . . . separation plays an integral part in the process of ego development. However, growth of ego boundaries cannot come into being without the experience of primary union or oneness which Jung has also referred to as *"abaissement du niveau mental"* [a lowering of the level of consciousness]. [Strauss, 1962, pp. 104–105].

In their different ways such theorists as Winnicott, Jung, Kohut, and even, it may be argued, paradoxically, Bion (although this list of theoreticians is by no means inclusive), recommend or implicitly encourage such identifications, or at least a certain "identificatory attitude" that amounts to a passivity and an identification with the patient's perspective. *These identifications certainly do produce powerful effects in the analysis,* but whether or not they are beneficial is another question. Such periods are usually understood in terms of regression.

Winnicott discussed regression in terms of *regression to dependence,* and he talked of an experience of a patient having regressed "as far as was necessary". He said that "there was a bottom to the regression and no indication of a need to return following the experience of having reached the bottom" (Winnicott, 1953). Winnicott saw this as part of the capacity of the individual to bring about a self-cure (Winnicott, 1959). Jung had also had a parallel intuition, writing *"reculer pour mieux sauter"* (go back in order to better go forward) (Jung, 1935, par. 19), and subtly recommended an analytic style that predisposes the analyst to a position of identification with the patient. Kohut (1971) also argued for such a position in relation to his understanding of narcissism.

These analytic styles led to regressions that were problematic at times. In response to these difficulties associated with regression, Balint (1968) differentiated benign from malignant regression. While Winnicott's, Jung's, and Kohut's theories were sometimes responses to analytic styles where reductionist, narcissistically wounding interpretations were being over-used, it is proposed here that they encourage the analyst to fall into identifications with the patient and to take on the role of operating as a self-regulating other. It is one thing for the analyst to recognize that their actions powerfully affect the patient, it is quite another to take on responsibility for ensuring that the patient has a good sense of being. There is, of course, a spectrum of positions in between.

In the analysis with Rachel I certainly fell into such an identification, although I must, of course, take responsibility for my own neurotic countertransference, which amounted to my own narcissistic preferencing of sameness and aversion to difference. With regard to Winnicott and this kind of identification with the patient, Green writes,

My main criticism of [Winnicott] is his belief that he should try unconditionally to cure his patients by representing—and to some extent creating—the image of a good-enough mother. It is my belief that Winnicott could not tolerate the situation where he would have to show the patient how destructive he himself was, despite the fact that . . . he systematically interpreted the positive function of destructiveness. [Green, 2005a, p. 27]

Such identifications and enactments by the analyst bring us back to Caper's argument about the analyst counter-identifying with the patient's phantasy of the analyst as omnipotent healer. The identity–affect model would understand such a counter-identification as the analyst, consciously or unconsciously, assenting to taking on the role of self-regulating other. Taking on the role of self-regulating other is, however, a broader categorization than counter-identifying with the patient's phantasy of the analyst as omnipotent healer.

Schore very much aligns himself with Kohut when it comes to the psychotherapeutic treatment of developmental psychopathologies. Describing the therapist's reaction when the patient's shame has been triggered, he writes,

In a timely fashion the therapist subsequently re-establishes comforting and mirroring functions, thereby enabling the patient to recover from depressed low-keyed states, and facilitating a transition from negative/passive to positive/active mood. These transactions disconfirm the patient's expectation of humiliation and intensification of negative affectivity during periods of helpless self-exposure. [Schore, 1994, pp. 460–461]

My experience would indicate that, ultimately, it is necessary to work through the maternal failure in the analytic relationship rather than being able to make good that failure through "comforting and mirroring". Caper's (1994, 2003) and Colman's (2003) linked papers further explore this issue.

Containment and engagement

Curiously, perhaps, Bion's concept of the container can also be taken to subtly recommend a passive attitude in the analyst, even if it is not a strictly identificatory one. Alvarez quotes Grotstein writing about containment: "(Bion's) concept, even at its most mental, tends to have metaphorical links with something concave, a lap-like mind, perhaps" (Grotstein, 1981 quoted in Alvarez, 1992). Alvarez, pursuing her thinking about reclamation, where the analyst may need to act to reclaim aspects of the patient that are not yet formed, comments, ". . . sometimes the container is seen as something much firmer. The maternal object needs also to be seen as pulling the child, drawing the child, attracting or interesting the child" (Alvarez, 1992, p. 77).

Alvarez is concerned with the passivity that she feels analysts can be drawn into if they see themselves as simply the recipient of the patient's projections and projective identifications (*ibid.*, Chapters 1–3). While thoroughly agreeing with what Alvarez says about projective identification, in my experience, if the analyst visualizes themself as a container, and if this is taken as a generalized principle, it concretizes the notion of the analyst as "lap-like" recipient and, in this regard, places the analyst in a passive role. Perhaps this difficulty is due to an ambiguity in the term container, which can be understood to be either a box/receptacle, or the *function* that organizes and integrates the contents of the box, relating the contained elements to each other. The latter use is more concerned with the active function of *digesting* the patient's projective identifications, whereas the former use is a passive function. Bion was very much aware of these different uses of the concept and he frequently used the term "with its military implication of one force containing another" (Bion, 1970, p. 112).[2]

This raises the question of how the analyst really "contains" affects. Due to this sense of "lap-likeness", containment can be taken to be something akin to "holding on to", "putting up with", and/or "surviving"—the box-like, receptacle qualities. What is actively "containing" is for the analyst to be able to remain himself, not unduly affected, not "taken possession of" nor having his "emotions exploited" (Little), but rather able to actively *engage* with the patient's material. Rather than the term containment, the term engagement captures a more active sense of the primary activity of the analyst—the patient's feelings, desires, needs, wishes, and process need to be *engaged* with. This term echoes Bion's military usage as different forces "engage" one another, although it is not used here specifically in that way. Bion's term containment, however, may also encapsulate the analyst's necessary "receiving" function, as described below.

This less "lap-like" attitude might appear to be cold or lacking in empathy on the part of the analyst. However, overtly "containing" (as in "warm" and "protective") behaviour can simply amount to a defence on the part of the analyst against exactly the feelings and situation with which the patient really struggles. It can be argued that a less lap-like attitude constitutes the analyst's proper empathy with the patient's painful and difficult struggles, for example, with early deprivation.

Regarding the issue of passivity, Bion, of course, understands that the analyst needs to be active in the process of digesting the patient's affects and returning them to the patient (the organizing, integrating, and relating qualities). The comments made here concern the way Bion's concept is sometimes misused. Britton (2003) perhaps puts it best when he states that it is the *ego* that acts as a container. It should be noted that in circumstances like those described in Chapter One, this needs to be the patient's *own* ego.

Certainly, however, the analyst must be able to make a sufficient identification to empathically pick up what is going on in the patient. Caper engages in a dispute with Ogden about how much identification needs to occur, writing

> It has been suggested by some authors—for example Ogden (1996)—that the analyst must become quite identified with the patient's projections and work through this illness laboriously if his understanding of the patient's projections is to be therapeutically effective. I disagree with this position. What is important is only the fact that the analyst has been able to think about the patient's projections, not how much (or little) trouble he has had to go to in doing so. [Caper, 1999, p. 114]

It could be argued that the issue is not simply whether the analyst has been able to *think about* the patient's projections, but how *full* the analyst's appreciation and understanding of the patient's projections have been.

Fordham described some patients with whom he found he had to modify his normal analytic attitude. He proposed, as a consequence, that "states of identity" precede projective identification. In such states of identity "understanding or insight in the ordinary sense of the word did not operate effectively". Fordham found that one patient complained that his interpretations "did nothing to alleviate his basic struggle which gave rise to much pain, suffering and despair". As a result Fordham found that he needed to work in such a way that his "communication was not made so much with [his] analytic mind as with emotional conviction". This, Fordham observed, "had an effect" (Fordham, 1994, p. 68).

While the patient frequently "gestures, prompts and primes" the analyst (Grotstein), it has been my experience that the analyst is sometimes drawn into a deeper affective engagement with the patient in response, for example, to the patient continually presenting a false front. My experience with Dorothy, described in detail in Chapter Eight, was that the deepening of the transference–countertransference was called forth by an organic process of engagement with the more malignant elements that lay *beneath* her bland, surface politeness, which had ceased to be convincing to me. The *analyst's* attempt to engage is key here. It may well be that this affective engagement is required to constellate early affective patterns in the transference–countertransference. These early affective patterns are stored in the right hemisphere of the brain as *implicit memory* (Fonagy, 1999; Stern et al., 1998), which would otherwise not be accessible to verbal analysis and interpretation, which can only access *explicit memory* (Andrade, 2005).

These are fluid areas of work where the analyst needs to remain sufficiently open to the affective experience with the patient but also to be able to think and interpret without over-identifying. Tansey and Burke (1989) describe three phases of any interaction, necessary for the processing of a projective identification: an initial countertransference act of *reception* (which concerns the analyst's "mental set"—free floating attention, interactional pressure (pressure to act), and awareness of the affect); this is followed by the analyst's *internal processing* (tolerating, examining, and arriving at a tentative understanding); and finally, a stage of *communication* (verbal, non-verbal, implicit and explicit communication to the patient concerning the extent to which their projective identification has been processed). It is important to stress, again, the wider issue of how the patient's *identity* is being affected by the transaction of any particular affect—that is to say, whether the affect constitutes the person's whole sense of being, and therefore whether the patient's *self*-regulation by the other is at stake.

In practice, there can also be a danger of *under*-identifying and knowing too much in advance. Winnicott described how sometimes trainee therapists work more successfully than experienced ones. Bion and Fordham both address this issue in their different ways. Bion talks of the need to approach a session without memory, desire, or understanding but, instead, with an act of faith (Bion, 1970, pp. 41ff.). Fordham talks of locking away knowledge in a "mental filing cabinet" so that the analyst can approach the patient with openmindedness, "not knowing beforehand" (Fordham, 1993). A repetitive, stagnant period in an analysis, where the patient seems to be bringing back the same difficulty over and over again, often indicates the need for the analyst to open theirself up to new experience and learning—for the analyst to keep their ego-functioning *flexible*.

In regard to Fordham's example, above, it could be argued that *all* interpretations should bear a certain amount of emotional conviction. With Rachel, we only really passed out of the most difficult phase of the analysis when I could properly *embody* the analytic position (with reference to my boundaries and personhood) in a particular way and "live through" the interpretations with emotional conviction.

In the end, the analytic process can be seen as a kind of dance that occurs between the two protagonists, with the analyst continually engaging with the patient and their difficulties and struggling to be able to think about them. It is an organic process that relies on the analyst's very personal position and their engagement with that of the patient. As Caper says,

> The analyst is not someone who maintains a "neutral" stance above the fray, but someone who is always being drawn into the fray, could not do analysis if he were not in the fray, and who does analysis largely by figuring out what kind of fray he is in. [Caper, 1994, p. 28]

The archaic superego and the moral defence

Let us return to the question of why it is so difficult to achieve and maintain an analytic attitude. Caper addresses the narrower question of the difficulty in making a mutative interpretation, by which he means an interpretation "which helps the patient to see the analyst as a real external object, and at the same time allows him to recognize a previously unrecognised aspect of his internal object world" (1995, p. 32). "Seeing the analyst as a real external object" amounts to the analyst manifesting himself as a separate individual not identified with the patient's perspective. Caper suggests that

> it is just when the analyst is on the verge of making a mutative interpretation that he is beset by the feeling that he is about to do something harmful, something that will jeopardize his "good" relationship to the patient. [Caper, 1995, p. 35]

Caper understands that the analyst is prevented from making the interpretation by guilt, which he believes follows from the projection into the analyst of the patient's "archaic superego". He follows Strachey's (1934) use of the term "archaic superego" and his original formulation of "mutative interpretation" (see quote above). The analyst's superego merges with this projection of the patient's superego, producing a state of mind in which "moral" considerations squeeze out "scientific exploration". Furthermore, the analyst's thinking capacities deteriorate, becoming dominated by beta elements unsuitable for thinking; they have this quality because beta elements are, to paraphrase Caper, persecutingly, monotonously moralistic, imbued with the sense that everything that happens is felt to be deliberate and that someone deserves the blame (or credit) for it. As Bion puts it,

> Invariant to beta elements . . . is the moral component [which] is inseparable from feelings of guilt and responsibility and from a sense that the link between one . . . object and another, and between these objects and the personality, is moral causation. [Bion, 1965, p. 64, in Caper, 1999]

In the identity–affect framework the patient is understood to be constantly filtering experience through the affective appraisal mechanism. Experiences of separateness when, and also *because*, ego-functioning is compromised or suspended, are flagged up affectively as "bad". The patient does not, therefore, want to be confronted by the analyst's separateness, and experiences real pain and damage from that separateness, which they feel to be really, *morally* wrong. This can be seen as a kind of "moral defence" that treats separateness in a moral frame. This moral defence is described further in Chapter Seven. This aversion to separateness can be understood to be the reason that beta elements have a moral component.

The identity–affect framework can also shed some light on the operation of the superego, as the affective appraisal mechanism can be understood to take on judging, moralizing qualities as the individual develops as a social being. The "moralizing" is the form that appraisal takes in the "social self" (Stern, 1985), that is to say, the categories of good and bad are applied to the *other*. This understanding of the superego also explains the, on the face of it, curious fact that the superego develops *before* the ego—curious in so far as the superego is a form of conscience, which might be thought to be a higher-order mental function. Britton's (2003, pp. 103ff.) understanding of the superego is that the ego needs to reclaim the right to form judgements from the superego; in other words, ego functions need to take over from primitive appraisals.

The patient, therefore, experiences the analyst as morally bad, but the question is why the analyst takes this on. There can be a number of reasons for this. First, because the patient experiences the analyst's badness with real conviction, and the analyst is affected through their natural identification with the patient (Caper). The more vehemently, insistently, and with greater conviction that the patient "accuses" the analyst of something, the more the analyst will be likely to take it on, at least for a while.

Second, it can be difficult to understand why the patient feels the analyst is bad (this book is an attempt to satisfactorily explain this phenomenon). This lack of understanding means that the analyst is left solely with the affective experience. The understanding outlined here can help the analyst to resist taking in this projection.

Third, as Caper says, the analyst's thinking capacities deteriorate. Put simply, this can be seen to be due to the analyst's intense concentration on the patient's material. This induces a hypnotic-like state in the analyst due to the suspension of their broader ego-functioning as they concentrate on, and become immersed in, what the patient brings. The analyst makes a shift from complex to simple self experience, in Bollas's terms.

Countertransference

Another vertex from which to look at this phenomenon of the analyst taking on the feeling of being bad is that of the counter-transference. As described in the first chapter, the biggest struggle I had in Rachel's analysis was to bear, deal with, modify, and digest the feelings of badness that she induced in me—in particular, feelings of being bad following her stating that I was being cruel, cold, mean, not understanding her, being heartless, sadistic, or murder-ous. This is a *characteristic* feeling of badness, recognizable in working with the narcissistic elements of patients, that corresponds with the "morally" bad that Caper and Bion describe. I came to see that between this kind of generalized badness, where I could not under-stand what I had done wrong, was intimately linked with sepa-rateness. In contrast, as Balint (1968, p. 140) points out, if I said something or acted in a way that pleased Rachel, she let me know that she felt I was good, kind, clever, warm, empathic, sensitive, and insightful.

It is important to stress that the analyst's countertransference does not just consist of feelings the analyst *has* but, in the three-dimensional spirit of this book, it also constitutes *who the analyst feels him/herself to be* and *how he/she feels about him/herself*. This came as something of a shock to me. It is one thing to recognize that uncomfortable (or comfortable) feelings are being engendered in us, or even that we are playing a part in someone else's drama, but it is another to realize that this can penetrate into the way we feel about ourselves, and how we see ourselves, in a deep and profound way. The countertransference goes much deeper than I had origi-nally thought.

This countertransference struggle was ultimately resolved by my *understanding* of the situation, an understanding that allowed me to interpret what was going on to Rachel. However, this came about only after I had discovered that I needed to *do active work* on my countertransference feelings. Specifically, I had to let myself *feel* them. That is, I had to let myself feel murderous, sadistic, physically violent, hateful, punitive, and so forth, and explore, work on, and work out those feelings, both accepting them and understanding to which part of Rachel they were responding. It was usually the case that such feelings were being called forth by the need to safeguard and respect my personhood/sense of self. These challenges to my identity were usually the same as those with which Rachel had had to struggle, unsuccessfully, in her childhood. Any successes I had in meeting these challenges would engender envy in Rachel as they made her feel worse about herself and how she had fared.

Perhaps this countertransference struggle is what Freud and Caper mean by the analyst needing to come to terms with their own omnipotently destructive impulses (Caper, 1994, p. 23), although I believe that there is an additional dimension to it. I found that feeling my feelings towards Rachel had a different quality once I had properly established my own integrative ego-functioning. Prior to that, earlier in the analysis, Rachel had been able to induce feelings of irritation, frustration, anger, and even suicidal feelings in me, and she would usually know that she had. These feelings would become problematic, not *particularly* because Rachel knew about them—although I believe this gave Rachel, on one level, a sense of satisfaction and excitement while, on another level, a sense of disappointment (and worse) because she had effectively lost her analyst, which *was* problematic. What was more problematic, from my point of view, was that to *really* get to the bottom of Rachel's difficulties, I sensed that we were going to have to get much deeper into feelings more powerful than irritation and anger. I did not feel that I would be able to manifest *those* in the analysis. Ultimately, this is saying that I was struggling with, I hope and presume, a milder version of Rachel's own difficulties.

This is an admission of the depth of my difficulties with my neurotic countertransference, although it would be more accurate to say my difficulties with my own narcissism, identity, and ego-functioning. The problem was therefore not primarily about my destructive impulses, but about establishing my own proper, broader, integrative ego-functioning, which would be able to better contain my affects and provide me with a more stable sense of identity and separateness. I mention this struggle here in order to be really clear about what went on/goes on with the analyst's countertransference and identity issues. When my separateness and integrative ego-functioning were established, feeling my feelings became, more properly, an instrument for investigating, understanding and knowing about my patients. If I could follow the feelings, I could see where they were leading.

Some analysts talk optimistically about the consequences of openly expressing their affects; Coltart (1986) gives an example of her angry outburst at a patient. This happened, inadvertently, with me in the analysis with Rachel. Ultimately, however, I believe, it was not helpful as it simply indicated my struggles in parallel with Rachel's. I needed to address those difficulties in myself or, perhaps I should say, Rachel helped and required me to address them in myself, before I could properly address them in her. It is not quite what Caper means, but I am reminded of him saying ". . . one of the peculiarities of analysis is that, if the analyst does it well, then even if the patient does not get better, the analyst will" (Caper, 1995, p. 44).

It is in the light of these considerations that the analyst needs *not* to contain, as in bear, put up with, or masochistically accept, destructive attacks by the patient. At least, this is helpful only while the analyst works through their countertransference feelings, works out what they mean, and can then interpret them to the patient. The analyst does, however, have to be able to bear to be thought of as bad, cruel, sadistic, or murderous. But, again, this is not a long-term situation to be tolerated, but rather something that the analyst is *continually and actively engaging with,* not least because it indicates the level of distress that *the patient* is experiencing.

The degree to which the progress of an analysis depends on the analyst's ability to do inner work on themselves, and their countertransference, is very sobering. These considerations set the difficulties of achieving and maintaining an analytic attitude in the context of the *analyst's* struggles with their *own* identity, narcissism, and affects.

Notes

1. Lacan (1966) added "Style is the man, *to whom one speaks*", which captures something more of the relational element and, in particular, here, the way the analyst may be affected by the patient (although Lacan believed we are powerfully influenced by others and held that there is no true core to the individual).
2. Bion delineated further forms of relationship between the container and the contained, for example, describing commensal, symbiotic, and parasitic forms (Bion, 1970, p. 106).

CHAPTER SIX

Jung, the self, and spiritual experience

Introduction

This chapter represents, to those who are not familiar with Jung's ideas, an introduction to Jung's concept of the self, and a demonstration of the breadth of the Jungian field. It also demonstrates, through the relationship to the identity–affect model, the way that Jung's psychology can be understood to articulate with psychoanalytic theory. In other words, it can be seen as a possible reconciliation of the "old split". To Jungians, the chapter offers an understanding of the mechanisms that might underlie and explain the phenomena that are traditionally ascribed to, and described by, Jung's concept of the self. In addition, however, in describing the mechanisms underlying these phenomena, it also represents a revisioning of the self and a critique of the concept as it is traditionally framed. This chapter represents another challenge, then, in terms of describing the elephant, because the description is likely to be received differently depending on where the reader stands.

In essence, this chapter proposes that Jung's concept of the self can be seen to follow from the opening up of the space between the non-verbal and verbal self, and to afford deep respect for what comes from the emotional core. It is argued that this respect amounts to an over-valuation, at times, which leads to a subtle over-identification with the contents that arise spontaneously from the non-verbal self. This is understood to be embodied in the Jungian concept of the self. It is argued, in parallel, that Jung has taken a very narrow view of the ego and ascribed all of the integrative functions of the psyche to the self. This chapter proposes a more limited view of the self, essentially equivalent to the self as central organizing and guiding principle of the psyche.

Overview of the concept of the self

The Jungian concept of the self is very different from the psychoanalytic concept of the self and bears little resemblance to the everyday, commonsense usage of the term. It is, possibly, nearest to Winnicott's term "the true self", although it has a much larger scope and field of application. To understand Jung's concept of the self is to understand the core concept of his entire psychology.

His concept of the self developed out of earlier concepts and formulations regarding individuality, and his understanding of the structure and operation of the psyche. In particular, it derives from his understanding of the experience of "an inner world of almost unlimited dimensions", to use Fordham's phrase (1985, p. 5). As such, the concept integrates Jung's understanding of spiritual experience into his understanding of the psyche. As a result, Jung's psychology has often been accused of being mystical. There is some justification in this charge, both in the fact that Jung did see spiritual experience as a vital part of human experience and embodied it in his central concept of the self, and also that he spent a good deal of time investigating and writing about mystical and spiritual experience. Such inclusiveness could, however, be thought to be an asset. It is argued here that Jung's formulation is only problematic in so far as he preferenced spiritual experience in a way that distorts his understanding of the psyche and the process of individuation, his allied concept of human development. This constitutes the critique of Jung's concept of the self presented here. Before coming to this critique, however, the chapter lays out the breadth and richness of Jung's psychology, as embodied in his concept of the self.

* * *

After the split with Freud in 1913, Jung underwent a deep personal crisis in which he was flooded by, and forced to confront, the contents of his own unconscious (Jung, 1963). This experience partly accounts for the "figurative" language (not to everyone's liking) and nature of Jung's psychology—for example, his concepts of the anima, the animus, the wise old man, and the archetypal mother. His immersion in the unconscious put him in touch with characters, forces, and figures characteristic of the non-verbal, affective–configurational, image-making, right hemisphere of the brain. He came to understand these figures as archetypes, reflecting in part, the generalizing, sameness-recognizing aspect of the right hemisphere; that is to say, the archetype is a distillation of the symbolic, generalized, essence of objects, for example, mother, father, child, and so forth; as this faculty inheres in every individual, archetypes are common to all (archetypal theory, however, encompasses much more than just these aspects of it).

The seeds of Jung's view of the psyche were presaged in the split with Freud over whether the libido is purely/essentially sexual in nature or whether the energy is more neutral—Jung did not see everything as reducible to the sexual sphere. Astor (2002) traces the origins of Jung's work back to his roots within the dissociationist psychological tradition, where spontaneous and autonomous expressions of the psyche are understood to be "attempts of the future personality to break through" rather than, necessarily, pathological organizations.

Essentially, Jung's work rests on the intuition, discovery, and experience that the unconscious is not just the "dustbin of the psyche", as he (unfairly) accused Freud of treating it, but rather that it is a "buried treasure" of the highest value that can be used to guide the individual, if treated in the correct manner. In *Modern Man in Search of a Soul* (1933) he argued that one of the ills of modern man was that he had become dissociated from his emotional and instinctual nature, rooted in the unconscious.

Jung experienced, in a thoroughgoing way, what he had previously intuited: that, *in terms of the identity–affect model*, the ineffable nature of the non-verbal self, and the space between non-verbal and verbal, can be "held", and that the non-verbal self is the core and source of our personhood.[1] He came to call this core *the self* (as defined below). What follows from the opening-up of this space is, however, "an inner world of almost unlimited dimensions", where consciousness and its contents are experienced as powerful, full of meaning, imbued with truth, wisdom, and beauty, and have a time-less, eternal, oceanic, "archetypal" quality. These experiences might also be terrible and fearsome, rather like the Old Testament God. Jung used the term *numinous* to capture these qualities and, in particular, the spiritual dimension of this kind of experience. Much of Jung's psychology goes on to elaborate his understanding of these experiences, their relation to the ego, and the ego's necessary relation to them. In essence, the characteristic experiences relating to the self are experiences that follow from *the suspension of ego-functioning*: as Jung wrote, "The experience of the self is always a defeat for the ego" (Jung, 1955, par. 778).

Definitions

Jung came to define the concept of the self in a number of ways, reflecting the different facets of this complex concept. He saw the self as the *centre of the psyche*. However, as he felt the self spoke with an authority over and above the particular elements available to the individual ego, he also defined it as the *totality of the psyche*. This ascription of totality also reflected the subjective experiences of totality, limitlessness, and wholeness ascribed to the self. Further-more, he also saw the self as the *organising and guiding principle of the psyche*, guiding the individual's development. As part of this process, the self has both the ability to resolve conflicts in the psyche by bringing together the conflicting opposites under its auspices, and represents the *union of* (those) *opposites*.

The self also represented, for Jung, the unconscious *goal of devel-opment*, a potential toward which the personality naturally unfolds. As the guiding principle of the psyche, Jung held that the self was never itself manifest, but remained an *archetype*, guiding the individual from the unconscious. Experiences representing or approximating to an experience of the self are imbued with a sense of *wholeness,* thought to represent the experience of the integration of the different parts of the personality.

Evidence for the self sometimes comes to the individual in the form of archetypal *symbols of the self,* most often met with in dreams, although also reflected, for example, in all art forms, fairytales, and myths. These have the characteristics of being particularly powerful and numinous symbols, having a totality greater than the individual themselves. (See Colman (2006) for an excellent overview of the concept of the self.)

For Jung, the ego is distinct from, and subject to, the self. In the process of development, if all goes well, the ego comes to reflect the underlying nature of the self. For example, through development the ego enlarges to include those aspects of the personality that were previously denied, unrecognized, or under-developed. The ego increasingly comes to approximate to the self through the process of development that Jung called *individuation.* The individual, embodied in the ego, must be careful not to identify with the self for fear of experiencing what Jung called *inflation* and, at the extreme, psychosis.

Jung was crucially aware of the "problematic" nature of the unconscious and, concomitantly, the self, not only due to his own experience, but also due to having worked for many years as a psychiatrist. He understood the unconscious to consist of powerful archetypes, which the ego cannot handle, and which the individual must come to terms with and *humanize,* through personal experience. For example, the infant comes to personalize the archetypal mother, experienced as wonderful or terrible, but overwhelming, through experience of their actual mother. These archetypes "reside" in the deepest layer of the unconscious, which Jung called the *collective unconscious,* as they are common to all.

This is a potentially perplexing array of characteristics for one concept and much thinking has gone into reconciling these different elements over the years. Some of the main difficulties involved with Jung's concept of the self are:

- the apparent contradiction between the self being the *centre* or a *central archetype, and* the *totality* of the psyche, embracing the individual's whole nature (and all the individual, archetypal elements of the personality);

- the apparent contradiction between the self being seen as the locus for experiences of universality and oneness, while at the same time representing the unique personality, developed through individuation;
- the location and mechanism of operation of the self, if it is not to be treated as simply a notional, mystical, "virtual" concept;
- the question of the uneven nature of individuation and the clarification of the "goal". For example, is it a goal or a process and why does the self as organizing and guiding principle so often lead us astray?;
- the idealization of the self and the process of individuation, and the destructive nature of the self (the self has typically been portrayed in glowing terms).

Before addressing these difficulties, the concept of the self will be explored further, especially in relation to its spiritual aspects.

The self and the spiritual

What is characteristic of, and innovative in, Jung's concept of the self is the way that the locus of control and "wisdom" for the individual is understood to reside beyond the ego in the self. The ego is seen as subject to the self and, in the "ideal" arrangement, naturally attentive to and attendant upon it. This recommends a natural humility to the individual—if they are to avoid the dangers of an inflationary identification with the self. It is, therefore, an implicitly *spiritual* position as the core of the individual is understood to be centred in the non-"I"/non-ego part of the personality. The concept of the self embodies the psychology of spiritual experience as, with the openness of the ego to the self, the individual becomes exposed to "not-I" experiences—to experiences from beyond the ego—rather than rooted in his/her (narrow) individuality. The individual becomes aware, as Jung put it, that "there are things greater than the ego to which we must bow" (1963). Although he stressed the importance of the ego as the seat of consciousness, *the ego has been relativized* and, says Jung, "it is questionable whether it is the centre of the personality" (Jung, 1951, par. 11).

Jung was aware of the dangers of the non-ego parts of the personality, writing "It must be reckoned a psychic catastrophe when the *ego is assimilated by the self*" (Jung, 1951, par. 45, original italics). As he put it in regard to the struggle between the individual and the unconscious, "Only the man who can consciously assent to the power of the inner voice becomes a personality; but if he succumbs to it he will be swept away by the blind flux of psychic events and destroyed" (Jung, 1934, par. 308).

This concern with the elements of the individual that lie beyond the ego coheres with the intuition about the autonomy of certain aspects of the psyche. To repeat the quote from Jung,

> The autonomy of the unconscious ... begins where emotions are generated. Emotions are instinctive, involuntary reactions which upset the rational order of consciousness by their elemental outbursts. Affects are not "made" or wilfully produced; they simply happen. [Jung, 1934/1954, par. 497]

And, as he said further, specifically discussing the self,

> ... the impulses which we find in ourselves should be understood as the "will of God" ... the term "God" to be understood not so much in the Christian sense as in the sense of ... a mighty daemon ... express[ing] a determining power which comes upon man from outside, like providence or fate, though the ethical decision is left to man. [Jung, 1951, par. 51]

This relativization of the ego is, it is argued here, what is both characteristic of, and problematic for, Jungian psychology. It is proposed that some characteristics that Jung ascribes to the self are, in fact, characteristics of the ego—in particular, that of the function of integrating the different parts of the individual, and the development of a representation of the whole person. This different ascription of characteristics is, perhaps, due to the fact that Jung adopts a limited view of the ego, seeing it primarily as "subjectivity", and excludes the integrative functions from his definition.

Examples of the operation of the self

First, here is an example of the experience of the self, as described by the Jungian analyst, Gustav Dreifuss, in a paper entitled "Experience of the self in a lifetime". He writes,

While listening to a concert at the age of 20, I suddenly was over-come by a feeling of oneness. The music had touched deeper levels of my soul, which much later I could understand as an experience of the Self . . . a mystical, numinous experience of the Self. [Dreifuss, 2001, pp. 698, 690]

Second, in regard to the self operating to guide the individual, Adams gives the example of a young man who is being beaten down by his family life and has a dream of a dragon with a unicorn's horn rising from the sea (Adams, 2001, p. 400). Such dreams can be seen as compensatory to the conscious attitude of the individual; for example, they represent (over-simplifying) a bringing together of his powerful aggressive (dragon) qualities and his sensitive and special (unicorn) qualities. The dreams also serve to bring these undeveloped elements of the personality to consciousness. As such, they represent a development of the personality through the emer-gence of a powerful symbol, representing the operation of the self.

If the individual becomes cut off from their core and ignores the voice of the self, however, the consequences can be terrible. Jung (1963) gave one example of a man who had become an alcoholic due, as Jung saw it, to having compromised himself through accepting a belittling position in the family business. He was not giving full rein to his personality and had reacted, as a result, by turning to alcohol. The self is a powerful force that must be able to find proper expression; if it cannot, it is likely to wreak destruction on the personality. In this frame, the alcoholism could be seen as a re-vitalizing crisis that demands the individual's attention and can lead to further change. Such symptoms and crises can therefore be seen to have a *prospective* function rather than being solely evidence of pathological functioning.

Jung frequently found that his patients had become bogged down in the mundane and cut off from their psychic depths. He wrote,

Among all my patients in the second half of life—that is to say, over thirty-five—there has not been one whose problem in the last resort was not that of finding a religious outlook on life . . . this of course has nothing whatever to do with a particular creed or membership of a church. [Jung, 1932, par. 509]

For Jung it was, therefore, important to link the patient once again to their autonomous, emotional core, operating beyond what had become their rigid egos/false selves. As this occurred they would gain access to an experience of affect, subjectively felt as infinite, perhaps in the form of "an inner world of unlimited dimensions". (Spiritual experience is differentiated from "pathological", infinite experience at the end of this chapter.)

The self and the identity–affect model

The identity–affect model can offer some resolution of the difficulties inherent in the concept of the self. In particular, this model describes the mechanisms, and functioning of the mechanisms, which generate and are responsible for: the experiences of totality and wholeness; the central organizing and guiding principle; the process of individuation; and the generation of symbols of the self, all of which are discussed in detail below.

Such an understanding, however, does represent some loss and alteration to the concept of the self as it is traditionally understood—specifically, in regard to the self as totality, and the wisdom and authority with which the self is understood to speak. This is understood, here, to be *relative* rather than *absolute*.

On the other hand, the development in the understanding of the unconscious, set under way by Freud's introduction of his concept of "id", and carried forward by others such as Bion and Matte Blanco and more recently attachment theory and neuroscience, offers good support for the notion of the unconscious as an organ of affective processing. As such, it is argued here, this corresponds well to Jung's view of a guiding, organizing self or, more precisely, to the pared-down version of Jung's concept of the self that is outlined below.

Totality, authority, and over-identification

One function of the self is to act as a container for the ego, with the self representing the sum total of parts of the whole person. This corresponds, in part (only), with the limited, psychoanalytic concept of the self, with the term "self" being used in parallel to the term "object", as Hartmann (1950) suggests. Klein also uses the term self in a similar way (see also Urban (2003, p. 44)). This use of the term represents the self as a container in the sense of an inert "box" that contains all the parts of the personality.

Jung, however, suggests that this "totality" refers both to those elements that have already been realized and made conscious, and those that are held as archetypal "potentials". He holds that this kind of totality gives the self a certain authority and wisdom and, furthermore, he ascribes the role of integrating the different parts of the individual to the self.

Jung came to this conclusion through his many personal experiences of "an inner world of almost unlimited dimension", through dreams, and the spontaneous emergence of "symbols of the self", and through listening to these factors in himself and his patients, which, he observed, could naturally lead the individual to a significant and characteristic development of the personality—one which recognized the existence of this second centre of the personality, the self—through the process of individuation.

The process of individuation and the self's role in integration is discussed later; however, there is a significant critique that can be made concerning the fact that Jung's conclusions rest heavily on these powerful, *subjective* experiences. Fordham (1985) recognized that Jung's definition(s) of the self mixed metaphor and subjective experience with abstract concepts derived from logical, directed thinking. This applies, in particular, to the self as totality. As Elizabeth Urban puts it,

> . . . thus an affective experience, such as experiencing God's love and feeling at one with the world, becomes a memory put in terms of an "as if", or metaphorical experience, which then becomes an abstract statement about the totality of the psyche. [Urban, 2004, p. 12][2]

The understanding of the self as totality of the psyche can, therefore, be understood to be derived from the subjectively felt experiences of wholeness, timelessness, truth, wisdom, infinity, and limitlessness which Jung then, mistakenly, ascribes to the abstract concept of the self.

This is to put the issue theoretically. However, the issue is of critical importance clinically and the ascription of this kind of authority leads, it is argued here, to an over-identification with the patient and the contents of the unconscious . With Rachel, I discovered that following the lead of the many powerful, numinous, archetypal feelings was leading us down a blind alley, as has been described in Chapter One. I had been taking these feelings, as a Jungian analyst, to be the voice of the self, guiding the process of the analysis. I was making the same mistake as Jung in thinking that these subjective experiences held a particular authority that should be followed.

The analytic attitude that I adopted towards Rachel was formed, and informed, in part, by Jungian theory and practice. As the self is understood to guide the process of development and the process of analysis, and bears a wisdom that the analyst is recommended to heed, the analyst is encouraged to value what emerges from the patient's unconscious. This can be seen to lead, subtly, to a passive, identificatory role, as these "expressions" are taken, in some sense, at face value. Although Jung did warn of the "tricksterish" quality of certain elements of the psyche, essentially the contents that emerge from the unconscious are treated uncritically. For example, while Freud distinguished the manifest content and the latent content of dreams, Jung felt there was no such disguise and did not subject dream images to "reductive" interpretation (Jung, 1917, pars 121ff.).

It would be incorrect to suggest that the classical Jungian position would not interpret and ascribe meaning to spontaneous expressions of the unconscious, but it would not be felt that these expressions had an innate bias or agenda to them. My experience with Rachel showed me that until spontaneous, affective expressions are integrated with ego-functioning, they have a powerful tendency to prefer sameness and to be averse to difference in a way that is potentially destructive to the individual. Jung, too, recommends that archetypal affects be integrated with the ego. There is one set of characteristics, however, that he specifically allows, and that is the subtle, sameness-recognizing element that gives an air of the *numinous* and the mystical and that Jung takes to indicate the effects of the self.

This attitude, it is argued here, serves to undermine ego-functioning, both in its function of forming second-order representations (which help to contain affect rather than being immersed in it) and in its integrative aspects of bringing different elements of the personality together. It can be seen that Jung's theorizing engenders a split between the *apparently* benevolent suspension of ego-functioning (with a potentially "ego transcending", mystical/spiritual nature) and the more clearly malevolent effects of such a suspension, for example, being overwhelmed by affect. The Jungian "technique", associated with this attitude toward the self, amounts to an identificatory attitude of "being on the patient's side" (see Chapter Five on technique). Jung, for instance, saw analysis as a process where analyst and patient proceed into a cave together with only a candle to shed light for both of them. In this vein, Jung's definitive work on the transference describes, with reference to a series of alchemical pictures, the manner in which the analyst becomes immersed in the transference relationship and loses their own separate identity. Discussing a series of pictures that depict the merging of a king and a queen figure into one, before evolving into a hermaphroditic figure and then a Christ figure, Jung comments,

> The doctor, *by voluntarily and consciously taking over the psychic suffering of the patient*, exposes himself to the overpowering contents of the unconscious and hence also to their inductive action . . . The patient, by bringing an activated unconscious content to bear upon the doctor, constellates the corresponding unconscious material in him, owing to the inductive effect which always emanates from the projections in greater or lesser degree. Doctor and patient thus find themselves in a relationship founded on mutual unconsciousness. [Jung, 1946, par. 364, my italics]

The analyst "consciously taking over the psychic suffering of the patient" amounts, it is argued here, to an over-identification with the patient. This technique has very definite, particular, and powerful effects, however, that appear not only to justify, but to *recommend*, its use. The analyst's identification leads to the patient experiencing their affects more powerfully, numinously, and infinitely, as the analyst comes to take over the ego-functioning and allow the patient to become immersed in affective experience. Some of these experiences can be sublime, others terrible. These outcomes are not solely the responsibility of the analyst's attitude, of course, although I believe that such an attitude can exacerbate, and certainly not help to resolve, such states.

An identificatory attitude is not exclusive to Jungian analysis. Winnicott's similarly "patient's-perspective attitude" has a parallel effect in *promoting* regression. It is important to stress that individual analysts of whatever persuasion will, of course, interpret the theoretical frame under which they work differently. Some may argue that an identificatory attitude is not necessarily recommended by Jung's concepts. Indeed, Jung spoke out against identification, saying the individual needs to distinguish themself from the collective. He also recommended that the patient should sit facing the analyst to emphasize the analyst's separate individuality—a practice often not followed by many contemporary Jungians who recommend use of the couch. While these are *overt* forms of emphasizing the analyst's separateness, a more subtle form of identification can be seen to occur, as has been described—identification comes in again "through the back door". The practice of facing the patient and seeing patients infrequently, adopted in classical Jungian analysis and by Jung himself, can be seen as a reaction formation against the natural tendency to identify and the consequences of that identification—a tendency that is strengthened and promoted by this particular Jungian style. Such reactions, it is argued here, do not properly help the patient to work through the fundamental issue of the analyst's separateness.

There is a long history of attempting to distinguish and characterize notional Jungian and psychoanalytic styles of practice. Zinkin (1969), for example, sees the contrast as based on the "Logos and Eros opposition". He writes,

> One emphasizes analysis as a science, the other as an art; one values "technique", the other values spontaneity; one values "making the unconscious conscious" or insight, the other "corrective emotional experience"; one values thinking, categorizing, drawing distinctions, reflection, the other feeling, relationship, growth and transformation. [Zinkin, 1969, p. 48]

Zinkin's proposed resolution accommodates both positions, recommending that the analyst "maintain a balance between distance and closeness to the patient, between separation and entanglement, between emotional response and detached interpretation" (*ibid.*, p. 60). While Zinkin accommodates both positions, he has not undertaken a thoroughgoing analysis of what leads to the Jungian attitude, as is outlined here.

Tellingly, the theory and lore of analytical psychology[3] is set up to deal with the kind of regressions and powerful affective experiences that occur, it is argued here, due, in part, to the analyst's identificatory attitude. Jung talked of the *Nekyia*, the "night sea journey", that patients undertake as they confront the unconscious. More contemporaneously, Nathan Field (1996) has written an influential book detailing the patient's need to *break down*, before there can be a *breakthrough*. These were initially welcome guide-posts in the, at times, *appalling* experiences in the analysis with Rachel. Both Rachel and I were keen to make sense of these experiences in whatever terms we could—if she was making, in classical Jungian terms, an "heroic journey into the underworld" with me as guide and companion, so be it. Unfortunately, I waited through all the breakdowns, hoping for the thoroughgoing breakthroughs to occur. While there were innumerable breakdowns, I came to understand these as breakdowns of her existing ego structure and functioning. Any breakthroughs were to chaotic and primitive states of mind—although there would be periods of calm after the storm. Every breakdown/breakthrough turned out to be a false dawn.

It could be cogently argued that the powerful, numinous, archetypal experiences that I was following in the analysis with Rachel were *not* experiences of the self, and were *not* related to the self as guiding principle or central organizing archetype. There *is* a certain, characteristic quality that is usually present when it is said that something is an "experience of the self". *On these occasions, there is an integration of the archetypal (affective) contents with the ego.* Here, the new material that emerges from a (brief) suspension of ego-functioning becomes integrated with the ego, entailing a new ego organization, and is subsequently enriching to the personality as a whole.

It might also be argued that the experiences that appeared to be due to the self were being distorted as Rachel was in a malignant regression, not reintegrating her affective experience with her own ego, as would occur in a benign regression. While this is true, clinical experience, such as with Rachel, shows that numinous material cannot be trusted as an effective guide within the process of analysis. It might be tempting to suggest that the "fault" was in Rachel (due to her malignant regression), or alternatively in me, through my coming to identify with the archetypal material rather than adopting a more sceptical and analytic attitude towards it. While this is also true, experiences such as those that I had with Rachel recommend a re-evaluation of numinous, infinite experiences taken to be indicative of the self. *The identity–affect model offers an alternate explanation for such experience—that it is due to the subjective experience of affect as infinite consequent upon the suspension of ego-functioning.* Such experience does not necessarily carry any overarching, *unequivocal* authority, although it will have significance, and perhaps very great significance, as explored in the section on individuation below.

While it could be argued that "bad infinite experience" is due to flooding by, and over-identification with, archetypal material, while "good infinite experience" represents exposure to the self, this understanding simply promulgates the split whereby the self is idealized and other material is conveniently left out. While Jung was adamant about recognizing the destructive, shadow side of experience—Christ vs. the devil, creation vs. destruction—he does not address the shadow of the self. Colman (2006) points out that, notably, only Kalsched (1996) investigates the destructive aspect of the self.

Wholeness and symbols of the self

The experience of wholeness can take different forms. First, there are experiences of wholeness that come from a simple immersion in affect, whereby the affective experience becomes the whole of a person's experience. The individual experiences a fullness of (the sense of) being. Fordham (1987) explains the way in which infants experience whole objects before they experience part objects that, he suggests, indicates the activity of the self. These kinds of experience could, in parallel, be understood to relate to the functioning of the non-verbal right hemisphere of the brain. The right hemisphere is understood to deal in "whole objects"—what Lezak (1976) calls "perceptual wholes"—so that there might well be a whole "take" on the individual, that might, for example, portray the individual's heroic/innocent/aggressive qualities as a dragon with a unicorn's horn.

The right hemisphere is *affective* and *configurational* in nature and can be understood to generate images and what Jung called *symbols of the self*. Dreams with significant symbols of the self are often accompanied by a powerful, affective component, and are sometimes called archetypal dreams. Fordham defines a symbol of the self as: "any symbol that carries the experience of or which is postulated as having a greater totality than man himself" (Fordham, 1985, p. 18). He adds also, "those archetypal images which have cosmic or other holistic references". A few of the innumerable, potential symbols of the self are: Christ, the child, the king, the hero, the philosophical tree, Mercurius, the bull, and the tortoise.

Redfearn's thoughts concerning symbols of the self are very relevant here. He writes,

> [Symbols of the self] are felt by the individual to represent the whole, especially if they are numinous symbols or experiences . . . the whole truth, the whole of himself, the will of God, ultimate good etc. In other words, parts of the total personality take over the feeling of myself and seem like the whole of the self or even of the cosmos. To the outside observer the individual may simply be in a "possessed" or regressed state. [Redfearn, 1985, p. 12]

Redfearn's understanding of the experience of wholeness stresses the powerful, total, affective nature of the subjective experience.

There is a second form of experience of wholeness that follows from *the experience of flexible and integrated ego-functioning*. Under these circumstances the individual is broadly in touch with all aspects of their personality, and also in touch and congruent with their emotional core. These are usually more stable, less ecstatic experiences. Experiences of wholeness of this form are sometimes felt more keenly, however, when a new integration is reached; that is, when new elements of the personality are integrated and added to the ego-representation, at which point the individual experiences themself differently.

The ego and the self

Experiences of wholeness and integration are usually understood as being due to the self in Jungian literature. It is argued here that this is due, in part, to the fact that Jung takes a very narrow view of the ego. As quoted above Jung sees the ego as the centre of the field of consciousness but says "it is questionable whether it is the centre of the personality" (Jung, 1951, par. 11).

Jung sees the ego as "the conscious personality" (*ibid.*, pars 7–8) while recognizing that the ego is not wholly conscious, by which he can be understood to mean that the ego includes all those elements of the personality of which the individual has become conscious, even though not all will be present to consciousness at any one moment. In contrast, he sees the self as "the total personality which, though present, cannot be fully known" (*ibid.*, par. 9).

While Jung's definition of the ego does recognize that the conscious personality is made up of different elements, he often does not apply it in this way but, instead, characteristically interprets the ego as the limited subjectivity—the impermanent, evanescent sense of "I". This is a "puny little ego", with the individual seen as being caught like a rabbit in the headlights, painfully aware of their fragile position in the universe.

For example, in *The Relations Between the Ego and the Unconscious* (1928), Jung describes the way that certain individuals identify (their ego) with particular elements of the unconscious with resulting "psychic inflation". He cites the optimist who becomes overweening and arrogant, and the pessimist who becomes overanxious and dependent. Jung writes, "each in his way steps beyond his human proportions, both of them seem a little 'superhuman' and therefore, figuratively speaking, godlike" (*ibid.*, par. 227). On the other hand, Jung gives the example of those who make one-sided identifications with the intellectual and rational aspects of their personality (*ibid.*, par. 347) and, as a result, need to acknowledge the limitations of those identifications by recognizing the unconscious.

Jung presents these examples as *limitations of the ego*, with the implication being that the ego needs to cede its unwarranted position of power to the authority of the self. While it is surely correct that the individual/ego needs to cede their/its attachment to the particular elements of the personality—the optimism, pessimism, or intellectual identifications—Jung's examples *do not demonstrate the limitations of the ego* per se, *but simply the narrowness of the particular ego identifications and self-representations that the individual has made.* The individual who identifies himself with his intellect, or with an optimistic or pessimistic point of view, is leaving out all the *other* aspects of their personality.

It may well be that sometimes the individual *is* unconscious of certain elements of their personality, and that can cause fundamental difficulties. For example, Rachel was not, at first, aware that the "forces" that were assailing her, as if from outside, were in fact her *own* rage or murderousness. When she became aware of these forces as elements of her own personality, however, her experience was not substantially or decisively different.

It could be asked whether the phenomenon of psychic inflation is due to the individual identifying with a part of the unconscious (or the self) that is powerful and archetypal in nature, that results in the individual becoming flooded with affect, inflated, and unrelated to reality, as Jung suggests, or whether, in contrast, the individual is disavowing substantial *other* elements of their personality, suspending the awareness of even the conscious elements of their ego, and thereby becoming immersed in the current experience which is, as a consequence, felt to be powerful, numinous, and archetypal. (This analysis demonstrates the way the individual's relationship to affect and current experience radically determines their sense of identity and subjective experience, and lies at the heart of the identity–affect model, so called for this reason.)

I would suggest that it is frequently the suspension of the integrative functioning of the ego that leads to the experience of being flooded with powerful, "archetypal" affect, and that once the integration between the conscious elements of the personality has been lost the individual can become dominated by whatever experience is central to consciousness, whether it is optimistic, pessimistic, intellect-based, or any other kind of experience. What Jung is referring to as problematic, therefore, is the *narrow unintegrated ego*, which desperately and defensively clutches on to current experience.

Jung is, however, making a vital observation concerning the need for this narrow ego to cede hold of the current experience (although he would describe these phenomena in terms of the ego "appropriating" qualities that "should remain outside our bounds" (*ibid.*, par. 227)). This can be accounted for, however, by understanding that the narrow ego needs to become both flexible and integrated; that is, *flexibly* open to the affective core and thus new experience, with the new experience being integrated with the existing self-representation, altering the individual's sense of self; as well as broadly inclusive of all elements of the personality rather than rigidly identified with a few (the optimistic, pessimistic or intellectual identifications, for example)—in other words, *integrated*. In both these situations the individual moves *beyond* the narrow and rigid ego identification.

As Jung takes a narrow view of the ego, there is consequently only the self to which to turn. However, as the self is essentially unconscious and beyond the "ownership" of the individual, there is no "substance" within the individual with which they could contain themself. This was exactly the difficulty I encountered with Rachel, as she felt she had no substance within herself and so required me to contain her.

Was I to take the traditional Jungian line and conclude, as Margaret Clark writes, that, "Many suffering people are not suited to psychoanalytic and psychodynamic psychotherapy, usually because their ego is not strong enough to sustain an increased awareness of their self" (Clark, 2006, p. xiv)?

This problematic conclusion can be seen to follow, in part, from the fact that Jung chose to work, latterly, predominantly with those in the second half of life, who had already well-developed, if perhaps over-rigid, egos. As Fordham observed in respect of the patients with whom Jung developed his concept of the self: most were "predominantly schizoid, mildly depressed or supposedly normal people" who, Fordham suggests, "might be thought to have narcissistic personality disorders" (Fordham, 1985, p. 15). In consequence the concept of the ego has not been fully developed in analytical psychology.

In situations like Rachel's it is traditionally understood that the self can only come into play when there is sufficient ego-functioning, but it is nevertheless held that it is the *self* that is the factor that integrates the different parts of the personality. For Jung "integration is the main function of the self" (Fordham, 1985, p. 31), while psychoanalysis ascribes the integrative powers to the *ego*; for example, see Klein (1955, p. 312). What was "beyond the ego", however, was certainly not functioning to integrate the different parts of Rachel's personality. The change in Rachel came through her coming to see herself more broadly and through being more in touch with the different parts of her personality, which served as a background to frame and contain her current experience. It is suggested here that this is due to the integrating faculty of the *ego*. The relation of the ego to the *unknown* elements of the personality, and whether there is another form of integration that could be understood to occur in addition, is dealt with in the next section.

This integrative faculty of the ego has the, often difficult, task of bringing together and reconciling the everyday sense of self and the more numinous aspects of self experience. While this process can be problematic, it is by no means impossible. The ego may be limited in its *form* of experience (it does not experience the limitless realms of "non-ego", affective experience), but it can nevertheless *represent* such experience. For example, I can picture many things, some of them impossible, such as being a dragon with a unicorn's horn rising out of the sea. Such an integrative faculty is vital to the personality as the more closely the self-representations reflect the individual's true nature and situation, including the numinous elements of the personality, the better the individual is able to deal with reality.

Fordham (1958. p. 45) argues that the ego is too limited a concept to perform the tasks described by psychoanalysis, specifically that of containing good and bad objects. His argument would also, presumably, apply to the position outlined here. In response, it can be argued that Fordham is similarly taking too narrow a definition of the ego, and that it is *exactly* under the auspices of the *broader* ego that good and bad objects are contained. When the individual becomes conscious of good and bad elements within themself and the object, it is the work of integration to accept that these elements co-exist—that the individual is themself both good *and* bad, or that the (m)other who loves them is *also* the (m)other who causes them pain. This is precisely the achievement of the depressive position, and it reinforces the argument that the achievement of the depressive position is equivalent to that of the achievement of flexible and integrated ego-functioning (see Chapter Four).

The central, organizing, and guiding principle and individuation

Having explored the notion of self as totality and outlined an expanded view of the ego, the question remains whether there are any other functions that correspond to the concept of the self, and to what mechanisms in the psyche they may refer. For example, Fordham has outlined the functioning of a "primary self", which he understands as the operation of the self from the beginning of life. This takes us directly to the question of the organizing principle of the psyche and the concept of individuation.

It is argued here that the non-verbal self and the right hemisphere of the brain, organized by the affective appraisal mechanism, represents the core construct of the self. The affective appraisal mechanism operates as the organizing principle of the developing personality, guiding the individual from the beginning of life, and is equivalent to the self as central, organizing principle of the psyche. Contact with this emotional core of the personality, centred in the right hemisphere, as opposed to the left hemispheric second-order representational functions of the developed ego, affords the individual experiences of an unlimited, infinite kind, as already described (see particularly Chapter Three). This definition of a "core self" is more limited than the concept of the self as it is traditionally framed. These propositions and functions of the self will now be explored.

The identity–affect model holds that elements of the personality that are not recognized in the current set of self-representations, and that are not integrated with the ego, will press for recognition and inclusion. Jean Knox (2004) describes the self-regulatory activity of the psyche (in the identity–affect model, the *auto*-regulatory activity) and its relation to the process of appraisal, in Bowlby's sense. She describes the "constant unconscious process by which experiences are constantly screened and evaluated to determine their meaning and significance" (Knox, 2004, p. 71). In the identity–affect framework, the affective appraisal mechanism, continually alert for samenesses and differences, continues to operate as a guiding principle in adults through the signalling of *dissonance* between the ego as it stands and the individual's affective response to their environment.

Such dissonances may be expressed in terms of dreams, phantasies, verbal slips, images, hallucinations, paranoid thoughts, moods, feelings, physical illness, or neurotic or psychotic symptoms. Symbols of the self would be examples of images that are generated in this way, while dreams are examples of affectively based patterns rendered into narrative image form by the affective–configurational right hemisphere. In effect, these are all expressions of the autonomous right hemisphere which, as they are not integrated with the ego, will have a different quality and will be experienced as dissonant. *These phenomena will, in their different ways, serve to draw attention to the dissonance from the ego and may function so as to lead the individual to a development of the personality.* This amounts to a description of the process that Jung called individuation, and can be seen as a different form of integration of the personality in which the core self is fundamentally involved. (Knox (2005) herself understands this as due to the activity of the transcendent function, a mechanism integral to the self.)

As the dissonance becomes conscious, the individual has some choice over whether and how to respond—they may do so by repression or denial of the new elements, or they may accept them as part of themselves, altering the existing ego structure, and integrating the new elements into their personality. Such an alteration may seem wholly unwelcome and be resisted—the growth of the personality can be difficult—or may be welcomed and integrated relatively easily.

The primary self

Fordham had a number of criticisms of the self that contributed to his developing a concept that he called *the primary self*. This concept sheds important light on the matters under discussion here. Fordham was not satisfied with Jung's understanding of the child and childhood development. Here, most of all, he felt, the central and organizing principle should be seen to be at work. Jung, on the other hand, did not see individuation occurring in childhood, rather he saw it as the work of later life. Furthermore, Jung did not see the child as an individual in their own right, but instead he understood the child's difficulties and personality to reflect the parents' unconscious.

Fordham, who worked with children and observed them closely, believed the child *was* an individual in their own right from the beginning of life. He also felt that the self, as Jung defined it, did not sufficiently take relationship into account—Fordham only found reference to the significance of relationship to individuation in Jung's work in one footnote (Fordham, 1985:17).[4] Finally, Fordham (1985, pp. 30ff) felt that the definitions of "self as totality" and "self as archetype" were incompatible. He tried to reconcile them by keeping the definition of "self as totality" for "the self", while he saw the "self as archetype" as a special "deintegrate" (see below), deriving from his concept of the primary self. (In contrast, the identity–affect model casts doubt on the "self as totality" and emphasizes the functions of right hemisphere of the brain and the affective appraisal mechanism, which correspond more closely to the self as central, organizing principle or archetype.)

Fordham's definition of the primary self not only answered the call of his observations, but elegantly responded to these criticisms of Jung, as well as extending Jung's thesis of the self back into childhood. Fordham started his investigations from the observations of a one-year-old boy who was absorbed in circular scribblings. These continued for some weeks until he "discovered" the word "I".

Fordham (1969) proposed that the self operated from the beginning of life in the form of the *primary self*. The primary self meant that the infant was an individual in their own right, able to distinguish self from other in rudimentary form. This primary self, the sum total of the individual's potential, unfolded through a process of *deintegration*, moving out from archetypal expectation to engage with the world, then returning in a process of *integration* to re-integrate the experience within the infant. This process corresponded to observations of the child engaging with the world before returning for periods of rest and assimilation. The central organizing and guiding principle corresponds to the observable fact that the infant has a dynamic core that guides the individual.

The self and individuation are thus not seen, by Fordham, as idealized concepts, coming into play in the higher reaches of adult development. They are down-to-earth, observable features of childhood, which are seen to be essentially relational (deintegration/integration), and to guide the individual's development and individuation from the beginning.

Elizabeth Urban, who has also worked extensively with children, cites three further pieces of evidence in support of the primary self (Urban, 1998):

- the infant's ability to distinguish abstract qualities, for example, shape, intensity and rhythm;
- "amodal perception", where objects are organised according to their affective quality over and above their particular experience as seen, touched or heard;
- the grouping of invariants, for example, affects such as goodness and badness.

The identity–affect model and the primary self

Beginning with Fordham's primary observation of the drawing of the circle and the discovery of the words "I" and "me": it is argued here that these do not necessarily indicate or require the concept of the self but, instead, are related to a certain degree of development of the *ego*. The growth of consciousness observable in a child of this age (twelve months) occurs because of the development of the left hemisphere and the beginnings of second-order representation—naming—that takes a leap forward at this time (Schore, 1994). The child is, for the first time, able to make a second-order representation that allows them to stand back from the affective experience and to name "I" and "me"—the move beyond the sense of being with the addition of a sense of "I". This development represents a category shift for the ego, allowing greater organization of consciousness and a partial escape from immersion in the particular, current experience.

The affective appraisal mechanism represents a dynamic core guiding the infant, preferencing sameness and averse to difference, from the beginning of life. This brings the rudimentary ability to distinguish self from other, and makes the infant an individual from the beginning. The infant's ability to distinguish abstract qualities, amodal perception, and the grouping of invariants (goodness and badness) can also be understood to follow from the functioning of the affective appraisal mechanism, as described more fully in Chapter Three.

The infant can be seen to deintegrate, in the sense of reaching out toward the other, because they are object-related from the start of life. The infant relies on the other to regulate their affect and their sense of self and, therefore, naturally and spontaneously relates to the other. The observation of integration would depend upon the level of ego development: at first, integration can be understood to be a pleasurable experience in harmony with the (m)other; later on, as ego-development proceeds, integration can be observed to be the experience of pleasurable affects and experiences that enhance and correspond with the child's self-representations, held in the ego.

The mechanisms described by the identity–affect model can be understood, therefore, to represent a possible mechanism for the operation of the primary self. The one element that is *not* covered and explained by this mechanism, however, is the notion that the primary self, and equally the self, represent the "totality of the individual in potential", waiting to unfold. A parallel criticism could be, and has been, made of the archetypes, that is to say, that they do not stand as fully furnished potentials waiting to unfold.

The identity–affect model is understood to be congruent with the view of archetypes as emergent, as outlined, for example, by Knox (2001, 2003) and Hogenson (2001). In this view the archetypes, and this would also apply to the self, are not understood to exist from the beginning of life, full of "content". Instead they are seen as patterns that naturally and inevitably emerge due to the dynamic interaction of the developing brain, the individual's environment, and the "narrative" they develop as a result. In this way, the phenomena and experiences related to the self would be the inevitable experience of being led and guided by something "beyond" the consciously known elements of the ego, that is to say, by the non-verbal self. As Hogenson writes, "The archetypes do not exist in some particular place, be it the genome or some transcendent realm of Platonic ideas. Rather, the archetypes are the emergent properties of the dynamic developmental system of brain, environment, and narrative" (Hogenson, 2001, p. 607).

Re-evaluation of the self

Reframing the self in terms of the identity–affect model still values the core insights of Jungian psychology. The mechanisms recommend that we listen to and respect "the voice from within", but propose that it should be treated with caution, not idealized, nor taken at face value, nor as an absolute authority. There is still a part of us, beyond the "I", to which we are subject, and to which we do well to listen and follow, and with which we should remain congruent—the emotional core and the affective appraisal mechanism, which is constantly unconsciously engaging with, registering, processing, and reacting to what is going on.

We can also account for those dreams or experiences that change the direction of our lives, as the ego, as it operates unconsciously, becomes aware of the dissonances in our lives, as generated by the core self; for example, the dream that leads us into analysis or to become a gardener, a writer, or a surgeon; the dawning realization that we are in the wrong place and need to be in a different relationship, job, or country; the events—a chance meeting, falling in love, an article in a newspaper—to which we intuitively respond and which take us in a new direction; the emergence of a part of ourselves from the shadow that changes our personality and our way of relating. These things sometimes happen against our will: we often do not *want* to be disturbed, or had not realized that we were ready to be disturbed. Having seen, or felt, or realized something, however, we cannot un-know it—or, if we do deny it, we do so at our cost and, perhaps, unsuccessfully, like Jonah and the whale.

We can *also* put our trust in the process of analysis—not to take place without the analyst having to play an active part, nor to lead to the full development and individuation of the individual, but as a space in which two people can work and see what emerges. This is a process where the analyst is active, putting forward their own understanding of the situation, yet balanced by periods of listening, feeling, not-knowing, thinking, and waiting.

In this model, what is lost from the traditional understanding of the self relates primarily to the "self as totality"; for example, "a healing image of wholeness, the union of opposites (including masculine and feminine, conscious and unconscious), which for (Jung) represented the inborn goal of psychic development" (McGlashan, 1997, p. 454).

While the mechanism outlined here *does* give experiences of wholeness and *is* healing and *can* bring resolution to warring opposites, the wholeness is recognized as either a subjective experience, or due to flexible and integrative ego-functioning, congruent with the emotional core, while the healing and resolution of conflict come through the ownership and integration of the feelings and reactions with the *ego*, facing the reality of the world and determining to live in that world. Both the ego and the core self are understood to play a role in integration of the personality: the ego draws together the different elements into a stable, linked set of self-representations, while the core self is responsible for the dissonant experiences, generated by the affective core and the affective appraisal mechanism, which are then integrated with/into the ego.

These mechanisms show how the same central, guiding and organizing principle—the preferencing of sameness and aversion to difference of the affective appraisal mechanism—is responsible for the organization of, and appraisal by, the psyche, and is *also* responsible for problematic and pathological outcomes due its narcissistic nature, as explored in the Part II of this book. The "guidance" of the core self is of a very particular nature and the individual cannot, therefore, simply put themself "in the self's hands", but must work to form a relationship with this core self through the development of flexible and integrative ego-functioning.

This chapter has offered a critique of the "self as totality" and described a pared-down understanding of a "core self", which is equivalent to the "self as central, organising principle". This concept can be seen to embrace many of the intuitions and functions of Fordham's primary self and Klein's early ego. Rather than seeing the self as superordinate to the ego, the division of ego and self can be seen as in some ways artificial, with the core self being an intrinsic and inseparable element of mature ego-functioning (see Chapter Two). This, perhaps, reflects the balance between the verbal and non-verbal selves implicit in what Edinger (1972) called a good ego–self relationship, as will be explored further below.

The core self can be seen as "primary" in the sense that Fordham's primary self, which he initially called the "original self", is primary and a precursor of developed ego-functioning. The phenomena associated with the "self as totality" can be seen to arise, primarily, from the underdevelopment or suspension of integrated ego-functioning, as encapsulated in Jung's quote: "The experience of the self is always a defeat for the ego" (Jung, 1955, par. 778). However, there is a specific set of experiences that are admirably accounted for by Jung's concept of the self: spiritual experiences, which must be further explored in order to justify and substantiate this reframing of the concept of the self.

Spiritual experience, the self, and the identity–affect model

The Jungian self is frequently idealized and taken to be somewhat like a benevolent and infallible God, with the fault lying only in the individual for not being able to properly manifest and live up to the self. For example, Edinger writes, "the Self is most simply described as the inner, empirical deity and is identical with the *imago Dei*" (1972, p. 3). It is an irony, but probably no surprise, that some of the obscurity and mystification that Jung once pared away from religious traditions has built itself up around his concept of the self.

Spiritual experience is understood here, as Jung understood it (1937, par. 4ff.), as being an incontrovertible "fact" alongside other facts of subjective experience such as perception, feeling, pain, or hallucination. Spiritual experience is simply a category of experience. The controversial issue is how we *understand* such experience, and to what we understand it to refer. One problem with discussions of spiritual experience is that some people have not, apparently, experienced it, just as some have not experienced hallucinations; this does not mean that such experience does not exist.

In regard to the question of whether there is "something" that corresponds to the inner, spiritual experience, this model is resolutely agnostic as, by and large, was Jung. Jung's answer to the question of *how* spiritual experience arises was to point to the structure of the self; this model, in parallel, points to the structures outlined here that, it is suggested, can adequately account for the subjective aspects of it.

Spiritual experience is seen, in part, as the outcome of the lowering or suspension of ego-functioning. Jung was very much aware of the consequences of such a phenomenon and writes of yogic practices, reflecting many of the elements described here:

> . . . the yogis, attain perfection in *samādhi*, a state of ecstasy, which so far as we know is equivalent to a state of unconsciousness. It makes no difference whether they call our unconscious a "universal consciousness"; the fact remains that in their case the unconscious has swallowed up ego-consciousness. They do not realize that a "universal consciousness" is a contradiction in terms, since exclusion, selection, and discrimination are the root and essence of everything that lays claim to the name "consciousness". . . . In the

end, consciousness becomes all-embracing, but nebulous; an infinite number of things merge into an indefinite whole, a state in
which subject and object are almost completely identical. This is all
very beautiful, but scarcely to be recommended anywhere north of
the Tropic of Cancer. [Jung, 1934/1954, par. 520]

Jung registers here the merging, sameness-recognizing link
between "unconsciousness" and this form of spiritual experience.

When the suspension of ego-functioning is short-term (inducing
"unconsciousness"), the individual may experience a feeling of
mystical one-ness or union with the other or the world. This represents getting in touch with the emotional core of the individual and,
as such, it may be vital and enlivening to the individual, bringing
new experience that may be integrated with the ego.

When the suspension of ego-functioning is long-term, the consequences are different. The individual will likely experience a weakening or loss of their broader, background sense of "I", an increase
in their sensitivity to others, and an increase in the power and intensity of their affects that can be overwhelming.

If such experience comes under the auspices of a particular religious tradition, the religious beliefs and practices may help frame
and contain those experiences, for example, understanding them as
an experience of grace from God. The religious tradition may also
direct the individual to turn toward others to express their love for
them, or to put less emphasis on individuality. In the long-term,
however, the individual will have to adjust to and accommodate
the lessening or loss of the sense of "I", and an increase in the sensitivity to others and of the intensity of feeling.

Of course, the loss of sense of "I" is the *sine qua non* of spiritual
experience and many religious traditions, from Buddhist to Christian, tell us that the self is a delusion (Humphreys, 1951, p. 119) or
recommend "crossing out the 'I'" (as in the orthodox Christian
traditions). What makes the loss of the sense of "I" more bearable
is that the "self-sacrifice" is chosen; this is very different, subjectively, to pathological states where the sense of "I" is lost predominantly against the individual's will—there is all the difference in the
world between giving money to charity and being mugged.

In this way the particular traditions help to frame the experience
and, indeed, such a loss of a sense of "I" will increase the sense of

closeness to others and may lead to an identification with, and a dependency on, the religious group. The individual becomes immersed in the group and gains their identity therefrom. They can become "full up" with religious experience which, being intoxicating, they will likely feel adequately compensates them for the loss of an individuality that only separated them from this powerful, mystical world of spiritual experience. Normal experience can seem pale and illusory in comparison.

The lessening of emphasis on, and even aversion to, the sense of "I", in some traditions, can mean that individuality is not respected, even one's own. An individual, full of religious feeling, may be happy to die for their cause or to kill others—individuality is cheap—for example, the Islamic suicide bomber or the Christian crusader.

The individual whose sense of "I" is weakened will be more sensitized to others, due to their greater sensitivity to sameness and difference. This is observed in religious groups becoming intolerant of otherness and requiring the compliance and adherence of their members. If the group is not actively intolerant it may be that others cease to be interesting and the individual comes to exist in a different "realm". Those not in the group do not "speak the same language" and do not "understand", so that they fall away, and friends and family are lost or rejected.

While in pathological forms of experience the sense of "I" is also lost, there are two further characteristics that set spiritual experience apart. First, the individual's sensitivity and dependence is, typically, not turned towards an individual as the self-regulating other, but rather to something other-worldly (spiritual). This may be interpreted as a spiritual being, God, the Universal Mind, or an inner part of the self other than the "I". If it is to a humanized figure it may be to Christ or the Prophet. This shift is likely to prove something of a development, as the individual is no longer dependent on the vagaries of another individual's actions, moods, and views, and the person may feel themselves more secure in being freed from an immediate, undependable, personal dependency. This does represent a shift in the "centre of gravity" back toward the individual.

The shift of dependence for self-regulation could also be, at least in part, towards the group, the priest, or the leader. This may still afford some sense of liberation for the individual unless, of course, the group or leader operates oppressively or malevolently. It can also be that the religious traditions' teachings themselves come to replace the "vagaries" of the other, and transgression of those teachings can lead to the threat of dire consequence. In this case, again, the new regime may not prove to be a liberation, and may not allow the individual greater self-possession.

Second, the other key change that is required for the individual to deal with the long-term suspension of their ego-functioning will, typically, be a different attitude to *suffering*. Being now exposed to the vagaries of the feeling world, and not expecting an *individual* to act as a self-regulating other, the individual has a number of options. They can either hope that God or the environment will bring good experience their way, and/or they can learn to accept whatever comes, whether good or bad. If the individual can learn to bear good and bad alike, that is, *to suffer*, then they are able to maintain their exposure to the world. They will become less split and will not need to try to avoid whole rafts of experience. They may become, however, at times, like Christ as bleeding heart, and find the demands of the world too much, sometimes needing to cloister themselves away for a while. There is a noble aspect to this life, and it may well be that the individual feels that the sacrifice of their self (their sense of "I") worthwhile for the fullness of their inner being and the spiritual life and sense of meaning that it brings. Something of their ordinary, everyday, human life will, however, have been sacrificed.

An alternate attitude to suffering is the Buddhist view, which understands suffering to come from attachment to the world and affective experience. This was the way which appears to have most struck a chord with Jung, as his writings in *The Secret of the Golden Flower* bear testament. The solution to attachment, says Jung, is to learn not to identify with what is experienced. Jung specifically says that he is labouring for such a detachment with his "students" and "patients" (1929, par. 66). He links this detachment with the "recognition of the unconscious", the cessation of the non-differentiation of subject and object, and the development of a "new centre . . . called the self". Jung writes of "the detachment of consciousness, thanks to which the subjective 'I live' becomes the objective 'It lives me'" (*ibid.*, par. 78).

As discussed above, the unintegrated ego does become "attached" to certain experiences in order to try to prolong the good and split off the bad. Flexible and integrated ego-functioning also offers a form of detachment from the immersion in any *particular* affect by keeping the individual in touch with the broader aspects of their personality. It is not, therefore, necessary to detach from the ego *per se*, as Jung appears to suggest. If this does occur, and at the extreme there can be a schizoid cutting off from affect and a limitation of ego-functioning, the individual then experiences the world in a very different way. The individual's field of experience becomes tinged with universal themes, and their struggles are seen in a different perspective, reflecting the detachment from the particular objects, drives, goals, and affects.

This extreme position does not necessarily follow, however, and the self-discipline and self-knowledge of these traditions does represent a form of ego development through broader self-representation (self-knowledge), which will afford greater containment of affects. Integrated ego-functioning (inclusive of all elements of the personality) and the sense of "I" is almost always sacrificed, however, due to the detachment from the everyday sphere and with the individual's identity set amongst the universal tides (" 'I live' becomes 'It lives me' ").

Transcendence of the ego and analytical psychology

This chapter began by claiming that analytical psychology preferenced spiritual experience in a way that distorted the psyche, as embodied in the concept of the self. It is time to make good that claim. Jung writes,

> If the unconscious can be recognized as a co-determining factor along with consciousness, and if we can live in such a way that conscious and unconscious demands are taken into account as far as possible, then the centre of gravity of the total personality shifts its position. It is then no longer in the ego, which is merely the centre of consciousness, but in the hypothetical point between conscious and unconscious. This new centre might be called the self. [Jung, 1929, par. 67]

While this could be taken as a recommendation to accommodate and respect the autonomous core self, Jung takes a more radical view, relativizing the ego, due to his narrow view of it—"*merely* the centre of consciousness"—and placing the centre of gravity *beyond* the ego, rather than integrated within it. This is a phenomenon that has been continued by later Jungians; here are two recent examples. First Nathan Field, in the conclusion of his book *Breakdown and Breakthrough*, writes,

> In its short history psychoanalysis has moved from drive theory to ego psychology, from ego psychology to object relations theory, and from object relations to individuation. Can it now go beyond? . . . The impulse to transcend the ego goes back to the beginnings of human society, and has been accomplished by a few people in every generation. But in our own historical period, with its capacity to poison and destroy most living forms on the surface of the planet, it has become a necessity. [1996, p.143]

It could be argued, in response to Field, that it is precisely the transcendence and *loss* of ego-functioning that has led to the destructiveness to which Field refers, as it is ego-functioning that lets us know our own boundaries and respect the boundaries of others. The "selfishness" that causes the individual to ruthlessly plunder the other and the planet comes from a "selflessness"; that is, the individual is identified with one aspect of their personality only, which gives a fullness of being but an unstable and precarious sense of "I". Field is describing the unintegrated ego, characteristic of analytical psychology, not the flexible and integrated ego that brings a stable, background sense of "I".

Corbett (1996, p. 171) describes a "mature" form of transcendence that properly only occurs when something has been completely "assimilated and outgrown". Even this form of transcendence, how-ever, implies a suspension of broader, integrative ego-functioning and fosters some kind of immersion in immediate experience. The identity–affect framework would suggest that the ego does not need to be transcended or, perhaps, rather, that the narrow unintegrated ego needs to be developed rather than transcended.

A second example is that of Young-Eisendrath's paper on the self, which characterizes what she describes as "our most complex and integrated stages of human subjectivity". She writes,

... one begins to experience directly the impermanent and fluid nature of Self (what Buddhists call no-self) in which one feels essentially connected to others, not only human beings but to all sentient beings. In this kind of state, one is freer in the way of not being ruled by self-centred desires, not being driven by one's complexes—ego or otherwise. [Young-Eisendrath, 1997, p. 165]

In Young-Eisendrath's description the emphasis on the connectedness to others sounds attractive. However, this connectedness can be seen as an aspect of flexible ego-functioning, with the individual retaining both a sense of "I" and emotional contact with others, so that the individual's relationships feel full, real, and meaningful.

While not all Jungians would share Young-Eisendrath's particular description of "our most complex and integrated states of human subjectivity", yet her description does capture something of Jung's preferencing of the spiritual over the everyday. Such spiritual experiences require a lowering or suspension of integrative ego-functioning and rational, second-order representational functioning, and bring a different sense of self (with primary emphasis given to the sense of being). Even if an individual is detached from the "pull" of the affective element of experience, they can still experience its infinite and numinous nature through immersion in the now.

It is not necessary to sacrifice ego-functioning in this process. It is still possible to recognize that the individual is guided by something not under their own control—that we have to adapt ourselves to, and value, our natural, spontaneous, emotional reactions. One of the best phrasings of this is Frieda Fordham's. She wrote, "If, however, the man can quietly 'listen' to the voice of the unconscious and understand that the power works through him—he is not in control—then he is on the way to a genuine development of personality" (Fordham, F., 1952, p. 60).

Here again, however, the contribution of the individual themselves is diminished. If the *ego* rather than the *self* is seen as the centre of gravity of the individual, then the control is understood to be under the individual's own auspices, although they must be open to the influences of their autonomous, affective core and be prepared to go beyond their "known self" at times. This requires an exercise of faith and the capacity to commit oneself to what is not known (see Chapter Three). In this configuration the individual can then better remain responsible for themselves, take action, and do active work to achieve their goals.

At worst the Jungian self can be taken to be a self-regulating other, like the God of the Garden of Eden, which allows the individual to give up their sense of self-determination and action, and to become passive and put themselves in the hands of this "other". Although Jung also sometimes stresses the individual's role, writing that the impulses we find in ourselves can be understood as the "will of God" though ". . . *the ethical decision is left to man*" (1951, p. 51, my italics), making an ethical decision is not necessarily the same as taking responsibility for oneself.

In regard to spiritual experience, a problem arises when it is seen as better or superior to everyday experience. Jung, for example, writes of a "superior personality", a "consciousness that is detached from the world" that he identifies with the self (Jung, 1929, pars. 67–68). Then a subtle, or not so subtle, form of splitting sets in. This is a form of splitting where the individual attempts to inhabit this part of themselves, limiting integrative ego-functioning that connects the individual to all aspects of their personality. This subtle preferencing thereby distorts the personality. When Jung writes " 'I live' becomes 'It lives me'" and "Individuation is a life in God" (Jung, 1956, par. 1642), he demonstrates that this preferencing of spiritual experience has occurred, and shows that integrative ego-functioning has been, at least partially, suspended. Spiritual experience, therefore, does not take its equal place as one among all other elements of experience, integrated into the personality.

The concept of individuation is, however, to some extent, an open concept that can describe human development in whatever form someone may understand it. There are many Jungian analysts who do not follow Jung's, Field's, or Young-Eisendrath's overt preferencing of the spiritual and relativizing of the ego. It is possible to argue for a rooted and stable ego position in relationship with the self. The concept of the ego–self axis (Edinger, 1972) could be seen to address exactly this difficulty. The ego–self axis depends upon the fact that "the integrity and stability of the ego depends in all stages of development on a living connection with the Self" (*ibid.*, p. 37). In the context of the identity–affect model this could be understood to mean that the ego needs to be connected to the affective core. As Colman (2006) notes, both Neumann and Edinger largely treat the concept of the self, in some important respects, as equivalent to the unconscious.

While the concept of the ego–self axis, understood in this way, is largely consonant with the identity–affect model, there is no escaping the fact that it is the *self* which is seen as the ultimate container and authority in the traditional Jungian frame. While the models, expressed in this manner, are not so very far apart, it is argued here that the traditional Jungian model does subtly militate against and undermine ego-functioning. The Jungian model shifts the emphasis away from the verbal self on to the non-verbal self— essentially identifying the ego with the verbal self, which can be "transcended" by moving to non-verbal experience, which is taken to be due to the self. While this shift can be a welcome reorienta- tion, compensating for an overweening rationality, at the extreme such a shift can undermine the individual and their sense of "I", with significant consequences for relationship, the quality of expe- rience, and the practice and experience of analysis. This traditional attitude can be counterbalanced by recognizing an expanded role for the ego, relinquishing the unequivocal authority of the "self as totality", and accepting a more limited version of the self.

Notes

1. This split between the verbal and the non-verbal self is also reflected in Jung's understanding of the different aspects of his own personal- ity, which he called his Number 1 and Number 2 personalities (1963, p. 75ff.). This difference is elaborated in his early formulations of directed thinking ("thinking in words") and non-directed, fantasy- thinking (including dreaming) in *Two Kinds of Thinking* (1912).

2. Urban has expanded on this in the published version of her paper (Urban, 2005, p. 573).

3. "Analytical psychology" is the term Jung coined to distinguish his ideas and form of practice from Freudian psychoanalysis.

4. The footnote reads: "wholeness is the product of an intrapsychic process which depends essentially on the relationship of one individ- ual to another. Relationship paves the way for individuation and makes it possible, but is itself no proof of wholeness" (Jung, 1946, p. 245, n.16).

PART II
PERSONALITY TYPES

Introduction

I t is frequently commented that, in practice, it can be difficult to clearly distinguish and delineate the four main personality types—narcissistic, hysteric, borderline, and schizoid. This difficulty is partly due to the characteristics that such personality types have in common, and partly due to the different classifications used by different practitioners. For example, what Kohut calls a narcissistic disorder, distinguishing it from borderline and schizoid disorders, is precisely what Britton calls borderline (Britton, 2003, p. 145); Rosenfeld often referred to borderline and narcissistic disorders collectively; and there is also the recently revitalized and updated term of hysteria that Bollas (2000) and Mitchell (2000), in particular, have made more clinically comprehensible. This is not to mention the wide range of understandings of any one disorder. Mollon (1993), for example, delineates nine major, representative models for understanding narcissism (surely the strongest candidate for inclusion in the tower of Babel), although there are certainly at least ten if not one hundred times that number, each emphasizing different characteristics and including different phenomena in their extension and definition.

Symington (1993) understands narcissism as the psychopathology that underlies all others. The identity–affect model follows Symington and understands that the affective appraisal mechanism, with its preferencing of sameness and aversion to difference, constitutes the basic narcissistic mechanism of the psyche, underlying the development and expression of the other personality types. This common "root" thereby explains the confusions, overlaps, and similarities between the different personality types. This Part outlines these different personality types in terms of this underlying root, relating them to the identity–affect model.

As an excellent example of the cross-fertilization between these categories, Britton expands on Rosenfeld's (1987) terms of "thick-skinned" and "thin-skinned" narcissism. Britton describes the thick-skinned narcissist as schizoid, having a "detached narcissistic disorder", and the thin-skinned narcissist as borderline, having an "adherent narcissistic disorder" (Britton, 2003, p. 169). Britton also comments that "inside every thick-skinned patient is a thin-skinned patient trying not to get out, and in every thin-skinned patient is a thick-skinned patient who is usually giving himself a hard time and periodically gives the analyst a hard time" (1998, p. 46). Britton also describes a third category of narcissistic disorder, the "as-if personality", where the patient appears to occupy physical space whilst actually being in another mental domain, giving the analyst the feeling that the patient is unreal (2003, pp. 147ff.).

There are clearly many different outcomes that can follow from the same underlying pattern. Indeed, it would have been possible to describe further personality types to the four outlined here, for example, the obsessional, the perverse, the somatizing, or the traumatized, dissociated individual. These four—narcissistic, borderline, hysteric, and schizoid—are the main types, however, and serve as an illustration of some of the ways the basic nature and functioning of the psyche and, in particular, the affective appraisal mechanism, can manifest and play out.

Terms

Britton suggests that there are three main uses of the term *narcissism*:

First, it describes *narcissism as a phenomenon*: an apparent lack of interest in others, combined with self-preoccupation. This can be seen in various psychological disorders and also in everyday life. Second, it is used to describe an imputed *force* or *innate tendency* within the personality that opposes relationships outside the self. Third, it is used to designate a specific group of personality dysfunctional cases called *the narcissistic disorders*. [Britton, 2003, p. 152, original italics]

This Part addresses all three uses of the term.

Bollas (2000, p. 4) distinguishes between a character state and a character disorder. He suggests that we each contain various states of mind—narcissistic, borderline, schizoid, and hysteric—but that a "normal" person shifts between such states fairly freely. Personality disorder occurs, Bollas suggests, when the individual becomes fixed in a particular character state. These fixed character states are the personality types described here.

The underlying narcissistic mechanism of the psyche

The affective appraisal mechanism, preferencing sameness and averse to difference when ego-functioning is undeveloped, suspended or disavowed, is understood to be *the basic narcissistic mechanism of the psyche*. This is the sensitive "emotional core" of the individual, which feelingly senses the world around, sometimes suffering narcissistic wounding. From this basic mechanism the different personality types follow.

The turning away from relationship, because it is too stressful, anxiety-provoking and painful, is the *schizoid solution*. Trying to dominate the relationship so as to try to ensure a positive sense of being is the *narcissistic solution*; here there is good contact with the affective core, though no stable or solid sense of "I", and the individual has a powerful sense of their "rightness". In contrast, when the individual has a poor sense of themselves (is identified with negative self-representations as the predominant part of their core identity), and feels that the other will not welcome relating to them, they relate, in desperation, by impact, requiring, demanding, or ensuring the other's reaction—this is the *borderline solution*. In the *hysteric solution* the individual tries to alter themself to fit in with what they think the other wants, thereby achieving a sense of sameness and union. *All of these are, in some sense, narcissistic solutions as the full, real relationship to the other is curtailed, and there is an overemphasis and preoccupation with the self and self states, with an aversion to difference and a desire for sameness.*

These pathological elements only emerge, however, when the affective appraisal mechanism is inadequately mediated by flexible ego-functioning. The emotional core, and the affective appraisal mechanism that structures it, are, in fact, essential, central, and embody our affective relation to reality, as has been described in previous chapters.

As has already been described in Chapter One, Fordham (1975) delineates "defences of the self", where the individual defends their core self and attacks anything experienced as other-than-self, which can be seen in the analysis as, for example, technique, method, and interpretation itself. These defences of the self can be seen as a form of narcissistic defence applying to all situations where there is either inadequate or rigid ego-functioning, that is to say, to all of the four personality organizations outlined above.

CHAPTER SEVEN

Narcissism and the narcissistic personality

Overview

T he outlines used in this and subsequent chapters draw substantially on Bollas's succinct and illuminating character sketches from Chapter One of his book *Hysteria* (Bollas, 2000). Bollas characterizes the different personality disorders very much in terms of the individual's particular history. Regarding the narcissistic personality type he writes,

> Experiencing the mother as uneven, the infant resolves the problem she poses by eradicating her and putting a part of the self in her place. This is the classic narcissistic pose: apparent infatuation with the self . . . the narcissistic strategy is to replace the other with some harmonic object that will support the narcissist's search for tran-quillity . . . *the narcissist's strategy is largely aimed at oblating the differ-ences between self and other.* [2000, p. 8, my italics]

act of
religion
offering

Mollon (1993) reviewed nine major and representative models of narcissism—those of Kernberg (1974), Kohut (1971, 1977), Robbins (1982), Gear, Hill, and Liendo (1981), Schwartz-Salant (1982), Rothstein (1980), Grunberger (1971), Rosenfeld (1971), and

203

Bursten (1973)—before synthesizing his own theory, calling on their findings and concepts. Mollon found that the themes of grandiosity and grandiose self-images and self-sufficiency were those most common amongst these models (though by no means universal—both occurring in five out of nine of the models). Further considerable areas of agreement were that in the childhood of narcissistic personalities the mother discouraged the child's own initiatives and failed to recognize and respond to the child's spontaneous gestures, often responding to the child in terms of their *own* agenda. This was understood to hamper the child's separation and the development of their autonomy (Mollon, 1993, pp. 101–103).

Mollon's own synthesis recognizes that narcissistic individuals have characteristic disturbances to their *self*, using Hartmann and Kohut's broader characterization of self in preference to the narrower term of ego (see Chapter Two, Section I). Mollon explores the disturbances of the self in terms of: differentiation of self from other; disturbances in the sense of agency, autonomy, and efficacy; disturbances in self-representation in terms of low-self esteem and grandiosity; disturbances in the structure and organization of the self in terms of cohesion, insubstantiality and dissociation; disturbance in the balance between the subjective and objective self—self-consciousness, false self, preoccupation with what others think, or little sense of others as real people; illusions of self-sufficiency; and, finally, disturbances in the sense of lineage—knowing who one is and where one has come from.

Out of this understanding of the self, and the disturbances of the self, Mollon distinguishes nine characteristics of narcissism: (1) the individual's illusion and captivation by a deceptive image—this is usually derived from the primary caregivers and reflects the myth of Narcissus and his captivation by his own image; (2) a lack of self-knowledge and knowledge of origins, for example, being trapped in illusion or simple lack of information; (3) the individual's difficulty with reflection and mirroring, for example, dependency on mirroring for a sense of self; (4) sado-masochistic interactions; (5) vanity, pride, and a turning away from object-relatedness; (6) the fear of being possessed; (7) envy; (8) self-absorption; (9) origins in a violent primal scene and the absence of a continuing parental couple (Mollon, 1993, pp. 139ff.).

Mollon's own model has two simple characteristics. First, it recognizes the failure of early communication between the infant and the primary caregiver, such as the mother discouraging the child's own initiatives, as described above. Second, it recognizes the failure to establish the triadic position due to the exclusion of the paternal dimension.

Mollon's descriptions and model admirably sum up the clinical picture of narcissism. Although he frames the core of his model in historical terms, like Bollas, it could be seen that he is essentially describing ongoing struggles with separation and the recognition of otherness. This is consonant with the identity–affect model's understanding of narcissism as the preferring of sameness and aversion to difference. While the identity–affect model describes a persistent psychic structure that continues to operate in this manner—the affective appraisal mechanism—it also recognizes that the narcissistic individual has been acted upon and developed into his/her particular personality organization (as opposed to a schizoid or hysterical form, for instance) due to the particular experiences of childhood. The particular outcome is the result of the interaction between inner structure and outer world.

Mollon's concern with the self reflects the identity–affect model's understanding of the individual's preoccupation with self states following the suspension of integrative ego-functioning. The grandiose elements of narcissism are understood to follow, not simply from historical/infantile experiences and phantasies of grandiosity, but from the powerful, *veridical* (i.e., real and true) experiences of affect, experienced as infinite, consequent upon the suspension of integrative ego-functioning.

There are many other formulations of narcissism, including Symington's[1] very particular, complex, and intriguing understanding. This section, and those which follow, are not, however, intended as exhaustive accounts of the fields but rather as basic orientations and introductions.

The narcissistic personality type

What characterizes the narcissistic, as distinct from the borderline, personality type is the degree of contact with the individual's emotional core and the generally good affective tone associated with the individual's self-representation. That is to say, the narcissistic individual feels essentially good about themself and primarily identifies themself with this good part—it is part of their core identity. Kernberg states that it is possible to identify a group of patients in whom there is almost a "pure culture of pathological development of narcissism" (Kernberg, 1975, p. 227), where there is a "fusion of ideal self, ideal object, and actual self images as a defense against an intolerable reality in the interpersonal realm, with a concomitant devaluation and destruction of object images as well as external objects" (*ibid.*, p. 231).

While the narcissist is identified with positive self representations—for Kernberg a fusion of ideal self, ideal object, and actual self images—this identification is unrealistic and requires that others support this self-representation (accounting for the narcissist's need for tribute from others), as well as requiring the oblation of any difference or dissent by/from others which might bring into question this unrealistic identification.

As Kernberg describes, such individuals may function socially very well, though their emotional life is shallow due to the lack of real consideration of others. A group of patients, who can be thought of as *successful* narcissists, is described here.

The "successful" narcissist

These individuals would fall into what Britton would call the group of *libidinal* narcissists. Britton describes libidinal narcissists as those individuals who are motivated by the wish to preserve the capacity for love by making the love-object seem like the self. He understands libidinal narcissism to derive from Freud's conception that self-love is a substitute for the absence of the mother's love, as "falling in love . . . depletes the self in favour of the object, whose reciprocal love is the only means of remedying this haemorrhage of libido" (Britton, 2003, p. 153). Without the reciprocal love from the mother the individual must withdraw their libido on to the self.[3]

The successful narcissist is, typically, accomplished in his career, sensitive, charming, engaging, and in touch with his affects, which are experienced deeply and expressed with conviction. The narcissist is tuned in to others and uses the power of his affects to have a big impact on others and to dominate the situation. He has a good feel for what is going on and is used to getting his way, either through political means or through the force of his personality.

The successful narcissist comes to analysis dissatisfied with his lot, not feeling properly understood, and unable to find a partner who really satisfies him. He is fiercely critical of others, who often find him "scary" and difficult to live up to. This puzzles him, as he sees himself as sensitive, although he recognizes that he does not suffer fools gladly. In fact, there are whole areas of his personality, typically the vulnerable parts, which are closed down. In analysis he is able to open up and really "be himself", for which he is grateful, and feels loving toward the analyst. He is, thus, able to become even more lively, spontaneous, and direct and, since he is used to the unconventional, he is not fazed by his erotic feelings towards the analyst, even if they are homosexual in nature. These feelings are acceptable to him as long as he remains in charge and sets the pace.

His openness can be refreshing and attractive for the analyst, who must beware of according the patient special status, underestimating his psychopathology, and not addressing his destructiveness. An example of these failures might be Winnicott's analysis of Masud Khan (see Green, 2005b; Sandler, 2004). This destructiveness emerges in full force when the analyst dares to challenge the patient and presents himself as a separate object, able to see the patient's sensitivities but without collusively protecting him from those sensitivities. A fearful negative transference can ensue where, as Fordham describes, the analyst's interpretations are subjected to the patient's re-interpretation; for example, that the analyst is "using his technique as a shield behind which to hide" (Fordham, 1974, p. 140), or as an example of the analyst's small-mindedness, timidity, or rule-bound nature.

The moral defence

The narcissist's sensitivities are often manifested as a *moral defence* that can be difficult to understand and in which the analysis can become stuck. While this defence is by no means confined to the narcissistic personality type, it is the narcissist who can put it into effect with the most certainty, conviction, and vehemence.

Fairbairn (1943, p. 65) describes a moral defence in regard to the child acceding to being morally bad in order to maintain the goodness of his/her objects. He argues that it is only on the institution of such a moral defence that the super-ego is established (1944, p. 93). While the moral defence that Fairbairn outlines is intrapsychic in nature, the moral defence described here is more directly interpersonal and puts considerable pressure on the analyst.

The characteristic of this defence, with which I have struggled in various analyses, including with Rachel, is the feeling that the analyst is doing, or has done, something *morally* wrong and has harmed/is harming the patient. The countertransference feeling is a deep, pervasive one of guilt. It is not necessarily linked to anything *specific* that the analyst has done, but is more akin to a generalized feeling of being bad, related somehow to the patient's suffering. For many years I was wrong-footed by such difficult and painful countertransference feelings and struggled to understand them. As soon as I felt "all right" about myself I would feel that I was again walking on eggshells, only to discover that I had mysteriously done something "wrong" without knowing what it was. At times I questioned whether my analytic technique was at fault. Fordham writes,

> Nor is it desirable to become excessively passive or guilty at the amount of pain, terror and dread that the patient asserts the analyst causes. It is important that the analyst should control any guilt he may feel about the patient's claim that he causes confusion, is sadistic, cruel and destructive, etc. [Fordham, 1974, p. 143]

Caper (1995, p. 35) describes the analyst's feeling that they will jeopardize the "good" relationship with the patient in making a mutative interpretation (i.e., one that will show the patient that the analyst is not what the patient takes them to be—see Chapter Five)—this is certainly one form of moral pressure on the analyst. The phenomenon is wider, however, and *the defence represents a continual pressure on the analyst to refrain from manifesting their separateness.*

While this defence might be familiar to practitioners in other forms according to their theoretical background, for example, as a form of superego activity, as one element of a defence of the self (Fordham, 1974), or as an aspect of beta functioning (Bion, see Chapter Five), or related to the aphorism which Kate Newton (personal communication, 1994) attributes to Money-Kyrle (1971): "oral bite is reversed into moral beat", it is here distinguished in its own right, as this moral quality is understood to be a significant, clinical phenomenon.

Another facet of this defensive phenomenon is the way in which narcissistic individuals like to remain on the "high moral ground" and are very sensitive to feeling that they are thought to have done wrong. Often this high moral ground represents, as my colleague Anne Ashley (personal communication, 2000) calls it, a *"living reproach"*. Here, the individual refuses to manifest the same "self-ish", separate, or hurtful behaviour that they experienced them-selves at their parents' hands. This refusal is often particularly telling when "selfish" behaviour is, in some ways, called for as a part of normal, assertive living, for example, in the individual considering their own needs, rather than being ministered to by others. The "martyr" is a good example of an individual employing a moral defence, as the other is left feeling bad for not doing enough to care for the martyr.

Notes

1.   Neville Symington (1993) offers a novel perspective on narcissism. Grotstein sums up Symington, writing,

> The infant/child becomes narcissistically disordered by making an unconscious choice either towards the *lifegiver* (its authenti-city or spontaneity) or to its disavowal and the use of magical pretence in order to evade psychic reality and to avoid external reality ... having partially abandoned the *lifegiver*, the hapless narcissistic subject becomes divided into dissociated sub-selves or alter egos that conflict with one another, defy integration, and forfeit their sense of a spontaneous agency or initiative. [Grotstein, pp. ix–x, in Introduction to Symington, 1993]

Symington's concept of the lifegiver is complex and not immediately accessible. Grotstein understands it as "an internal, phantasmal, transitional-like object that is composed of aspects of the self and of the external life-supporting object. It is an object that personifies the 'act of faith'" (*ibid.*).

Symington's concept could be "translated" into the terms of the identity-affect model, as follows: turning towards the lifegiver amounts to staying in touch with the (authentic, spontaneous) emotional core/affective appraisal mechanism, which connects the individual *both* to his own feelings *and* to reality, while, *at the same time*, maintaining broad ego-functioning. The maintenance of broad, integrative ego-functioning connects the individual to all parts of his personality, rather than splitting into conflicting "dissociated sub-selves or alter egos". In flexible ego-functioning there is both life-giving vitality and integrity (in the sense of authenticity and wholeness).

2. Britton distinguishes libidinal from destructive narcissists. The latter aim to annihilate the object as the representative of otherness. He understands this concept to derive largely from Abraham's (1908, 1917, 1924) conception of narcissism as a form of hostility to transference objects, where envy retards object-love; i.e., the narcissism is an aversion to the object *per se*. This conception, Britton holds, was the basis for Rosenfeld's concept of destructive narcissism. These two conceptions of narcissism express a different balance in respect of the desire for sameness (libidinal narcissism) or the aversion to otherness (destructive narcissism).

CHAPTER EIGHT

The borderline personality

Overview

O f the borderline personality type Bollas writes,

> The borderline person . . . has experienced the primary object as causing so much turbulence to the self that inner states of mental turmoil have become equivalent to it . . . [due to an uneven experience of the mother, the person] construct(s) an ideal object—stitched together out of bits of the good mother—as a fragile alternative to the other mother. Unfortunately, this solution is always a temporary one, because the borderline feels that his or her core object is to be found only through turbulent states of mind. Unconsciously, therefore, the borderline character seeks out turbulence, turning molehills into mountains, and escalating irritations into global states of rage . . . in the transference they will split the analyst, between a fragile idealised object and a denigrated object that feels more true, more primary. [Bollas, 2000, p. 9]

Gunderson and Singer (1975), who offer a classical approach in their overview of the use of the term borderline, bear witness to the disagreement in the term's use. They recognize, however, some characteristics that are fairly consistent among authors. They describe the borderline individual as typically forming an intense relationship with the therapist and having a strong tendency to regress. The individual's affective state is characterized by the prominence of anger and depression, with varying degrees of anxiety and anhedonia (lack of pleasure). Impulsive and self-destructive acts are also characteristic, although these tend to co-exist, perhaps curiously, with good social functioning. This is a "stably unstable" (Schmideberg, 1959) organization, although there can be transient, reversible, limited, psychotic symptoms that are usually stress-related. Borderline individuals tend to be "over-ideational", over-elaborating the affective meaning of their experiences.

Kernberg (1975) offers a comprehensive analysis of what he calls the borderline personality organization. He describes a characteristic ego pathology where there are manifestations of "ego weakness"—lack of anxiety tolerance, impulse control, and developed subliminatory channels (capacity for enjoyment or creative achievement)—a shift toward primary process thinking, and the presence of specific defensive mechanisms, in particular splitting, as well as primitive idealization, projection, projective identification, denial, and omnipotence. The identity–affect model would stress how such ego pathology would profoundly influence the individual's subjective sense of self, which would itself play a significant role in affecting and determining their behaviour.

Other features of the organization that Kernberg describes are powerful, pregenital, aggressive needs, and pathology of internalized object relationships, where splitting interferes with the normal integration of self and object representations. These characteristics are typically accompanied by many of the features that Gunderson and Singer describe. Kernberg cites the following symptomatic constellations which, if more than two or three are present and are allied with the ego pathology described, indicate a borderline personality organization: chronic, diffuse, free-floating anxiety; phobias; obsessive-compulsive symptoms; dissociative reactions; paranoid and hypochondriacal trends; polymorphous perverse sexual trends; schizoid and hypomanic personality; addictions; and chaotic and impulsive behaviours.

In contrast to these descriptions, Britton emphasizes the quality of the transference, writing, "I now realise that the term borderline is most commonly used to describe a particular sort of patient with a distinctive transference pattern, not a theoretical 'borderline position'" (Britton, 2003, p. 147).

Britton's understanding of the quality of the borderline transference is described in the following chapter, in contrasting borderline and hysteric functioning.

The borderline personality type

There are a number of particular features of borderline individuals that go to make up their personality structure and significantly impact on their object relations. Among the most significant are: negative feelings about the self (identification with negative self-representations), malignant regression, a tendency to pathologize the contents of their minds, panic, envy, passivity, and depressive traits, in particular, hopelessness, despair, and isolation. Their poor self-image makes them "thin-skinned narcissists" (Britton, 1998, p. 46). Feeling that the other will be unlikely to respond positively to their approach, and sensitive to separateness and rejection, they come to dominate their relationships indirectly, by impact, demanding that the other "pick up the pieces" (the turbulent relationships of the borderline is contrasted with that of the hysteric personality type in the following chapter). For the borderline individual their nihilism *is* the link to the other.

Dorothy

My patient, whom I will call Dorothy, illustrates many of these features of the borderline personality. She was in her late thirties, single and childless, with a pressing sense of time and opportunity passing her by. Dorothy had been low and depressed, feeling intensely bad about herself since her teens. She was desperately envious of those who had partners and whom, she felt, must have good relationships. She felt she needed and wanted others to appreciate and respond to her, and was angry and resentful when she felt they did not. Others did, however, usually respond with concern to her depression. Dorothy felt that in her childhood the only times that her parents had responded to her had been when they were concerned about her, and that this had been their only overt form of expression of their love and care.

Dorothy had little sense of "I" and no sense of security or of a secure centre. She was significantly passive and reliant on others; hence, what others did had a big impact on her and was experienced intensely. All her feelings could be frighteningly intense at times. She was concerned about these extremes, feeling unable to contain them herself, and despairing of there being anyone else who would contain them. She felt that almost any feeling she had was *wrong*, in particular, her need, anxiety, anger, bitterness, fear, and envy. She took these feelings to be signs of her indisputable, irredeemable pathology and badness. Even if a feeling was experienced mildly it would often give rise to a characteristic panic, as Dorothy would fear that it would escalate and, fearing this, it would usually do so and, in this way, she would become immersed in the affect. Her integrative ego-functioning can be understood as being compromised both by this immersion in affect and by her primary identification with painful, negative, and nihilistic states that represented her core identity. Some of these early states might have been due to the fact that her father had a depressive breakdown just before she was born, which left her already fragile mother even less able to relate to her.

When Dorothy first came to analysis she was in deep crisis, having been sacked from her job. She was immensely grateful and relieved that I was not fazed by the depth of her distress and predicament. Indeed, she looked back on this period fondly and ruefully as a particularly good one, despite the severity of her difficulties. She said she felt secure and cared for by me, and that she had known the purpose of what she was doing—surviving and working on something that felt important with me. As Bollas says, the borderline individual "finds their object through turbulent states of mind", and this period was certainly turbulent.

This pattern of crisis amounted to relating by impact as, completely broken down, and despairing of her terrible situation, she felt contained by my responses as I picked up and explored the pieces of her life with her. She felt secure in her dependence upon me, and was adhesively related to me. This profound sense of need and helplessness, with little integrative ego-functioning and no sense of "I", allowed her to feel that she could approach me, feeling that it was this part of herself that might interest me.

The sense of crisis continued, however, long after what seemed warranted by the situation, when many improvements were taking place in her life, notably her getting a better job, having her skills properly recognized, becoming much more stable, making new friendships, and breaking down with her friends much less frequently. At these times her internal structure, as described here, became clear, as did the extent to which her experience of the world was dominated by this psychic organization.

Over a one year period I made a note of all the ways I addressed her certainty that nothing would ever improve, and her continued experience of anxiety, panic, despair, loneliness, depression, and deep nihilism. I interpreted, primarily, her wish to remain adhered to me and her fear of survival without this form of relationship. To this she responded mournfully, and occasionally scornfully, that it was not the same as it had been, that I did not offer her any reassurance that things would be all right, and that she now felt more profoundly alone and did not know why she was coming to analysis any more.

What was most striking was the way in which any session's insights were completely wiped away by the next day, when I would be presented with the near-same level of panic and despair. On one occasion when I addressed this, Dorothy told me, with her usual wry, self-deprecating humour, that she had been trying to engage in a meditation to build a sense of stability by imagining a mountain that would be able to withstand wind, rain, storm, and hurricane, but that she could not manage it as she kept changing the mountain she was visualizing! She could not identify with stable, benign elements in her personality that would have given her a stable sense of "I" and would have given some containment to these continually shifting states. Sometimes, as her outer situation improved, her panic and despair worsened as, she said, she felt more isolated and lonely. I understood this, in part, to be due to the pain and loss of giving up some of the intensity of her adhesive relating to me and her friends.

It became clear that Dorothy's passivity held a deep wish to be, and expectation of being, looked after and made to feel good, a bitter resentment that this had not occurred early in her life, a deep envy of those who appeared to have achieved this, and a furious refusal to give up the expectation of, and desire for, self-regulation by the other. She was wedded to her view of herself as an unviable victim. By wiping away any insights in the analysis, I was left as the ever-necessary, thinking-container for her broken-down, envious, feeling self. This wiping away also represented an envious attack on me, and the powerful position she had accorded me, as well as an attack on my, and her own, ego-functioning.

Over time a number of things began to be, importantly, constellated in the analysis. Dorothy would often not talk to me or engage me directly, but would talk about the trials of her day, sometimes losing me in the detail of the account, or sinking me in the tone, mood, and spirit of what she was saying. When I did not engage with what she brought in the way she wanted, for example, by making encouraging extra-transference "reframings" of the situation, Dorothy would feel unattended to and uncontained. She became increasingly convinced that I did not care about her. In this spirit her nihilism deepened and the depth and power of the envy she expressed took on an increasingly bitter and powerful tone. Interpreting this envy, especially as it related to me, simply led to a bitter acknowledgement that "Yes, I am a very envious person".

This brought us to the recognition that her bitterness and envy were core parts of her personality, present from early in life, that she felt were unacceptable but with which she identified. She had felt that she irritated others and that her approach would be unwelcome. This pattern was set up and enforced, like a self-fulfilling prophecy, by the fact that she did not engage me directly in the first place. My pointing this out and exploring the lack of self-belief behind this did not, however, shift the pattern. It seemed important that I could relinquish any optimism I might have had and accept and allow myself to be penetrated by the despair that Dorothy undoubtedly felt and, indeed, allow in the irritation as she expected. In this way we penetrated beneath the "pleasant" but unconvincing way she tried to put herself across at times, which overlaid her feeling of being unacceptable.

Continuing to accept, explore, and interpret these experiences in the analysis from within the transference–countertransference constellation and linking them to early experience seemed, finally, more effective. Perhaps we had constellated the early affective patterns, held as implicit memory, that were inaccessible to verbal analysis and interpretation alone (see Andrade, 2005, and Chapter Five on technique). It also signified to Dorothy, I believe, that I was engaging with this core part of her, and was not unduly put off by it; I did not cut off from her as her mother, in particular, had. Exploring the negative identifications she made with certain parts of her personality and making clear the way she discounted other "positive" elements of her personality that were evident from her experience, for example, that people warmed to her, liked her, and valued her and her friendship, also seemed useful.

Most important of all was investigating the way she did not allow herself to acknowledge her desire and capacity to relate to me more directly. The *lack* of acknowledgement had previously left her feeling that she got nothing from me at all, as she had not allowed herself to believe that she was "in a relationship" with me (a characteristic borderline feature). Not relating to me directly also precluded grieving for what was *not* possible in the relationship.

As well as engaging with these core parts of her, I was also aware that all the while that I had been prepared to act as the "helpful analyst", making encouraging extra-transference reframings, Dorothy's own ego-functioning (by which I mean thinking, holding the broader picture, and containing herself) remained devolved into my hands. While this occurred, her *own* ego-functioning did not develop: she had little sense of "I" and she remained bound to an unstable sense of being. Had I been prepared to continue to take on this role of analytic container (see the discussion on containment in Chapter Five, on technique) we would not, I believe, have reached this traumatic core complex of unrelatedness, uncontainment, and poor self-image. Britton (2003, pp. 88ff.) describes the ego as that which offers containment to the individual—this is, crucially, the individual's *own* ego.

As Dorothy's position shifted she commented, significantly, that she "hadn't realized changing was so hard when I had thought that was exactly what I wanted"; in other words, she began to see her intense resistance to change. She also said that she realized she had been "more afraid of living than of dying". Her life had been a hard struggle, from which she had got little pleasure, as it never provided the care that she wanted—her passivity had been, largely, "emotional" as she had worked hard to achieve things materially. She had to force herself to act over the top of her resentment, however, as she could not allow herself to properly grieve for what she had not had.

Dorothy always felt "outside", different, and that she did not fit in. I came to understand her focus on difference as being the basis of her envy. She always noticed the discrepancy between her own situation and that of others, feeling intensely bad about it, almost always interpreting her situation as the worse. I came to see her envy as, simply, a powerful, adverse reaction to difference, as well as a communication to me to address the ways in which she felt different and cut off from me.

The choice of the name Dorothy is deliberate as, like Dorothy in *The Wizard of Oz*, my patient felt she had to get to the "Emerald City" (where everyone else lived) and where the wizard/analyst would make things better, while all the while battling against the Wicked Witch of the West (!). Along the way, however, she developed the qualities in herself—bravery (the lion), intelligence (the scarecrow), and feeling (the tin man)—so that the goal of finding the wizard was proved to be illusory and unnecessary. My patient had developed her own faculties and began to believe in herself, act from herself, and relate to others in a way that was, ultimately, much more stable, satisfying, and fulfilling.

While Dorothy's aggression was expressed towards me largely indirectly, some borderline individuals are much more overtly aggressive toward the analyst, perhaps reflecting more profoundly negative self representations, as well as more direct expressions of the rage at others' separateness, felt as indifference (or worse), and at the narcissistic wounding that is experienced at the hands of an uncaring, frustrating world. This results in a certainty that the analyst would not want to relate to them. In so far as the borderline individual's nihilism *is* the link to the other, their aggressive attacks do form some kind of attempted penetration of the other. As such they are an expression of their need, desire, and even love for the other, or at least an expression of the frustration of that need and desire. It is important for the analyst to recognize the wish for connection implicit in the nihilism.

CHAPTER NINE

The hysteric personality

Overview

R egarding the hysteric, Bollas writes,

> The mother is in conflict over her child, whom she knows she has failed. In the presence of this primary object, the child seeks out who he or she is to the mother and then tries to identify with this object of desire and to represent it to the mother. The hysteric's ailment, then, is to suspend the self's idiom in order to fulfil the primary object's desire. [Bollas, 2000, p. 12]

Kohon sees the hysteric from a different perspective. He understands that the hysteric individual cannot choose whether to identify with mother or father. This follows from a natural "divalence", representing a hysterical stage, common to all, which the hysteric is unable to move through. As a result the hysteric

> creates the game of multiple identifications, which ultimately leaves the hysteric empty and desperate: the labyrinths of her

desire lead nowhere—except to the preservation of that very desire.
... She will reject whoever loves her and will die in desperate
passion for an inaccessible other. [Kohon, 1999, p. 20]

Mitchell understands the key factor in the aetiology of the
hysteric to be the individual's awareness of the presence of siblings.
This produces a catastrophic experience of displacement: "confronted with a sibling the infant regresses to wanting to be the
unique baby it previously was" (Mitchell, 2000, p. 27). This regression to a fantasized merger with mother—a craving for union,
fusion, identification, and "sameness" (*ibid.*, p. 219)—takes the form
of an infantile hypersexuality. However, the death drive also plays
an important part, for Mitchell, as the infant, craving for mother,
finds father, not to mention the other sibling(s), in the way (*ibid.*,
p. 23). Mitchell also touches on the emptiness and fragmentation
the hysteric experiences:

... since the mind is part of the body, if the psyche, soul or mind is
not recognized, the body cannot flourish. Even if it has been well-
tended, the body, along with the "soul", will feel non-existent. ...
the shock of sibling substitutability for the subject leads to fragmentation and even to multiple personalities as avoidance of the
absence underneath. (Mitchell, 2000, pp. 220, 230]

The hysteric personality type

The hysteric has been unable to safely express their authentic
emotional responses due to the caregivers' limited empathy, self-
preoccupation, neglect, or abuse, or the child's particular sensitivity or sense of displacement. The child's need for contact and
sameness with their caregivers leads them to suspend their own
idiom and to become, superficially, compliant. One result of this
compliance is the hysteric's bitter resentment when they themselves
are not satisfied, which might be understood to be what Khan
(1975) refers to as the hysteric's "grudge". The adult hysteric's sense
of entitlement follows from the compliance and the often complete
sacrifice of themselves to the other in order to please them. This sacrifice carries the expectation that the other will respond in like
manner. If and when this response does not follow, the hysteric is

mortified and furious. The analyst with the hysteric often becomes sensitive to inflicting such a "mortal" narcissistic wound on the patient and this becomes a powerful, unconscious means by which the analyst is induced to comply with the hysteric's wishes.

The hysteric, out of touch with their emotional core, becomes lost in their multiple, mobile identifications. They have suspended their own ego-functioning to better fit in with others, and they become confused and desperate, with no stable sense of "I". They feel continually isolated and unseen because they cannot make real contact with the other as their authentic core is not being articulated. As a result they will regularly explode into affective expression, usually instigated by some narcissistic wounding, in an attempt to achieve contact with the other and, ideally, to come to inhabit the other in the mode of a claustrum (Meltzer, 1992), having little or no interest in developing their own independent self. The hysteric comes to hate themself for their inauthentic way of being and their mode of relating.

The consolations of this way of being are the moments or periods of union with others, achieved either through the suspension of their own self (an adhesive identification with the other) or through the compulsion or seduction of the other. Having embarked on this way of being, the hysteric becomes trapped in a vicious cycle of dependency, unable to conceive of relating differently and with no confidence in themself or their ability to change.

Eleanor

My patient, whom I will call Eleanor, was a compliant child, clinging to her mother, and anxious to get things "just right". She was expected not to be jealous of her younger brother, who had profound special needs (Mitchell's catastrophic displacement). Her compliance took a different, angry, despairing turn when, one day at the age of eleven, very distressed, she finally concluded that her mother was not interested in what she *really* felt, but just wanted her to be quiet.

In her late teens Eleanor had a powerful sexual experience that may have made her feel that this could be the way to achieve the desired intimacy, aliveness, self-worth, and excitement that she craved, although she was powerfully conflicted about her sexual nature, and came to express it indirectly in the manner described below.

Eleanor came to analysis after the breakdown of her previous therapy and following a period in a specialist psychiatric unit. When I first began seeing her, she was going through periods at home where she would just "fit in" with what she felt was expected of her, either by her husband or the values of her strict upbringing, in a deadening and stultifying way until she could stand it no longer and something would trigger her rage and despair. She would then run down to the local pier, sometimes as many as a couple of times a week, and wait in a dangerous and exposed position until the police came and physically rescued her. She would then be taken to a psychiatric unit where she would be given medication and hospitalized for a few days, sometimes longer, or discharged if the psychiatrists had become fed up with this pattern of behaviour.

Sometimes when the police came she would struggle and fight against them until she achieved the experience that she longed for—to be overpowered by them, to be taken control of, to be made to feel safe and that she was "inside" them. She could see what she was doing throughout all of this—there was a part of herself that would be watching—but she could do nothing about it as everything was driven by her need for this experience, even if its achievement lasted for just a few moments.

Eleanor said that she did not want to exist but wanted to be safe inside someone. Increasingly this came to be me. Britton writes that the "death wish in hysteria is meant to lead to the consummation of a greatly desired sexual union: it is not intended to separate but to end all separation" (2003, p. 3). Eleanor had little or no sense of "I", due to the "suspension of her own idiom", her out-of-touchness with her everyday affects, her identification with others, and the suspension of her ego-functioning. This ego-functioning could become overwhelmed by the immersion in powerful, uncontained affect, for example, as she ran, pell-mell, down to the pier. She wanted to achieve a "sense of being" inside me, in what Meltzer (1992) would describe as a claustrum. She also wanted to escape the rigid, dead, compliant false self that was, in fact, so precarious.

In the analysis Eleanor was appreciative of feeling understood and was at a point where she was ready to work, perhaps due to the time she had spent with previous therapists. One of her fears was of acting out her desire to be inside me by rushing at me, so she would sometimes rush out of the room instead. She was able to talk with some difficulty about what was going on, and about what she wanted from me. This made some difference, as she was soon running down to the pier only occasionally, and then not at all. Her difficulties had become partially "gathered into the transference" (Meltzer, 1968). She still operated a split, however, between the mostly good, understanding me, to whom she presented, to some extent, the "good girl"/"good patient", and the frustrating others. This meant that the violence of her affects remained substantially outside of the analysis for a time.

In the transference the problem became her passivity as, like Dorothy, Eleanor expected and demanded that the world act to regulate her benevolently and, when it did not, she would have furious outbursts, usually at her husband. Also, as with Dorothy, the analysis itself provided a claustrum-like, understanding "container" which, as long as she remained broken down, enabled her to exist substantially without a sense of "I" and to feel that she existed, to some extent, under my auspices. Masud Khan describes how the hysteric "beseeches (the other) to take over the necessary and required ego-functions" (Khan, 1975, p. 53).

Unlike Dorothy, however, Eleanor had more faith in herself and her ability to affect others and she was prepared to engage in dramas that gave her some gratification. The split meant that she could, for a time, avoid giving up the highs of powerful affective experience, and avoid the painful working-through of this loss in the transference or, at least, this working through took place more slowly than with Dorothy.

An important element of the analysis with Eleanor was the recognition of the more everyday, tender feelings, for example, the wishes for love and care. These had not been expressed or satisfied as a child, and were being transposed into the dramatic actings out. Eleanor was terrified of expressing them more directly. Discussing and exploring these feelings, with much difficulty, began to ground her in a more ordinary, real and, ultimately, more satisfying way of being, and led to her developing her own place in the world and her own individuality, which had previously been disowned.

The differentiation of the borderline
from the hysteric personality

This brings us to the difficult question of the differentiation of the borderline from the hysteric position. Eleanor certainly had many features that could be thought of as borderline, for example, relating by impact and turbulent relationships, while Dorothy could also be seen as compliant, taking some pains to fit in, in part to disguise what she felt was unacceptable.

Britton argues that although hysteria and the borderline syndrome have features in common, they are distinct syndromes. The essence of the difference, for him, is that, in hysteria, priority is given to the claim to "possess the object in the realm of love". Here there is a transference "illusion" that ignores the importance of any reality other than love, and annihilates the analyst's erotic bonds with anyone else. In contrast, in the borderline syndrome "the claim is to possess (the object) in the realm of knowledge"; here the insistence is on complete inter-subjective understanding (Britton, 2003, pp. 24–25).

This difference, it could be argued, is largely related to the hysteric being able to express their positive affect more openly and fully (the realm of love), while borderline individuals feel that they have to make do, due to their negative self representations, with taking possession of the analyst, and being understood by them, in the verbal sphere. While the hysteric can achieve these levels of intensity with others, it is through substantially suspending their own idiom, so that they are significantly incongruent with their "true" nature. The hysteric is more flighty in their identifications (Kohon), leaving greater scope for reality to be avoided and for the analyst to be lulled along. Borderline individuals, on the other hand, stay more true to their nature, being more genuine, so that it can be easier to work through their core experience.

In contrast to Bollas, turbulence is not seen here as a definitive characteristic of borderline individuals. Hysterical individuals are also intent on turbulently involving the analyst, but frequently do so in a more direct and personal way (the realm of love), with the turbulence following particularly from the inevitable frustration of this involvement. For the borderline individual the turbulence is focused more in crises in the outer world (apparently) which involve the analyst in picking up the pieces and coming alongside to assist, or in failing to do so.

Anne Tyndale (2002) suggests that the hysteric "finds consecutive meaning in life and the palaver, bamboozlement and determination to make others love them", while the borderline patient gives the analyst a feeling of "being drawn into chaos, not being able to make sense of the world". My experience very much mirrors this distinction.

Britton also writes from the perspective of the countertransference. With the hysteric, he says, "the analyst's feeling is most often of being regarded as an important person by an interesting patient" (2003, p. 83), while with the borderline patient the characteristic countertransference "is one of being constrained: either feeling tyrannized by the patient or of having misgivings about being tyrannical" (*ibid.*). With Eleanor, as with Rachel, I felt that I was regarded as important, while with Dorothy's sense of being a victim, pushed around by the world, I was often sensitive to feeling tyrannical.

Rachel—the hysteric and borderline elements

Although, with Rachel, early on in the analysis, I felt substantially tyrannized, Rachel can be thought to be, primarily, hysteric. A dream she had a number of years into the analysis particularly captures this element: she dreamt that there was a young girl aged three or four years and an old man standing by the window. The girl was impaled on the man's penis. They were surrounded by cockerels, which were all facing them, motionless. The pair also did not move, although the man occasionally lifted the girl off his penis or put her back on. Rachel looked through a glass panel in the door in horror, and rushed off in a taxi to try to get help from me.

This was a key dream that we returned to again and again, understanding it variously as the terrible penetration and control of the innocent, young Rachel by her parents; her use of her sexuality as the means of getting attention; her moulding herself around and on to the other, including me as analyst; her impalement on my analytic penis and the ensuing stuckness of the analysis; and her own impaling of the other with her need and demand for attention.

It also bears out Khan's, Kohon's, Bollas's, and Mitchell's understanding of the role of sexuality in hysteria, particularly that the sexuality which appears adult is, in fact, infantile.

Working through the hysteric elements of Rachel's personality continued the work with separation and difference, although the atmosphere became less fraught and life-or-death as time went on. The pace became slower and the work more painstaking, as the intricacies of what was going on in the relationship had to be unpicked. The slow and painstaking nature of this period of the analysis fulfilled, at times, Rachel's desire to remain adhered to me and itself had to be analysed and understood.

Ultimately, Rachel was able to relinquish much of this form of relating, although it could appear again at times of stress. She became much more in possession of herself and confident in her own abilities—an integration of the range of self representations—to the extent of being able to set an end date for the analysis. This was a watershed experience that allowed her to acknowledge, test out, and take pride in her own abilities. She became increasingly able to relate to others more directly, openly, honestly, effectively, and straightforwardly. She was also able to bear, respect, and value others' separateness—an integration of object representations so that her objects were no longer crudely split into good and bad.

CHAPTER TEN

The schizoid personality

Overview

In regard to the schizoid personality Bollas writes,

> The schizoid turns the relational space into something of a labora-
> tory where the self becomes a research scientist. . . . Each intense
> experience of a life is repeatedly examined in the mind until grad-
> ually the mind becomes (the) fundamental object of dependence
> . . . The schizoid wants to talk and explain his or her inner world to
> the analyst, and dreads emotional experience as it usually brings
> closer a form of surrender to the primary object, which, for the
> schizoid, it is preferable to keep at a distance. [Bollas, 2000, p. 10]

Guntrip (1952/1980), calling on Fairbairn's ideas, describes a
range of manifestations of schizoid phenomena, from the everyday
to the *overtly* schizoid; in the latter the individual feels shut off, out
of touch, strange, unreal, and with things seeming futile and meaningless. Guntrip describes the characteristics of the schizoid individual as introversion, withdrawnness, narcissism (the individual's

love-objects all being inside, with the individual greatly identified with them), self-sufficiency, a sense of superiority, loss of affect, loneliness, depersonalization (loss of sense of identity and individuality, and loss of oneself), and regression. He writes,

> We may finally summarize the emotional dilemma of the schizoid thus: he feels a deep dread of entering into a real personal relationship, i.e. one into which genuine feeling enters, because, though his need for a love-object is so great, he can only sustain a relationship at a deep emotional level on the basis of infantile and absolute dependence. [1980, p. 48]

Guntrip emphasizes that Fairbairn regarded infantile dependence (by which Fairbairn meant states of identification), not the Oedipus complex, as the basic cause of psychopathological developments. This is in line with the fact that Fairbairn saw object-relations, not instinctive impulses, as the primary and important element in psychic functioning.

Frances Tustin, investigating the most profound of all schizoid formations, that of autism, found that the autistic individual forms a rigid "protective shell". Tustin quotes Olin, who writes,

> The autistic child's identity problem is one of feeling so small and insignificant that he hardly exists. So he defends against feelings of non-existence by using all his strength and ability to try to be a shell of indestructible power. [Olin, 1975, in Tustin, 1990, p. 5]

On this Tustin comments, "Such a child may feel that he *becomes* a car, a light switch, a pavement or a record player. He becomes *equated* with such things instead of identifying with living human beings" (Tustin, 1990, p. 5). This primitive identification with inanimate objects provides the individual with an impenetrable shell, in which the vulnerable feeling core can remain protected.

Job, Oedipus, and reality: the schizoid struggle

The figure I meet in my consulting room as frequently as Oedipus, is Oedipus's dark cousin, Job. While Oedipus "gets his girl" (with appalling consequences), Job's life takes a darker route, although there is a better ending for him. Kate Newton (1993) points out, illu-minatingly, that Job starts his journey as "perfect and upright", fitting in with his "good God", expecting and receiving his reward, *at first*. This "fitting in" might sound like the hysteric, but Job is passive and does not deem to engage directly with God, as the hysteric would. By the end of the story, as Newton describes, after his many trials and losses, Job has been transformed from someone who dutifully followed the prescribed rituals into a much more developed and integrated person.

The story of Job can be seen to signify the schizoid individual's struggle with reality and, in particular, the struggle with potency, efficacy, and impotence in the face of an encounter with reality that nearly destroys him/her. Job has done everything he thinks he should to have ensured a good life, and yet is denied it. He loses everything he has—family, possessions, and rank—and, in the desert, covered with boils, he is humiliated by his friends, who tell him he must have done something wrong to deserve all his losses. Job, however, has not done anything wrong and I would argue that the moral element in the story is an example of a moral defence, a moral raging against the "unfairness" of Job's losses. It is also an example of the intentionality of the psyche, where purpose is attrib-uted to any event impinging on the individual.

Job endures, he suffers, he does not complain, he continues to be hopeful. As long as he does this, there is no change in his position. Finally, he has had enough and he rails against his fate. This is the crucial point of the story for me—this is where Job comes into the consulting room. The schizoid element in the personality (not just the schizoid personality type) "dreads emotional experience", to use Bollas's phrase. He/she asks, "What is the point of railing against your lot when it will (*apparently*) do no good, and when nothing will change?" This meeting with what seems like the insu-perable power of the other/reality is what destroys the individual. But the power of the other is experienced as *insuperable* precisely because the individual has absented his feeling self from the equa-tion, so he has nothing to "fight" with.

And the schizoid patient is *right*, nothing does change, *out there*. When Job finally does rail at God, God does not throw up his hands and say, "Yes, you are right Job, I was wrong, I am sorry." On the contrary, God appears out of a whirlwind and tells Job, repeatedly (and significantly), to "brace [himself] and stand up like a man" (Job, 38: 3). God then describes his own "insuperable" power in his creation and knowledge of everything—the earth, the stars, the elements, and all living things. But something *has* changed in this process *in Job*: he has faced and expressed his feelings. He has been pierced to his vitals (to use Jung's phrase) by what has occurred, and has spoken from there. He has "stood up like a man". It is not a question, ultimately, of right or wrong, winning or losing; Job has gained *not* because he has triumphed over God—he has not (he "repents in dust and ashes")—but because he has become congruent with, and has integrated, his emotional core.

Jung (1952) sees Job as achieving a moral ascendancy over God in this process, and Jung joined Job in railing against God. This says more about Jung than Job. While Jung, at least, allowed himself to be pierced "to the vitals", he was not prepared to relinquish this superior position and submit to reality again. Newton (1993) points out that what Jung rails against are *separations* (the expulsion from Eden, the crucifixion, and Job's ordeals) and links these to Jung's own narcissistic wounds.

Britton sees the struggle between Job and God as a struggle between the ego and the superego. His view directly addresses the preoccupation of the Book of Job with the moral dimension. Britton concludes that it is a crucial moment "when the ego takes the super-ego to task and, still afraid of its power, claims the right to question its judgement and to doubt its motives" (2003, p. 111).

Britton is, surely, exactly right in stressing the role of the ego in claiming its proper position. Job, however, did not begin the story in the borderline or narcissistic position, railing against his unfair lot. He was a satisfied, dutiful subject. Indeed, his name is synonymous with patience, forbearance, and acceptance. It is only on *relinquishing* that forbearance that he becomes properly human. Job's becoming narcissistic and self-centred was the (interim) *achievement*. In contrast to Britton, then, the *affective* element of Job's story could be emphasized, as it is the inclusion of the dissociated, affective elements and their containment under the auspices of the ego that is the essence of the story. As Jung says,

> ... the violence is meant to penetrate to a man's vitals, and he to succumb to its action. He must be affected by it, otherwise its full

effect will not reach him. But he should know, or learn to know, what has affected him, for in this way he transforms the blindness of the violence on the one hand and of the affect on the other into knowledge. [Jung, 1952, par. 562]

At the beginning of the story the violence is dissociated, and is seen only as God/the devil's attacks on Job, but by the end Job has gone through a period of being attacking and full of rage himself. This is the resolution of the schizoid dilemma—allowing the hurt to hurt, not avoiding it through dissociation or rationalization, experiencing the impotence, as well as the rage in response, and knowing that there is no redemption of the pain through supremacy. To be able to integrate loss (and losing), that is to say, giving up a powerful identification with it, enables the schizoid individual to move beyond their schizoid block.

The schizoid personality

In the consulting room the schizoid patient finds the reality of analysis painful. They are "thick-skinned narcissists" who have grown a "thick skin" to protect them from the pain and power of the other. While the schizoid individual wants to fit in (like the hysteric), unlike the hysteric they do not feel that they can influence the other, so want to "talk and explain his or her (*own*) inner world to the analyst" (Bollas, 2000, p. 10). I have been surprised to find, almost invariably, just how *compliant* and *eager to please* schizoid individuals are, or, at least, have been at some point in their lives.

Like the narcissist, borderline, and hysteric, the schizoid individual cannot bear the separateness of the analyst and feels criticized by their interpretations. The schizoid patient, however, feels mortified that they have not thought of the interpretation first, as this would have pre-empted expression of the analyst's separate position. They do not rail against the analysis openly. For example, they do *not* say, "Why won't you make up the time if I am late?" What would be the point? It would only be too painful to do so as it would remind and confirm them in their feelings of impotence. The schizoid patient knows this, so does not ask. They have internalized "the rules", in an identification with the aggressor, so that they can avoid painful conflict.

Malcolm

Malcolm was in his mid thirties, lacking in confidence, harsh, and self-critical. His wife, as he portrayed her, was troubled and demanding and he, on some level, had dedicated himself to her care. Malcolm's acceptance of this role with his wife had not led to the resolution or reward that he had wanted—mutual harmony and satisfaction. His acceptance meant, however, that he could avoid conflict and avoid facing his own reactions towards her, which would have made him bad and blameworthy (Job, at first, used to make sacrifices to allay the guilt from his children's imagined transgressions!). Malcolm did not rail against his fate, rather he was the good one on the high moral ground. One might speculate what effect this had on his wife.

Malcolm's project of dedicating himself to his wife had not, therefore, been a success. He had been unable to make her happy and satisfied. He was bitterly resentful of all the care he had given and confused that this had made no substantial difference. He felt himself to be a failure and impotent. Malcolm's troubled relationship was the focus of what he brought to the analysis, interspersed with self-criticism. It became clear, however, that the marriage had served to put him in touch with his feelings and engage him in relationship.

In the analysis there were a number of conflicting forces upon me. On the one hand I was invited to join in with the criticism of Malcolm and his inadequacies (if he had not already got there first): his not feeling a success, not feeling powerful, not able to get in touch with his feelings, and not being able to stand up to his wife. It was tempting for me to make such comments as "You are afraid of expressing your anger". While true, this kind of interpretation carried an implicit pressure for Malcolm to change, and would have reinforced his feelings of failure and his sense of my power. Such interpretations are not, consciously, meant punitively; however, they often come out of frustration with the patient. They can sometimes be attempts to "make something happen" in the face of countertransference feelings of deadness and uselessness, like those that Malcolm sometimes induced in me, rather than understanding them as a communication of his sense of powerlessness. Such interpretations reinforce the schizoid patient's defences against expressing his feelings, which go even deeper "into hiding". The exchange confirms that the individual is not a likeable person and cannot make a good impact on the other—the very issue they have been working on in their "relational space"/"laboratory" (Bollas).

Another pressure of which I was aware, in the face of all Malcolm's self-criticism, was a tendency to take a more gentle line and focus on the difficult narcissistic wounds of his childhood—a strict but generally absent father, boarding school, and experiences of humiliation. It could have become my role to "coax out" the wounded emotional core through understanding and patience.

Finally, there was Malcolm's attempt to enlist me into the role of helper with his difficult relationship, which would have kept me safely "on his side", in what O'Shaughnessy (1993) would call an extra-transference "excursion". All these roles avoided my difference. In the case of enlisting me as a critic, this represented a pseudo-separateness that, in fact, fitted in with his internal world.

While such pressures on me could be seen in terms of projective identifications, I found it more helpful to keep in mind the wider perspective of the kind of object relationship in which Malcolm wanted to enlist me, rather than to get caught up in my interpretation of any particular deadness (for example) that I experienced. The pressures he was putting on me were ways in which the schizoid individual attempts to avoid what they really fear, which is the analyst's proper separateness, experienced as power. The patient is frightened of the otherness of relationship as it calls up their genuine reaction which, they fear, will be either unbearable, or lead to the loss of the relationship due to the strength of their "real" feelings.

If the analyst colludes with the patient in avoiding separateness he is secretly despised for doing so, partly because the schizoid patient sees the analyst adopting their own despised methods of identification with the other. The patient is also genuinely disappointed in the analyst because they know that, ultimately, this will not help them.

I found with Malcolm that it was necessary, as always, to stick exactly and only with what he was doing in the here and now of the analysis, to eschew all thoughts of what he might be "supposed" to be doing (mostly by him), and to find the threads of what was going on in his relationship with me. In this way I was respecting the freedom and autonomy of his feelings and the way that they were expressing themselves. I felt that he would have been prepared to exploit these essentially autonomous feelings (from the non-verbal, right hemisphere) if he had been able to do so. I saw his feeling self as having to protect itself against his verbal self, as if, in some Faustian pact, he was prepared to "sell his soul to the devil" to achieve the power over, and security from, others (indeed, perhaps Job had, at the beginning of his story, "sold his soul to God").

The most difficult element in the analysis was also, naturally enough, the most important: dealing with the countertransference feelings of powerlessness and uselessness that Malcolm induced in me. These could either come through my feeling his critical eye on me and his demands and questions about "what I was going to do" to make a difference, or through my frustration with him and his lack of change, which tempted me to interpret what he was *not* doing, thereby ejecting my own feeling of impotence. It could feel that we were stuck in a sado-masochistic clinch at times. Interpreting and exploring Malcolm's feelings of impotence was the most effective and helpful intervention.

The other main focus of my interpretations with Malcolm was his extreme sensitivity to otherness, which lay beneath his thick-skinned exterior, and the way in which he reacted, in particular, to *my* otherness. As a result of such interpretations the analysis usually remained vital, meaningful, and alive, rather than feeling cut-off and dead. In time Malcolm became more effective and fulfilled in his life, and made positive changes in his relationship with his wife.

Conclusion

These analytic sketches have, I hope, demonstrated the differences between the four main personality types—narcissistic, borderline, hysteric, and schizoid—and the overlap between them due to their common root in the sensitivity to sameness and difference, when ego-functioning is disavowed, under-developed, or suspended. This suspension of ego-functioning, and consequent loss of sense of "I", explains the disturbances in the sense of self common to all four personality types. This substantiates the claim, in line with Symington, that narcissism is the pathology underlying all others. Each particular personality type represents a different "solution" to the problems of the pain, fear, and loss involved in separation and the recognition of otherness, the sensitivity of the emotional core, and the establishing of the person as an individual, in touch with their emotional core yet also contained by their broader experience; in other words, a response to the difficulty of developing flexible and integrative ego-functioning.

This book has traced the significance of shifts in self-experience—distinguished into a sense of being and a sense of "I"—and related those shifts to the differing relationships to, and subjective experiences of, affect. The object has been shown to have a profound influence on the individual through being a self-regulating other who, at times, will regulate the individual's whole sense of self. Identity, affect, and object relations have, therefore, been shown to be intimately linked and interrelated.

These phenomena have been shown to be underpinned and put into effect by the affective appraisal mechanism. This mechanism provides the missing link between the understanding of consciousness, early development, and normal and pathological forms of psychic experience. It is a link which threads together subjective experience—from the everyday to the spiritual, psychoanalytic phenomena—from separation to narcissism, and a neurobiological function that can support and structure these subjective phenomena.

The identity–affect model throws a whole host of clinical and theoretical issues into a different light, from the personality types just outlined to the ego—distinguishing the integrative and flexible elements of ego-functioning, with the affective appraisal mechanism shown to be the precursor or early operative of ego-functioning, akin to the Jungian self as central organizing principle. The book has also offered a new perspective from which to view such cornerstones of analytic thinking as the pleasure principle, primary and secondary process, the transference, separation, destructiveness, envy, paranoid experience, omnipotence, the superego, projective identification, analytic technique, spiritual experience, and the Lacanian subject.

I have trailed the analytic elephant through the heartland of analytic theory and hope that not too much has been trampled underfoot along the way. I suggest, boldly, that the identity–affect model offers a skeleton framework and architecture against which the main analytic models—Freudian, Kleinian, Jungian, and Lacanian—can be seen to articulate with each other.

REFERENCES

Abraham, K. (1908). The psycho-sexual differences between hysteria and dementia praecox. In: *Selected Papers on Psychoanalysis* (pp. 64–79). D. Bryan & A. Strachey (Trans.). London: Hogarth, 1973.

Abraham, K. (1917). Ejaculatio praecox. In: *Selected Papers on Psychoanalysis* (pp. 280–298). D. Bryan & A. Strachey (Trans.). London: Hogarth, 1973.

Abraham, K. (1924). A short study of the development of the libido, viewed in the light of the mental disorders. In: *Selected Papers on Psychoanalysis* (pp. 418–502). D. Bryan & A. Strachey (Trans.). London: Hogarth, 1973.

Adams, M. V. (2001). *The Mythological Unconscious*. New York: Karnac.

Alcoholics Anonymous, (1939). *The Big Book*. Center City: Hazelden Publishing and Educational Services; www.aa.org/bigbookonline.

Alvarez, A. (1992). *Live Company: Psychoanalytic Psychotherapy with Autistic, Borderline, Deprived and Abused Children*. Hove: Brunner-Routledge.

Andrade, V. M. (2005). Affect and the therapeutic action of psychoanalysis. *International Journal of Psychoanalysis, 86*: 677–697.

Arnold, M. B. (1960). *Emotion and Personality*. New York: Columbia University Press.

Astor, J. (2002). Analytical psychology and its relation to psychoanalysis. A personal view. *Journal of Analytical Psychology, 47*(4): 599–612.

Balint, M. (1937). Early developmental states of the ego. Primary object-love. In: *Primary Love and Psycho-Analytic Technique* (pp. 74–90). London: Tavistock, 1965.

Balint, M. (1960). Primary narcissism and primary love. *Psychoanalytic Quarterly, 29*: 6–43.

Balint, M. (1968). *The Basic Fault—Therapeutic Aspects of Regression.* London: Tavistock.

Bergoyne, B (1998). Lacan. Lecture given at the Brighton Association of Analytic Psychotherapists.

Bion, W. R. (1957). Differentiation of the psychotic from the non-psychotic personalities. *International Journal of Psycho-Analysis, 38*(3–4). Reprinted in *Second Thoughts* (pp. 43–64). New York: Jason Aronson, 1967.

Bion, W. R. (1959). Attacks on linking. *International Journal of Psycho-Analysis, 40*(5–6). Reprinted in: *Second Thoughts* (pp. 93–109). New York: Jason Aronson, 1967.

Bion, W. R. (1962a). *Learning from Experience.* London: Heinemann.

Bion, W. R. (1962b). Theory of thinking. *International Journal of Psycho-Analysis, 43.* Reprinted in: *Second Thoughts* (pp. 110–119). New York: Jason Aronson, 1967.

Bion, W. R. (1963). *Elements of Psycho-Analysis.* London: Heinemann.

Bion, W. R. (1965). *Transformations.* London: Heinemann.

Bion, W. R. (1967). *Second Thoughts.* New York: Jason Aronson.

Bion, W. R. (1970). *Attention and Interpretation.* London: Karnac.

Bion, W. R. (1980). *Bion in New York and São Paulo.* F. Bion (Ed.). Strathtay, Perthshire: Clunie Press.

Bion, W. R. (1992). *Cogitations.* London: Karnac.

Bollas, C. (1987). *The Shadow of the Object: Psychoanalysis of the Unthought Known.* London: Free Association Books.

Bollas, C. (1992). *Being a Character—Psychoanalysis and Self Experience.* London: Routledge.

Bollas, C. (2000). *Hysteria.* London: Routledge

Borch-Jacobsen, M. (1991). *Lacan—The Absolute Master.* Stanford, CA: Stanford University Press.

Bowlby, J. (1969). *Attachment and Loss, vol. 1. Attachment.* London: Hogarth.

Bowlby, J. (1980). *Attachment and Loss, vol. 3. Loss: Sadness & Depression.* London: Hogarth.

Brierley, M. (1937). Affects in theory and practice. In: *Trends in Psychoanalysis*. London: Hogarth, 1951.

Britton, R. (1998). *Belief and Imagination—Explorations in Psychoanalysis.* London: Routledge.

Britton, R. (2003). *Sex, Death, and the Superego—Experiences in Psychoanalysis.* London: Karnac.

Broucek, F. (1979). Efficacy in infancy: A review of some experimental studies and their possible implications for clinical theory. *International Journal of Psycho-Analysis, 60*: 311–316.

Burr, V. (1995). *Social Constructionism* (revised 2003). London: Routledge.

Bursten, B. (1973). Some narcissistic personality types. *International Journal of Psycho-Analysis, 54*: 287–300.

Campos, J. J., Barrett, K. C., Lamb, M. E., Goldsmith, H. H., & Stenberg, C. (1983). Socioemotional development. In: P. H. Mussen (Ed.), *Handbook of Child Psychology* (4th edn, pp. 783–815). New York: Wiley.

Caper, R. (1994). Does psychoanalysis heal? A contribution to the theory of psychoanalytic technique. *International Journal of Psycho-Analysis, 73*: 283–292. Reprinted in: *A Mind of One's Own* (pp. 19–31). London: Routledge, 1999.

Caper, R. (1995). On the difficulty of making a mutative interpretation. *International Journal of Psycho-Analysis, 76*: 91–101. Reprinted in: Caper, R. *A Mind of One's Own. (pp. 32–44)* London: Routledge, 1999.

Caper, R. (1999). *A Mind of One's Own.* London: Routledge.

Caper, R. (2001). The place of affect in the representational world: In memory of Joseph Sandler. *International Journal of Psychoanalysis, 82*: 597–600.

Caper, R. (2003). Response to Colman. In: R. Withers (Ed.), *Controversies in Analytical Psychology* (pp. 338–351). Hove: Brunner-Routledge.

Carvalho, R. (2002). Psychic retreats revisited: binding primitive destructiveness or securing the object? A question of emphasis. *British Journal of Psychotherapy, 19*(2): 153–172.

Chiland, C. (2005). *Exploring Transsexualism.* London: Karnac.

Clark, M. (2006). *Understanding the Self–Ego Relationship in Clinical Practice: Towards Individuation.* London: Karnac.

Colman, W. (2003). Interpretation and relationship: ends or means? A commentary on Caper. In: R. Withers (Ed.), *Controversies in Analytical Psychology* (pp. 352–361). Hove: Brunner-Routledge.

Colman, W. (2006). The self. In: R. Papadopoulos (Ed.), *Handbook of Jungian Analysis* (pp. 153–174). Hove: Routledge.

Coltart, N. (1986). Slouching towards Bethlehem . . . or thinking the unthinkable in psychoanalysis. Reprinted in: *Slouching Towards Bethlehem . . . and Further Psychoanalytic Explorations* (pp. 1–14). London: Free Association, 1992.

Corbett, L. (1996). *The Religious Function of the Psyche*. Hove: Brunner-Routledge.

Damasio, A. (1994). *Descartes' Error—Emotion, Reason and the Human Brain*. New York: HarperCollins,

Damasio, A. (1999). *The Feeling of What Happens—Body, Emotion and the Making of Consciousness*. London: Vintage.

Davis, F. (1961). Deviance disavowal: The management of strained interaction by the visibly handicapped. *Social Problems*, 9: 120–132.

Davis, M. & Wallbridge, D. (1981). *Boundary and Space—An Introduction to the Work of D. W. Winnicott*. London: Karnac.

Dreifuss, G. (2001). Experience of the self in a lifetime. *Journal of Analytical Psychology*, 46(4): 689–696.

Edinger, E. F. (1972). *Ego and Archetype*. Boston, MD: Shambhala.

Emde, R. N. (1983). The prerepresentational self and its affective core. *The Psychoanalytic Study of the Child*, 38: 165–192.

Erikson, E. (1956). The problem of ego identity. *Journal of the American Psychoanalytic Association*, 4: 56–121. Reprinted in: E. Erikson, *Identity and the Life Cycle*. New York: Norton, 1980.

Fairbairn, W. R. D. (1943). The repression and the return of bad objects (with special reference to the "War Neuroses"). In: W. R. D. Fairbairn, *Psychoanalytic Studies of the Personality* (1990) (pp. 59–81). Hove: Brunner-Routledge.

Fairbairn, W. R. D. (1944). Endopsychic structure considered in terms of object relationship. *International Journal of Psycho-Analysis*, 25: 70–92.

Field, N. (1996). *Breakdown and Breakthrough—Psychotherapy in a New Dimension*. London: Routledge.

Fliess, R. (1953). Countertransferences and counteridentification. *Journal of the American Psychoanalytic Association*, 1: 268–284.

Fonagy, P. (1991). Thinking about thinking: some clinical and theoretical considerations in the treatment of a borderline patient. *International Journal of Psycho-Analysis*, 72: 639–656.

Fonagy, P. (1999). Memory and therapeutic action. *International Journal of Psychoanalysis*, 80: 215–222.

Fonagy, P., & Target, M. (1995). Understanding the violent patient: The use of the body and the role of the father. *International Journal of Psycho-Analysis*, 76(3): 487–502.

Fonagy, P., Gergely, G., Jurist, E., & Target, M. (2002). *Affect Regulation, Mentalization and the Development of the Self.* London: Karnac.

Fordham, F. (1952). *An Introduction to Jung's Psychology.* Harmondsworth: Penguin.

Fordham, M. (1958). *The Objective Psyche.* London: Routledge & Kegan Paul.

Fordham, M. (1969). *Children as Individuals: An Analytical Psychologist's Study of Child Development.* London: Hodder and Stoughton.

Fordham, M. (1974). Defences of the self. *Journal of Analytical Psychology* 19: 2. Reprinted in S. Shamdasani (Ed.) *Analyst–Patient Interaction—Collected Papers on Technique* (1996) (pp. 139–146). London: Routledge.

Fordham, M. (1985). *Explorations into the Self.* London: Karnac.

Fordham, M. (1987). Action of the self. In: P. Young-Eisendrath & J. A. Hall (Eds.), *The Book of the Self* (pp. 345–365). New York: New York University Press.

Fordham, M. (1993). On not knowing beforehand. *Journal of Analytical Psychology, 38*(2): 127–136. Reprinted in S. Shamdasani, (Ed.). *Analyst–Patient Interaction—Collected Papers on Technique* (pp. 199–207). New York: Routledge, 1996.

Fordham, M. (1994). *Freud, Jung, Klein—The Fenceless Field: Essays on Psychoanalysis and Analytical Psychology.* R. Hobdell (Ed.). London: Routledge.

Foucault, M. (1973). *The Birth of the Clinic: An Archaeology of Medical Perception.* London: Tavistock.

Freud, A. (1936). *The Ego and the Mechanisms of Defence.* London: Karnac.

Freud, S. (1894a). The neuro-psychoses of defence. *S.E., 3*: 43–61. London: Hogarth.

Freud, S. (1895d). Studies on hysteria. *S.E., 2*: 1–240. London: Hogarth.

Freud, S. (1900a). *The Interpretation of Dreams. S.E., 5.* London: Hogarth.

Freud, S. (1912e). Recommendations to physicians practising psychoanalysis. *S.E., 12*: 109–120. London: Hogarth.

Freud, S. (1914c). On narcissism: An introduction. *S.E., 14*: 67–104. London: Hogarth.

Freud, S. (1915c). Instincts and their vicissitudes. *S.E., 14*: 111–142. London: Hogarth.

Freud, S. (1915e). The unconscious. *S.E., 14*: 161–262. London: Hogarth.

Freud, S. (1916–1917). *Introductory Lectures on Psycho-Analysis. S.E., 15–16.* London: Hogarth.

Freud, S. (1923b). *The Ego and the Id. S.E., 19*: 3–108. London: Hogarth.

4242424242

Freud, S. (1924c). The economic problem of masochism. *S.E.*, *19*: 157–172. London: Hogarth.

Freud, S. (1926d). Inhibitions, symptoms and anxiety. *S.E.*, 20: 77–175. London: Hogarth.

Freud, S. (1933a).The dissection of the psychical personality. *S.E.*, 22: 57–80. London: Hogarth.

Freud, S. (1937c). Analysis terminable and interminable. *S.E.*, 23: 216–254. London: Hogarth.

Gazzaniga, M. S. (1985). *The Social Brain: Discovering the Networks of the Mind*. New York: Basic Books.

Gear, M. C., Hill, M. A., & Liendo, E. L. (1981). *Working through Narcissism, Treating its Sado-masochistic Structure*. New York: Jason Aronson.

Gergely, G., & Watson, M. (1999). Early social-emotional development: Contingency perception and the social biofeedback model. In: P. Rochat (Ed.), *Early Social Cognition: Understanding Others in the First Months of Life* (pp. 101–137). Hillsdale, NJ: Lawrence Erlbaum.

Gergen, K. (1999). *An Invitation to Social Construction*. London: Sage.

Gerhardt, S. (2004). *Why Love Matters—How Affection Shapes a Baby's Brain*. London: Routledge.

Green, A. (1977). Conceptions of affect. *International Journal of Psycho-Analysis*, *58*. Reprinted in: *On Private Madness* (pp. 174–213). London: Karnac, 1986.

Green, A. (1999). *The Fabric of Affect in the Psychoanalytic Discourse*. London: Routledge. First published as *Le Discours Vivant*. Paris: Presses Universitaires de France, 1973.

Green, A. (2005a). Winnicott at the start of the third millennium. In: L. Caldwell (Ed.), *Sex and Sexuality—Winnicottian Perspectives*. London: Karnac.

Green, A. (2005b). Addendum to lecture. In: *Play and Reflection in Donald Winnicott's Writings* (The Donald Winnicott Memorial Lecture) (pp. 29–38). London: Karnac.

Grinberg, L. (1962). On a specific aspect of countertransference due to the patient's projective identification. *International Journal of Psycho-Analysis*, 43: 436–440.

Grinberg, L., Sor, D., & Tabak de Bianchedi, E. (1971). *New Introduction to the Work of Bion*. Northvale, NJ: Jason Aronson.

Grotstein, J. (1981). *Splitting and Projective Identification*. London: Aronson.

Grotstein, J. (2005). Projective *trans*identification: An extension of the concept of projective identification. *International Journal of Psychoanalysis, 86*(4): 1051–1070.

Grunberger, B. (1971). *Narcissism.* New York: International Universities Press.

Gunderson, J. G., & Singer, M. T. (1975). Defining borderline patients: An overview. *American Journal of Psychiatry, 132*: 1–10. Reprinted in: M. H. Stone (Ed.), *Essential Papers on Borderline Disorders* (pp. 453–474). New York: New York University Press, 1986.

Guntrip, H. (1952/1980). *Schizoid Phenomena, Object-Relations and the Self.* London: Hogarth.

Hartmann, H. (1939). *Ego Psychology and the Problem of Adaptation.* New York: International Universities Press.

Hartmann, H. (1950). Comments on the psychoanalytic theory of the ego. *Psychoanalytic Study of the Child, 5,* 74–97.

Heimann, P. (1950). On counter-transference. *International Journal of Psycho-Analysis, 31*: 81–84.

Heimann, P. (1960). Counter-transference. *British Journal of Medical Psychology, 33*: 9–15.

Hinshelwood, R. D. (1989). *A Dictionary of Kleinian Thought.* London: Free Association.

Hogenson, G. B. (2001). The Baldwin effect: A neglected influence on C. G. Jung's evolutionary thinking. *Journal of Analytical Psychology, 46*(4): 591–612.

Holmes, J. (2001). *The Search for a Secure Base—Attachment Theory and Psychotherapy.* New York: Brunner-Routledge.

Humphreys, C. (1951). *Buddhism.* Harmondsworth: Penguin.

Isaacs, S. (1952). The nature and function of phantasy. In: M. Klein, P. Heimann, S. Isaacs, & J. Riviere (Eds.), *Developments in Psycho-Analysis* (pp. 67–121). London: Hogarth.

Jackson, J. M. (1988). *Social Psychology: An Integrative Orientation.* Hillsdale, NJ: Erlbaum.

Jacobson, E. (1965). *The Self and the Object World.* London: Hogarth.

James, W. (1890). What is emotion? *Mind, 9*: 188–205.

James, W. (1892). *Psychology: The Briefer Course.* New York: Henry Holt.

Johnson, M. (1987). *The Body in the Mind. The Bodily Basis of Meaning, Imagination and Reason.* Chicago, IL: Chicago University Press.

Joseph, B. (1978). Different types of anxiety and their handling in the clinical situation. In: M. Feldman & E. Spillius (Eds.), *Psychic Equilibrium and Psychic Change* (pp. 106–115). London: Tavistock/ Routledge, 1989.

Joseph, B. (1982.) Addiction to near-death. *International Journal of Psycho-Analysis*, 63: 449–456. Reprinted in: *Psychic Equilibrium and Psychic Change* (pp. 127–138). New York: Brunner-Routledge, 1989.

Joseph, B. (1984). Projective identification: Clinical aspects. In: J. Sandler (Ed.), *Projection, Identification, Projective Identification* (pp. 65–76). London: Karnac, 1987.

Jung, C. G. (1912). Two kinds of thinking. *C.W.*, *5*, R. F. C. Hull (Trans.). London: Routledge & Kegan Paul.

Jung, C. G. (1917). On the psychology of the unconscious. *C.W.*, *7*, R. F. C. Hull (Trans.). London: Routledge & Kegan Paul.

Jung, C. G. (1921). *Psychological Types*, *C.W. 6*, R. F. C. Hull (Trans.). London: Routledge & Kegan Paul.

Jung, C. G. (1928). The relations between the ego and the unconscious. *C.W.*, *7*, R. F. C. Hull (Trans.). London: Routledge & Kegan Paul.

Jung, C. G. (1929). Commentary on *The Secret of the Golden Flower*. *C.W.*, *13*, R. F. C. Hull (Trans.). London: Routledge & Kegan Paul.

Jung, C. G. (1932). Psychotherapist or the clergy. *C.W.*, *11*, R. F. C. Hull (Trans.). London: Routledge & Kegan Paul.

Jung, C. G. (1933). *Modern Man in Search of a Soul*. London: Routledge & Kegan Paul.

Jung, C. G. (1934). *The Development of Personality*, *C.W.*, *17*, R. F. C. Hull (Trans.). London: Routledge & Kegan Paul.

Jung, C. G. (1934/1954). *The Archetypes and the Collective Unconscious*, *C.W.*, *9(i)* , R. F. C. Hull (Trans.). London: Routledge & Kegan Paul.

Jung, C. G. (1935). Principles of practical psychotherapy. *C.W.,16*, R. F. C. Hull (Trans.). London: Routledge & Kegan Paul.

Jung, C. G. (1937). *Psychology & Religion: West and East*, *C.W.*, *11*, R. F. C. Hull (Trans.). London: Routledge & Kegan Paul.

Jung, C. G. (1946). The psychology of the transference. *C.W.*, *16*, R. F. C. Hull (Trans.). London: Routledge & Kegan Paul.

Jung, C. G. (1951). *Aion—Researches into the Phenomenology of the Self*, *C.W.*, *9(ii)*, R. F. C. Hull (Trans.). London: Routledge & Kegan Paul.

Jung, C. G. (1952). Answer to Job. In: *Psychology and Religion: West and East*, *C.W.*, *11*, R. F. C. Hull (Trans.). London: Routledge & Kegan Paul.

Jung, C. G. (1955). *Mysterium Coniunctionis*, *C.W.*, *14*, R. F. C. Hull (Trans.). London: Routledge & Kegan Paul.

Jung, C. G. (1956–1957). Jung and religious belief. In: *Symbolic Life*, *C.W.*, *18*, R. F. C. Hull (Trans.). London: Routledge & Kegan Paul.

Jung, C. G. (1963). *Memories, Dreams, Reflections*. A. Jaffe (Ed.). London: Collins and Routledge & Kegan Paul.

Kalsched, D. (1996). *The Inner World of Trauma—Archetypal Defences of the Personal Spirit*. London: Routledge.

Kernberg, O. (1974). Further contributions to the treatment of narcissistic personalities. *International Journal of Psycho-Analysis, 55*: 215–240.

Kernberg, O. (1975). *Borderline Conditions and Pathological Narcissism*. New York: Aronson.

Khan, M. (1975). Grudge and the hysteric. *International Journal of Psycho-Analysis 56*(4). Reprinted in: *Hidden Selves: Between Theory and Practice in Psychoanalysis* (pp. 51–58). London: Karnac, 1989.

Klages, M. (2001). Jacques Lacan. [Online] Available at www.colorado.edu/English/ENGL2012Klages/lacan.html; [February, 2005].

Klein, M. (1935). A contribution to the psychogenesis of manic-depressive states. *International Journal of Psycho-Analysis, 16*:145–174. Reprinted in: *The Writings of Melanie Klein*, vol. 1 (pp. 262–289). London: Hogarth Press (1975).

Klein, M. (1940). Mourning and its relation to manic-depressive states. *International Journal of Psycho-Analysis, 21*: 125–153. Reprinted in: *The Writings of Melanie Klein, Vol. 1* (pp. 344–369). London: Hogarth, 1975.

Klein, M. (1946). Notes on some schizoid mechanisms. *International Journal of Psycho-Analysis, 27*. Reprinted in: Klein, M., *Envy and Gratitude and Other Works 1946–1963* (pp. 1–24). London: Virago, 1988.

Klein, M. (1952). Mutual influences in the development of ego and id. In: *Envy and Gratitude and Other Works, 1946—1963*, pp. 57–60. London: Hogarth, 1984.

Klein, M. (1955). On identification. In: M. Klein, P. Heimann, & R. E. Money-Kyrle, (Eds.), *New Directions in Psycho-Analysis: The Significance of Infant Conflict in the Pattern of Adult Behaviour* (pp. 309–345). London: Tavistock.

Knox, J. (2001). Memories, fantasies, archetypes: An exploration of some connections between cognitive science and analytical psychology. *Journal of Analytical Psychology, 46*(4): 613–636.

Knox, J. (2003). *Archetype, Attachment, Analysis—Jungian Psychology and the Emergent Mind*. New York: Brunner-Routledge.

Knox, J. (2004). Developmental aspects of analytical psychology: New perspectives from cognitive neuroscience and attachment theory. In: J. Cambray & L. Carter (Eds.), *Analytical Psychology—Contemporary Perspectives in Jungian Analysis* (pp. 56–82). New York: Brunner-Routledge.

Knox, J. (2005). Sex, shame and the transcendent function: the function of fantasy in self development. *Journal of Analytical Psychology*, 50(5): 617–640.

Kohon, G. (1999). *No Lost Certainties to be Recovered*. London: Karnac.

Kohut, H. (1971). *The Analysis of the Self*. New York: International Universities Press.

Kohut, H. (1977). *The Restoration of the Self*. New York: International Universities Press.

Kristeva, J. (1974). *La Révolution du Langage Poétique*. Paris: Editions du Seuil. English edition (M. Waller, Trans.), *Revolution in Poetic Language*. New York: Columbia University Press, 1984.

Krystal, H. (1978). Trauma and affects. *Psychoanalytic Study of the Child*, 33: 81–116.

Lacan, J. (1949). The mirror stage as formative of the function of the I as revealed in psychoanalytic experience. Reprinted in: *Écrits: A Selection* (pp. 1–7). London: Routledge.

Lacan, J. (1966). *Écrits*. Paris: Seuil.

Lacan, J. (1977a). *Écrits: A Selection*. Trans. Alan Sheridan. London: Routledge.

Lacan, J. (1988). [1953–54] *The Seminar. Book 1: Freud's Papers on Technique*. J.-A. Miller (Trans.). With notes by J. Forrester. Cambridge: Cambridge University Press.

Laplanche, J., & Pontalis, J.-B. (1973). *The Language of Psychoanalysis*. London: Karnac.

LeDoux, J. E. (1989). Cognitive-emotional reactions in the brain. *Cognition and Emotion*, 3: 267–289.

LeDoux, J. E. (1996). *The Emotional Brain: The Mysterious Underpinnings of Emotional Life*. New York: Simon & Schuster.

Lezak, M. (1976). *Neuropsychological Assessment*. New York: Oxford University Press.

Little, M. (1981). *Transference Neurosis and Transference Psychosis: Towards a Basic Unity*. New York: Aronson.

Magyar, J., & Gergely, G. (1998). The obscure object of desire: "Nearly, but clearly not, like me". Perceiving self-generated contingencies in normal and autistic children. Atlanta, GA: Poster, International Conference of Infant Studies.

Mahler, M. (1963). Thoughts about development and individuation. *The Psychoanalytic Study of the Child*, XVIII: 307–324.

Mahler, M., & Gosliner, B. (1955). On symbiotic child psychosis. *The Psychoanalytic Study of the Child*, X: 195–212.

Mahler, M., & La Perriere, K., (1965). Mother–child interaction during separation–individuation. *Psychoanalytic Quarterly*, 34: 483–489.

Mahler, M., Pine, F., & Bergman, A. (1975). *The Psychological Birth of the Human Infant*. New York: Basic Books.

Mangabeira, W. (2000). Constructing theory—Freud's concepts of the "ego" and the "self" and post-Freudian developments. In: *Who am I? The Ego and the Self in Psychoanalysis* (pp. 23–60). London: Rebus.

Matte Blanco, I. (1975). *The Unconscious as Infinite Sets*. Maresfield Library. London: Karnac.

Matte Blanco, I. (1988). *Thinking, Feeling and Being*. London: Routledge.

McCauley, J. (1994). Finding metrical structure in time. In: M. C. Mozer, P. Smolensky, D. S. Touretzky, J. L. Elman, & A. S. Weigend (Eds.), *Proceedings of the 1993 Connectionist Models Summer School*. Hillsdale, NJ: Erlbaum.

McGlashan, R. (1997). Comment on Eli Weisstub's "Self as the feminine principle". *Journal of Analytical Psychology*, 42(3): 457–459.

Meissner, W. W. (1980). A note on projective identification. *Journal of the American Psychoanalytic Association*, 28: 43–67.

Meltzer, D. (1968). *The Psycho-Analytic Process*. Strathtay, Perthshire: Clunie Press.

Meltzer, D. (1975). Adhesive identification. *Contemporary Psycho-Analysis*, 11: 289–310.

Meltzer, D. (1992). *The Claustrum: An Investigation of Claustrophobic Phenomena*. London: Clunie Press, Karnac.

Mitchell, J. (2000). *Mad Men and Medusas—Reclaiming Hysteria and the Effects of Sibling Relations on the Human Condition*. New York: Basic Books.

Mizen, R. (2003). A contribution towards an analytic theory of violence. *Journal of Analytical Psychology*, 48(3): 285–306.

Mollon, P. (1993). *The Fragile Self—The Structure of Narcissistic Disturbance*. London: Whurr.

Money-Kyrle, R. (1971). The aim of psycho-analysis. *International Journal of Psychoanalysis*, 51. Reprinted in: *The Collected Papers of Roger Money-Kyrle* (pp. 442–449). Strathtay, Perthshire: Clunie Press, 1978.

Newton, K. (1993). The weapon and the wound: The archetypal dimensions in "Answer to Job". *Journal of Analytical Psychology*, 38(4): 375–397.

Nobus, D. (2000). Why I am never myself: On presence and absence in Lacanian theory. In: *Who am I? The Ego and the Self in Psychoanalysis* (pp. 181–198). London: Rebus.

Ogden, T. H. (1982). *Projective Identification and Psychotherapeutic Technique*. New York: Jason Aronson.

Ogden, T. H. (1986). *The Matrix of the Mind: Object Relations and the Psychoanalytic Dialogue*. Northvale, NJ: Jason Aronson.

Ogden, T. H. (1989). *The Primitive Edge of Experience*. London: Karnac.

Ogden, T. H. (1996). The perverse subject of analysis. *Journal of the American Psychoanalytic Association, 44*(4): 1121–1146.

Ogden, T. H. (2004). On holding and containing, being and dreaming. *International Journal of Psychoanalysis, 86*(6): 1349–1364.

Ohman, A. (1986). Face the beast and fear the face: Animal and social fears as prototypes for evolutionary analyses of emotion. *Psychophysiology, 23*: 123–145.

Olin, R. (1975). Differentiating the psychotic child from the mentally retarded child. *Minnesota Medicine, 58*: 489–492.

O'Shaughnessy, E. (1993). Enclaves and excursions. *International Journal of Psycho-Analysis, 73*: 603–611.

Panksepp, J. (1998). *Affective Neuroscience: The Foundations of Human and Animal Emotions*. Oxford: Oxford University Press.

Perlow, M. (1995). *Understanding Mental Objects*. London: Routledge.

Plaut, A. (1956). The transference in analytical psychology. Reprinted in: M. Fordham, R. Gordon, J. Hubback, & K. Lambert (Eds.), *Technique in Jungian Analysis* (pp. 152–160). London: Karnac, 1974.

Port, R., Cummins, F., & McCauley, J. (1995). Naïve time, temporal patterns and human audition. In: R. Port & T. van Gelder (Eds.), *Mind as Motion*. Cambridge, MA: MIT Press.

Potter, J., & Wetherell, M. (1987). *Discourse & Social Psychology: Beyond Attitudes and Behaviour*. London: Sage.

Ramachandran, V. S. (2003). Hearing colors, tasting shapes. *Scientific American, 288*(5): 52–59.

Rayner, E. (1995). *Unconscious Logic*. London: Routledge.

Redfearn, J. (1985). *My Self, My Many Selves*. London: Karnac.

Rizzolatti, G., & Arbib, M. A. (1998). Language within our grasp. *Trends in Neuroscience, 21*: 188–194.

Robbins, M. (1982). Narcissistic personality as a symbiotic character disorder. *International Journal of Psycho-Analysis, 63*: 457–473.

Rosenfeld, H. A. (1971). A clinical approach to the psychoanalytic theory of the life and death instincts: An investigation of the aggressive aspects of narcissism. *International Journal of Psycho-Analysis, 52*: 241–251.

Rosenfeld, H. A. (1987). *Impasse and Interpretation*. London: Routledge.

Rothstein, A. (1980). *The Narcissistic Pursuit of Perfection.* New York: International Universities Press.

Sandler, A.-M., with Godley, W. commentator (2004). Institutional responses to boundary violations: The case of Masud Khan. *International Journal of Psychoanalysis, 85*: 27–43.

Sandler, J. (1960). On the concept of superego. *Psychoanalytic Study of the Child, 15*: 128–162.

Sandler, J. (1976). Countertransference and role responsiveness. *International Review of Psychoanalysis, 3*: 43–47.

Sandler, J. (1987). The concept of projective identification. In: J. Sandler (Ed.), *Projection, Identification, Projective Identification* (pp. 13–26). London: Karnac.

Sandler, J., & Joffe, W. (1969). Towards a basic psychoanalytic model. *International Journal of Psycho-Analysis, 50*: 79–90.

Sandler, J., & Rosenblatt, B. (1962). The concept of the representational world. *Psychoanalytic Study of the Child, 17*: 128–148.

Sandler, J., & Sandler, A.-M. (1998). *Internal Objects Revisited.* London: Karnac.

Sartre, J.-P. (1943). *L'Etre et le Neant.* English edition, Hazel Barnes (Trans.), *Being and Nothingness.* New York: Simon & Schuster, 1969.

Schore, A. N. (1994). *Affect Regulation and the Origin of the Self.* Hillsdale, NJ: Lawrence Erlbaum Associates.

Schore, A. N. (2001). Minds in the making: Attachment, the self-organising brain, and developmentally-oriented psychoanalytic psychotherapy. *British Journal of Psychotherapy, 17*(3): 299–328.

Schmideberg, M. (1959). The borderline patient. *American Handbook of Psychiatry,* vol. 1, S. Arieti (Ed.), New York: Basic Books.

Schwartz-Salant, N. (1982). *Narcissism and Character Transformation.* Toronto: Inner City Books.

Segal, H. (1983). Some clinical implications of Melanie Klein's Work. *International Journal of Psycho-Analysis, 64*: 269–276.

Silberman, E. K., & Weingartner, H. (1986). Hemispheric lateralization of functions related to emotion. *Brain & Cognition, 5*: 322–353.

Solms, M., & Turnbull, O. (2002). *The Brain and the Inner World: An Introduction to the Neuroscience of Subjective Experience.* New York: Other Press.

Spillius, E. (1988). *Melanie Klein Today, Vol. 1.* London: Routledge.

Steiner, J. (1993). *Psychic Retreats: Pathological Organisations in Psychotic, Neurotic and Borderline Patients.* London: Routledge.

Stern, D. N. (1998). *The Interpersonal World of the Infant* (revised edn). New York: Basic Books.

Stern, D. N., Sander, L., Nahum, J., Harrison, A., Lyons-Ruth, K., Morgan, A., Bruschweiler-Stern, N., & Tronick, E. (1998). Non-interpretive mechanisms in psychoanalytic therapy: The "something more" than interpretation. *International Journal of Psychoanalysis, 79*: 903–921.

Stoller, R. J. (1968). *Sex and Gender. Vol. 1*. New York: Science House.

Stoller, R. J. (1975). *Sex and Gender. Vol. 2*. London: Hogarth.

Strachey, J. (1934). The nature of the therapeutic action of psychoanalysis. *International Journal of Psychoanalysis, 50*: 275.

Strauss, R. (1962). The archetype of separation. In: *The Archetype*, Procedures of the 2nd International Congress on Analytical Psychology, Zurich 1962 (1964). Basel: S. Karger.

Symington, N. (1983). The analyst's act of freedom as agent of therapeutic change. *International Review of Psycho-Analysis, 32*: 218–220.

Symington, N. (1993). *Narcissism—A New Theory*. London: Karnac.

Tansey, M. J., & Burke, W. F. (1989). *Understanding Countertransference—From Projective Identification to Empathy*. Hove: The Analytic Press.

Torras, C. (1985). *Temporal-Pattern Learning in Neural Models*. Amsterdam: Spring-Verlag.

Tronick, E. Z. (1989). Emotions and emotional communication in infants. *American Psychologist, 44*: 112–119.

Tustin, F. (1990). *The Protective Shell in Children and Adults*. London: Karnac.

Tyndale, A. (2002). Modern views of hysteria with special focus on how they influence the way we work. Unpublished paper given to the Brighton Association of Analytic Psychotherapists, February 2002.

Urban, E. (1998). States of identity: A perspective drawing upon Fordham's model and infant studies. *Journal of Analytical Psychology, 43*(2): 261–276.

Urban, E. (2003). With healing in her wings: integration and repair in a self-destructive adolescent. In: R. Withers (Ed.), *Controversies in Analytical Psychology* (pp. 9–22). Hove: Brunner-Routledge.

Urban, E. (2004). Fordham and the self. Unpublished paper presented to the Analytic Group of the Society of Analytical Psychology. 1 March 2004.

Urban, E. (2005). Fordham, Jung and the self: a re-examination of Fordham's contribution to Jung's conceptualisation of the self. *Journal of Analytical Psychology, 50*(5): 571–594.

Verhaeghe, P. (1998). Causation and destitution of a pre-ontological non-entity: On the Lacanian subject. In: D. Nobus (Ed.), *Key Concepts of Lacanian Psychoanalysis* (pp. 164–189). London: Rebus.

Watson, J. S. (1994). Detection of self: The perfect algorithm. In: S. Parker, R. Mitchell, & M. Boccia (Eds.), *Self-Awareness in Animals and Humans: Developmental Perspectives* (pp. 131–149). New York: Cambridge University Press.

Watson, J. S. (1995). Self-orientation in early infancy: The general role of contingency and the specific case of reaching to the mouth. In: P. Rochat (Ed.), *The Self in Infancy: Theory and Research* (pp. 375–393). Amsterdam: Elsevier.

Weil, S. (1956). *The Notebooks of Simone Weil.* London: Routledge & Kegan Paul.

Weininger, O. (1996). *Being and Not Being.* London: Karnac.

West, M. A. S. (2004). Identity, narcissism and the emotional core. *Journal of Analytical Psychology, 49*(4): 521–552.

Winnicott, D. W. (1953). Letter to Clifford Scott. Extract reprinted in Davis, M. & Wallbridge, D. *Boundary and Space—An Introduction to the Work of D. W. Winnicott.* London: Karnac, 1981.

Winnicott, D. W. (1958). Mind and its relation to the psyche-soma. In: *Through Paediatrics to Psycho-Analysis* (pp. 243–254). London: Hogarth.

Winnicott, D. W. (1959). Classification: Is there a psycho-analytic contribution to psychiatric classification? In: *The Maturational Processes and the Facilitating Environment* (pp. 124–139). London: Hogarth, 1987.

Winnicott, D. W. (1960a). The theory of the parent–infant relationship. *International Journal of Psycho-Analysis, 41*: 585–595.

Winnicott, D. W. (1960b). Ego distortion in terms of the true and false self. In: *The Maturational Processes and the Facilitating Environment* (pp. 140–152). London: Hogarth, 1987.

Winnicott, D. W. (1969). The use of the object and relating through identification. *International Journal of Psycho-Analysis, 50*: 711–716.

Winson, J. (1990). The meaning of dreams. *Scientific American,* November: 86–96.

Withers, R. (2003). The demonisation of the body in analysis. In: R. Withers (Ed.), *Controversies in Analytical Psychology* (pp. 236–248). London: Routledge.

Yorke, C. (1991). Freud's "On Narcissism": A teaching text. In: J. Sandler, E. S. Person, & P. Fonagy (Eds.), *Freud's On Narcissism: An Introduction* (pp. 35–53). Yale: Yale University Press.

Young-Eisendrath, P. (1997). The self in analysis. *Journal of Analytical Psychology, 42*(1): 157–166.

Zajonc, R. (1980). Feeling and thinking: Preferences need no inferences. *American Psychologist, 35*: 151–175.

Zinkin, L. (1969). Flexibility in analytic technique. *Journal of Analytical Psychology, 14*(2). Reprinted in: M. Fordham, R. Gordon, J. Hubback, & K. Lambert (Eds.), *Techniques in Jungian Analysis* (pp. 45–61). London: Karnac (1989).

Zinkin, L. (1987). The hologram as a model for analytical psychology. *Journal of Analytical Psychology, 32*(1). Reprinted in: H. Zinkin, R. Gordon, & J. Haynes (Eds.), *Dialogue in the Analytic Setting— Selected Papers of Louis Zinkin on Jung and on Group Analysis* (pp. 116– 134). London: Jessica Kingsley.

INDEX

integrative, xiv–xvii, 11–12,
14–15, 17, 19–20, 31, 35, 37,
43–44, 46, 49–50, 52, 54, 64,
68–69, 71, 73, 76, 78–79, 85–86,
99–101, 111, 118, 125, 137, 139,
143, 146, 148, 158, 167, 176, 178,
180, 186–187, 192–195, 205, 210,
214–215, 235
elephant and the blind men, xii, 80,
84, 161, 235
Emde, R. N., xvii, 59, 240
engagement, 150–154, 216
envy, 65–66, 71, 76, 107, 126, 158,
204, 210, 213–214, 216, 218, 235
Erikson, E., 50, 240

Fairbairn, W. R. D., 18, 114, 123,
208, 227–228, 240
Field, N., 86, 174, 193, 195, 240
Fliess, R., 24, 240
Fonagy, P., 9, 13, 16, 21, 38, 42–43,
46, 51, 53, 58, 63, 67–70, 72–75,
87, 89–90, 96, 110, 113–114,
116–117, 127, 129, 146, 153,
240–241
Fordham, F., 194, 241
Fordham, M., 8, 12, 29, 35, 42,
152–154, 162, 170, 175–176,
179–184, 187, 202, 207–209, 241
Foucault, M., 78–79, 241
Freud, A., 45, 241
Freud, S., xvi, 6–7, 18, 20, 39–45, 47,
49, 52–53, 55, 63, 69, 73, 82,
84–85, 87, 98, 100–104, 113, 145,
158, 163, 169, 171, 206, 241–242
Freudian, xiv, 37, 42, 53, 56, 58, 196,
236
fusion, 35, 73, 147, 206, 220

Gazzaniga, M. S., 49, 91, 242
Gear, M. C., 203, 242
Gergely, G., 13, 42–43, 46, 51, 53, 58,
63, 67–70, 72–75, 87, 89–90, 96,
110, 113–114, 116–117, 127, 129,
146, 241–242, 246
Gergen, K., 78, 242

Gerhardt, S., 116, 242
Godley, W., 207, 249
Goldsmith, H. H., 115, 239
Gosliner, B., 55, 246
Green, A., xvi, 91, 100–102, 149–150,
207, 242
Grinberg, L., 128, 130, 145, 242
Grotstein, J., 121, 124, 133, 145, 151,
153, 209–210, 242–243
Grunberger, B., 203, 243
Gunderson, J. G., 109, 211–212, 243
Guntrip, H., 227–228, 243

Harrison, A., 16, 153, 250
Hartmann, H., 39–40, 46, 170, 204,
243
Heimann, P., 142, 145, 243
hemisphere of the brain,
left, xvii, 11, 13, 16, 32, 38, 43,
45–46, 49–50, 91, 107–108, 181,
184
right, xiii, xvii, 10–11, 32, 42–43,
49, 91, 95, 105, 107–108, 136,
153, 163, 175–176, 181–183, 234
Hill, M. A., 203, 242
Hinshelwood, R. D., 43, 55, 123, 125,
243
Hogenson, G. B., 185, 243
Holmes, J., 15, 61, 243
humility, 89, 107, 109–110, 145, 166
Humphreys, C., 189, 243

id, xiv, 40–41, 45, 47, 52–53, 102–104
identity, xii–xvi, xviii, 10, 16, 20–24,
33–87, 100, 102, 107, 109,
111–112, 123–124, 130–131,
135–136, 141, 144, 146–148,
152–153, 158–159, 172, 178, 190,
192, 201, 206, 214, 228, 235
-affect model, xvi, 3, 10–11, 29, 33,
37–38, 42–44, 49–51, 53, 61, 63,
68–70, 72–75, 78–79, 82–85, 89,
91–94, 97–99, 103–104, 111, 118,
122, 126–127, 129–130, 135–136,
141, 144, 150, 155–156, 161, 163,
169, 175, 178, 181, 183–185, 188,